Wissenschaftliche Beiträge aus dem Tectum Verlag

Reihe Wirtschaftswissenschaften

Wissenschaftliche Beiträge
aus dem Tectum Verlag

Reihe Wirtschaftswissenschaften
Band 111

Isabelle Hinsche-McLardy

Unlocking the Potential of Sustainable Finance

Tectum Verlag

The open access publication of this book was funded by the Open Access Publication Fund of Goethe University Frankfurt am Main.

The Deutsche Nationalbibliothek lists this publication in the Deutsche Nationalbibliografie; detailed bibliographic data are available on the internet at http://dnb.d-nb.de

a. t.: Frankfurt/Main, Johann Wolfgang Goethe-Universität, Diss., 2024

ISBN 978-3-68900-464-4 (Print)
ISBN 978-3-68900-465-1 (ePDF)

DOI: https://doi.org/10.5771/9783689004651

Online version

1st edition 2025

Cover illustration created by the author with the assistance of AI

Overall responsibility for manufacturing (printing and production):
Tectum – ein Verlag in der Nomos Verlagsgesellschaft mbH & Co. KG
Waldseestraße 3–5 | 76530 Baden-Baden | Germany
www.tectum-verlag.de | www.nomos.de

Table of Content

Acknowledgments

This dissertation is the result of three years of intensive research, inspiring discussions and conferences, countless long nights and work-filled weekends, as well as the highs and lows of life as a doctoral candidate. But most important for the success of my doctoral journey were the incredible people that supported me along the way.

First and foremost, I would like to thank my doctoral supervisor Prof. Dr. Rainer Klump for his excellent guidance, his interest and belief in my research ideas and for opening many doors to wonderful opportunities throughout my doctoral journey, including workshops, conferences and the implementation of fantastic research projects. Additionally, I would like to thank my further evaluators Prof. Dr. Hackethal, Prof. Dr. Gründl and Prof. Dr. Schefold for their valuable time and support.

Furthermore, I would like to thank the Konrad Adenauer Stiftung for their financial support in the form of a doctoral scholarship, which allowed me to fully focus on my research and to enrich my research with practical experiences in the field of sustainable finance. I am also incredible grateful for having been selected to join the Promotionskolleg Soziale Marktwirtschaft during my time as a scholarship holder, which allowed me to participate in intriguing seminars, as well as valuable discussions and exchange with other doctoral students, who have become lifelong friends.

I was able to complement my research with a practitioner point of view, which was an important aspect for me during my doctoral time. I would like to thank the DZ Bank Stiftung, which financially enabled an extensive survey research project, as well as in particular Tim Buchholz, Marcus Pratsch, Bettina Streiter, Florian Moser and Jasmin Tur for their support and time. Moreover, throughout my doctoral journey I was lucky enough to meet many extraordinary researchers and doctoral students, who have inspired me and provided guidance when needed. A special thank you to Anna Maurer, Christian Zürpel, Phillip Schirmer and Dr. Florian Rester for sharing their experience and their valuable suggestions.

Finally, I would like to express my deepest gratitude to my fiancé, my parents and my sister, for their tireless encouragement, support, feedback and empathy during my dissertation: Without you this would have not been possible!

Summary of the Thesis

The severity and magnitude of the global climate crisis is becoming more apparent every year. The most recent Intergovernmental Panel on Climate Change (IPCC, 2023) report states that global warming might already reach 1.5°C in the near term, between 2030 and 2035, and that approximately 45 % of the world population live in an environment that is highly vulnerable to climate change (IPCC, 2023), which emphasizes the pressure to take action. In order to contribute to the global efforts against climate change, the European Union (EU) has adopted the European Green Deal in December 2019, with the aim to reach climate neutrality by 2050 (European Commission, 2024a). This also translated into country-level targets, for instance, Germany adopted the Climate Change Act in 2021 (Bundesregierung, 2021) determining that Germany is to achieve greenhouse gas neutrality already by 2045.

The market mechanisms of a social market economy, as in the EU, are insufficient to establish a systemic climate protection, as part of our current system, as long as environmental pollution does not have a price. This is reflected by the lack of private sector investments necessary for the transformation towards an ecologically sustainable economy (Georgieva & Adrian, 2022). The EU alone needs additional annual investments of up to €290 billion, to achieve its climate targets and thereby contribute to limiting global warming to 2°C (European Commission, 2019), whilst estimated necessary global annual investments reach up to $8.1 trillion (Buchner et al., 2023). Therefore, the state has to intervene by complementing the market process and market mechanisms for the transformation to an ecologically sustainable economy, which the EU intends to do with the EU Green Deal. In a market-oriented economy, the financial sector is responsible for providing the economy with liquidity in the form of financial resources. Consequently, the financial sector was chosen by politicians as a fundamental driving force for the implementation of sustainability disclosure regulations and acceleration of sustainability investments.

The financial sector is responsible for companies' financing and thereby offers an attractive channel to incentivize companies to become more sustainable. Moreover, financing frameworks, requirements and instruments allow for an adaptation to sustainability criteria. The process of incorporating sustainability criteria into investment and credit decisions has been termed sustainable finance and aims to support the achievement of the set sustainability targets (European Commission, 2024b). In order to successfully integrate sustainability criteria into financial decision-making, two main conditions have to be fulfilled:

Firstly, there has to be a common understanding regarding what relevant sustainability criteria are and they have to be provided by companies in the form of comparable measures. The European Commission introduced the EU taxonomy, to establish a common definition of sustainability and sustainability metrics (European Commission, 2024c). Furthermore, sustainability disclosure regulations such as the corporate social responsibility directive (CSRD) and the sustainable finance disclosure regulation (SFDR) make the reporting of sustainability criteria mandatory for companies and financial institutions, creating the desired sustainability performance transparency (European Commission, 2024d; European Commission, 2024e).

Secondly, authorities have to determine how sustainability criteria should be integrated into the existing decision-making and risk-assessment methods. On the EU level, the European Central Bank (ECB, 2022) published a guideline on climate-related and environmental risk integration and expects banks to comply with it by the end of 2024. On the national level, for example in Germany, the Federal Financial Supervisory Authority (BaFin, 2023) published binding recommendations on how to integrate ESG risks into risk management practices for banks. So far, regulatory risk adjustments are focused on pillar II and pillar III of the Basel framework, whilst the integration of sustainability risk criteria into pillar I, which calculates banks' capital requirements based on banks' risk, is still being discussed (Deutsche Bundesbank,

2023). As long as the existence of a risk differential between green and non-green assets is not proven, the European Banking Authority (EBA, 2023) recommends to incorporate sustainability risks into established pillar I risk categories, but currently refrains from supporting the introduction of risk-weighted adjustment factors, such as a green supporting factor.

Sustainability criteria are increasingly also integrated into established financial instruments directly. The most prominent examples are green (use-of-proceeds) or sustainability-linked bonds. Additionally to the characteristics of a conventional bond, these instruments can restrict the use of proceeds to green investment projects or link bond characteristics to sustainability criteria on the company-level (Hinsche, 2021). Sustainable finance structures can also be applied to other financial instruments, such as schuldscheindarlehen and loans, which are overall termed sustainable finance instruments (SFIs). Their aim is to strengthen sustainability investments and encourage the achievement of company-level sustainability targets.

Regarding the progress of integrating sustainability criteria into investment and credit decisions, the EU taxonomy is still being further developed and sustainability disclosure regulations have become binding since January 2024 (European Commission 2024c; European Commission 2024d). Thus, sustainability transparency is being established, but will need time to reach full scale. Furthermore, as the existence of a risk differential between green and non-green assets is still being debated in practice and science, no financial consequences in the form of green supporting or brown penalizing factors have been introduced yet (EBA, 2023). Instead, companies are currently primarily incentivized and guided, in the form of establishing sustainability targets and reporting frameworks, to invest into their sustainability transition by the use of SFIs and their potential benefits.

Consequently, expectations are very high regarding SFIs' potential to effectively incentivize companies to invest into their sustainability transition and thereby achieve the set sustainability targets. The most recent IPCC (2023) report findings underline that sustainability investments cannot wait until the desired sustainability transparency is achieved and more binding risk regulations based on the established sustainability transparency are introduced, but need to be implemented now. In order to raise the necessary sustainability investments, the full potential of sustainable finance has to be unlocked. This dissertation aims to provide a piece of the key to the solution and thereby support the efforts to increase sustainability investments and to ultimately reach the global climate targets.

In order to unlock the potential of sustainable finance, two overarching questions have to be answered. Firstly, whether SFIs work well in terms of generating the necessary sustainability investments and secondly, how the financial sector can support this process. This dissertation contributes to these research questions by analyzing the effectiveness of the sustainable finance market in regard to incentivizing companies to transition and by taking a closer look at the potential of the company-bank relation in the context of SFI use. The first research paper evaluates the effectiveness of the sustainability-linked bond (SLB) market in attracting those companies that are crucial for a successful sustainability transition, namely carbon-intensive companies and companies that are lagging behind in their sustainability transition. The second research paper investigates how banks can improve and tailor their SFI support to their customers, and the third research paper analyzes how SFIs and the incentive structure need to be adapted to small and medium-sized companies (SMEs) and companies relying on bank-based financing.

The first paper offers important insights into the SLB market, which offers a promising approach to incentivize companies to implement their transition strategy and is growing rapidly. Sustainability-linked instruments require companies to set company-level sustainability targets and implement a financial consequence, for example in the form of a coupon step-up, should the company fail to achieve its set sustainability targets. Thereby, companies are encouraged to develop a credible transition strategy with a transparent reporting mechanism, as well as to ensure the achievement of their transition strategy. From a company perspective, sustainability-linked instruments offer the opportunity to transparently communicate their transition strategy and a potential pricing advantage, so-called premium, compared to a conventional financing instrument. Consequently, sustainability-linked instruments are a promising SFI. *But does the SLB market efficiently attract companies that are crucial for a successful sustainability transition, namely companies that are carbon-intensive and are lagging behind in their sustainability transition, thereby promising the largest emission reduction potential?*

In order to assess the SLB markets' mechanism and accessibility, the paper develops a conceptual framework and analyzes companies' probability to issue a SLB by running probit and logit regressions based on the framework and subsequently calculating the respective risk ratios. The research results demonstrate that the SLB market indeed attracts carbon-intensive industries, but fails to attract companies that are lagging behind in their sustainability transition, termed ESG laggards. In fact, ESG laggards and companies without an ESG rating have a significantly lower probability to issue a SLB. This indicates a SLB market entry barrier for companies that are lagging behind in their sustainability transition, likely caused by the fact that they are faced with extensive data collection and reporting requirements, which are costly to implement and can prevent them from entering the SLB market. However, it would be especially important that those companies start to transition.

In fact, SLBs offer an attractive opportunity for companies that are carbon-intensive and companies that are lagging behind in their sustainability transition to transparently communicate their transition strategy, which becomes increasingly important in terms of financing access and financing conditions. Furthermore, the results suggest that a sustainability-linked structure can be particularly beneficial for companies that have a low credit rating, as it can improve a financial instrument's attractiveness compared to a conventional instrument with a higher credit rating.

Nevertheless, the research results demonstrate that the SLB market must not only improve its accessibility, but also its transparency and credibility. Greenwashing and credibility concerns are currently among the biggest barriers to SLB use. The results indicate that companies should start with short-term sustainability targets, in line with a long-term transition plan, rather than directly setting long-term climate-neutrality target claims. This could also help lower the entry barrier for companies lagging behind in their sustainability transition, as setting and reaching short-term sustainability targets could appear more feasible to them.

Despite the identified challenges, the results confirm the SLB market's growth potential. Furthermore, the paper finds that the EU legislations have successfully established a common sustainability investment environment and the paper therefore recommends that any adjustments regarding the accessibility and transparency of SLBs should be implemented on the EU level rather than the country level. Overall, the results contribute to the literature on sustainability-linked instruments, which has so far been primarily focused on pricing, by focusing on the effectiveness of the market, incentivization and implementation mechanisms.

The second research paper complements the findings of the first paper that SFI use and needs might differ for companies based on their sustainability transition progress. In fact, sustainability regulations apply to companies depending on their company size and whether the company is listed. Moreover, the increase in transparency regarding companies' sustainability performance can have different effects on their financing, depending on the company's industry, as for instance carbon-intensive industries are more often subject to divestment and exclusion criteria. Based on these observations, banks should provide more tailored sustainable finance support in line with companies' individual sustainable finance needs. *But how do companies differ in their sustainable finance interests and needs, and how can banks provide tailored sustainable finance support to their credit customers accordingly?*

The research question is answered by applying a mixed method approach, using regression and thematic content analysis, as well as by conducting a survey with 700 corporate customers of a large German bank. Based on the recorded observations, the research paper identifies and analyzes seven push and pull factors, as well as barriers to SFI use, in regard to differences between company sizes, sectors and capital market activity. The research results demonstrate that SFI use indeed significantly differs between company sizes, sectors and capital market activity. Furthermore, the analysis indicates significant differences in companies' SFI interests and needs particularly with respect to company sizes, emphasizing that banks should tailor their sustainable finance support accordingly.

In fact, smaller companies demonstrate a lower awareness and knowledge regarding how sustainability regulations and transparency can affect their financing access and conditions, as well as how SFIs work and how they can be beneficial. Moreover, in regard to SFI use barriers, smaller companies state predominantly insufficient consulting and the applicability of SFIs. Both observations indicate that smaller companies might need a more fundamental consultation than larger companies, supporting a more tailored sustainable finance support.

Additionally, the research paper shows that companies in general, irrespective of size, sector and capital market activity, experience regulatory and transformative pressure, but are not sufficiently aware of how this can impact their financing access and conditions. The qualitative evaluation supports this observation, as companies demand more information regarding SFI use from their banks, as well as clear expectations how sustainability performance measures might affect their financing access and conditions.

In regard to SFI barriers, companies predominantly report bureaucracy, lack of sustainability data and choice of sustainability targets. In order to overcome these barriers they would like to receive best practice examples from their financing partners and see their bank as a sparring partner that supports them in financing their sustainability transition. Furthermore, the analysis results demonstrate the need for a more simplified and standardized SFI process, but also show that proactively suggesting SFI use can be a first step to increase SFI use. Overall, this research paper contributes to the literature on companies' SFI use and behavior by identifying companies' individual sustainable finance interests and needs, as well as by formulating three recommendations on how banks can advance and support SFI use by tailoring their sustainable finance support to smaller companies accordingly, improving sustainable finance awareness and knowledge, and simplifying the implementation of SFIs.

The third research paper adds to the findings of the second research paper, that companies differ significantly in their SFI needs and interests, by taking a closer look at companies that rely on bank-based financing. Companies that are not active in capital markets are not exposed to the same sustainability regulations and market environments as companies active in capital markets. This could influence how they can be successfully incentivized to use SFIs. Furthermore, in Germany's bank-based financial system, companies that rely on bank-based financing predominantly have a house bank relation, which can be defined as a long-term, close relation with a bank that provides all core financial services (Behr & Schmidt, 2016; Hackethal, 2004). The characteristics of a house bank relation can also influence whether and how companies use SFIs. Consequently, this research paper analyzes *whether and how the currently implemented sustainable finance incentivization scheme might need to be adapted for companies not active in capital markets and how the characteristics of a house bank relation can be utilized for an efficient SFI use.* Both evaluations are performed with a special consideration of SMEs not active in capital markets.

The research paper applies a mixed method approach, using logistic regression and thematic content analysis, and uses the same database, collected through a survey with 700 corporate customers of a large German bank, as the second research paper. The results confirm that companies not active in capital markets have a significantly lower share of SFI users. Furthermore, companies not active in capital markets differ in regard to their motivational, implementation and enabling factors to use SFIs, compared to companies active in capital markets. In fact, companies that rely solely on bank-based financing perceive a lower regulatory pressure and transition risk. Moreover, compared to companies active in capital markets, they cannot benefit from reputational advantages resulting from SFI use in capital markets, in the same manner. Consequently, the research results indicate that companies not active in capital markets can be predominantly incentivized to use SFIs through a pricing advantage.

Green and sustainability-linked loans can potentially offer such a pricing advantage, in the form of a premium, but also have precise and binding sustainability data and reporting requirements. The research results show that this poses a challenge to companies not active in capital markets, as they report insufficient data availability and monitoring, as well as a lack of sustainable finance knowledge and experience as barriers to SFI use. This observation suggests that SFIs should be adapted for companies not active in capital markets, and particularly SMEs not active in capital markets, taking their current level of data availability into consideration. Based on the research results, a form of SFIs that could be an, at least temporary, efficient alternative for companies not active in capital markets, that are currently unable to meet sustainability data requirements of sustainability-linked or green loans, could be promotional loans. They foster investments into companies' sustainability transition, offering a clear pricing or risk advantage compared to conventional instruments, but have lower sustainability data requirements.

Regardless of whether the intended instrument is a green, sustainability-linked or promotional loan, banks play a crucial role in advising and supporting companies in regard to their SFI use. However, the research results demonstrate that companies not active in capital markets experience a high uncertainty regarding their banks' role and potential support. Furthermore, the research paper shows a very low recommendation of SFI use by banks for companies not active in capital markets, and the effect is even stronger for SMEs not active in capital markets. The analysis indicates that banks are not making sufficient use of their long-term relations with their corporate customers, including benefits such as an in-depth knowledge of companies' business and an established trust, which could be used to foster investments into companies' sustainability transition. Consequently, the paper emphasizes the importance of banks, and particularly regional banks, to advance and improve their sustainable finance support.

Overall, the third research paper contributes to the current literature on sustainable finance in bank-based financial systems by identifying how companies not active in capital markets differ in their motivational, implementational and enabling factors to use SFIs, as well as by formulating recommendations on how SFIs can be adapted accordingly and how the benefits of house bank relations can be utilized.

This dissertation has developed three main calls for action, based on the findings of the three research papers, that can provide a piece of the key to unlock the full potential of sustainable finance and thereby contribute to the overarching goal of mobilizing the necessary sustainability investments.

Firstly, sustainability disclosure regulations are necessary to create a common basis for comparable sustainability performance measures. However, they should not paralyze companies in regard to their sustainability transition. The risk of a potential adverse effect is imminent and particularly in regard to SMEs should be evaluated carefully.

Secondly, it is crucial to recognize companies' individual sustainable finance interests and needs, and to adapt SFI requirements and structure accordingly. SFIs need to be able to grow in terms of their binding requirements and structures in line with companies' data availability and reporting progress.

Thirdly, existing and established structures, such as long-term house bank relations and their benefits, have to be leveraged to foster sustainability transition investments. The financial sector should not be reduced to implementing sustainability disclosure regulations, but given the room to utilize its established infrastructure to support an efficient and effective SFI use.

The research and findings of this dissertation are equally relevant for banks, companies and politics. For policy makers, as they emphasize the need for sustainable finance instruments and regulations that are more adapted to companies' level of sustainability data availability and reporting. This is particularly important for companies relying on bank-based financing and SMEs. Furthermore, the results demonstrate that promotional loans can be an, at least temporary, efficient instrument to foster sustainability transition investments for those companies. However, the findings also emphasize the need for determining a price for environmental pollution and in this context the introduction of, for instance, risk-weighted adjustment factors to capital requirements, in order to ensure an effective SFI, whilst returning to market-based structures.

Regarding the relevance for companies, the research results demonstrate that they need to improve their sustainable finance awareness and knowledge, as well as that they still need to catch up in terms of the required sustainability data collection and monitoring. Finally, the results of this dissertation are especially relevant for the financial sector, in particular banks, as they point out that banks need to improve their sustainable finance support in terms of consultation, actively advising companies on SFI use, and becoming a sparring partner for companies in their pursuit to finance their sustainability transition.

References

Behr, P., & Schmidt, R. H. (2016). The German banking system: Characteristics and challenges. In T. Beck and B. Casu (Eds.), *The Palgrave handbook of European banking (pp. 541–566).* Palgrave Macmillan London. https://doi.org/10.1057/978-1-137-52144-6

Buchner, B., Naran, B., Padmanabhi, R., Stout, S., Strinati, C., Wignarajah, D., Miao, G., Connolly, J., & Marini, N. (2023). *Global landscape of climate finance 2023.* Climate Policy Initiative. https://www.climatepolicyinitiative.org/wp-content/uploads/2023/11/Global-Landscape-of-Climate-Finance-2023.pdf

Bundesregierung. (2021). *Climate Change Act 2021: Intergenerational contract for the climate.* Retrieved June 7, 2024, from https://www.bundesregierung.de/breg-de/schwerpunkte/klimaschutz/climate-change-act-2021-1936846

Deutsche Bundesbank. (2023). *Nachhaltigkeitsrisiken in der Bankenaufsicht.* https://www.bundesbank.de/resource/blob/908142/135778eb15c61c27b515e2ba955aa176/mL/2023-04-nachhaltigkeit-bankenaufsicht-data.pdf

European Banking Authority. (2023). *On the role of environmental and social risks in the prudential framework.* https://www.eba.europa.eu/sites/default/files/document_library/Publications/Reports/2023/1062711/Report%20on%20the%20role%20of%20environmental%20and%20social%20risks%20in%20the%20prudential%20framework.pdf

European Central Bank. (2022). *Walking the talk – banks gearing up to manage risks from climate change and environmental degradation.* https://www.bankingsupervision.europa.eu/ecb/pub/pdf/ssm.thematicreviewcerreport112022~2eb322a79c.en.pdf

European Commission. (2019). *Financing sustainable growth.* https://finance.ec.europa.eu/system/files/2020-01/200108-financing-sustainable-growth-factsheet_en.pdf

European Commission. (2024a). *The European Green Deal.* Retrieved June 7, 2024, from https://commission.europa.eu/strategy-and-policy/priorities-2019-2024/european-green-deal_en

European Commission. (2024b). *Overview of sustainable finance.* Retrieved June 7, 2024, from https://finance.ec.europa.eu/sustainable-finance/overview-sustainable-finance_en

European Commission. (2024c). *EU taxonomy for sustainable activities.* Retrieved June 7, 2024 from https://finance.ec.europa.eu/sustainable-finance/tools-and-standards/eu-taxonomy-sustainable-activities_en

European Commission. (2024d). *Corporate sustainability reporting.* Retrieved June 7, 2024, from_https://finance.ec.europa.eu/capital-markets-union-and-financial-markets/company-reporting-and-auditing/company-reporting/corporate-sustainability-reporting_en

European Commission. (2024e)._*Sustainability-related disclosure in the financial service sector.* Retrieved June 7, 2024, from https://finance.ec.europa.eu/sustainable-finance/disclosures/sustainability-related-disclosure-financial-services-sector_en

Federal Financial Supervisory Authority. (2023). *Minimum requirements for risk management.* Retrieved June 19, 2024, from https://www.bafin.de/SharedDocs/Downloads/EN/Rundschreiben/dl_rs_0523_marisk_ba_en.html

Georgieva, K. & Adrian, T. (2022). *Public sector must play major role in catalyzing private climate finance.* International Monetary Fund. https://www.imf.org/en/Blogs/Articles/2022/08/18/public-sector-must-play-major-role-in-catalyzing-private-climate-finance

Hackethal, A. (2004). German banks and banking structure. In J. P. Krahnen and R. H. Schmidt (Eds.), *The German financial system* (pp. 71–105). Oxford University Press.

Hinsche, I. C. (2021). A greenium for the Next Generation EU Green Bonds analysis of a potential green bond premium and its drivers. *Center for Financial Studies Working Paper,* (663). https://dx.doi.org/10.2139/ssrn.3965664

Intergovernmental Panel on Climate Change. (2023). Summary for policymakers. In H. Lee & J. Romero (Eds.), *Climate Change 2023: Synthesis Report. Contribution of Working Groups I, II and III to the Sixth Assessment Report of the Intergovernmental Panel on Climate Change (pp. 1–34).* https://www.ipcc.ch/report/ar6/syr/downloads/report/IPCC_AR6_SYR_SPM.pdf

Chapter 1 Mirror, Mirror on the Wall, Who Is Transitioning Amongst Them All?

An Analysis of the Sustainability-Linked Bond Market's Efficiency in Attracting the Most Crucial Companies for a Successful Sustainability Transition

Isabelle Cathérine Hinsche and Rainer Klump[*+]

Abstract

In order to reach climate neutrality by 2050, the European Union is taking action in the form of extensive sustainability regulations with the aim to push the private sector towards sustainable economic activities. In this context, a new instrument to finance a company's sustainability transition has been developed: the sustainability-linked bond (SLB). This paper analyzes the SLB market's efficiency in attracting those companies that are most crucial for a successful sustainability transition, namely carbon-intensive companies and companies that are lagging behind in their sustainability transition, defined as ESG laggards. By developing a conceptual framework for the SLB market and running a probit and logit regression estimation, this paper shows that the SLB market efficiently attracts carbon-intensive companies, but fails to attract ESG laggards. Moreover, the paper identifies four success factors for the SLB market to improve its future accessibility and credibility.

JEL Classification: C25, G10, G14, G18, G38, Q01, Q58

Keywords: Sustainable Finance, Sustainability-Linked Bonds, Transition Financing, Sustainable Investing, ESG, Market Efficiency

---

* We would like to thank Marcus Pratsch, Bettina Streiter, Franziska Lamprecht, Klaus Thuß, Jasmin Tur, Florian Moser and Anna-Maria Maurer for intriguing discussions, valuable input and support. Furthermore, we thank participants in the DIW/DSGV-Workshop in Berlin, May 11–12, 2023 for their helpful comments and suggestions. The usual disclaimer applies.

+ Published in a similiar version in DIW Vierteljahresheft zur Wirtschaftsforschung, Volume 3, 2023.

1.1 Introduction

The nations of the world are confronted with the challenge of climate change, as well as its ecological and societal consequences. They therefore increasingly make use of policy tools that try to achieve a transition towards more sustainable economic activities. The development of public policies to address climate change is known in the United States as the Green New Deal, whilst the European Union (EU) has adopted the European Green Deal. The latter, with a total promised budget of €600 billion, has set the political goal to reduce greenhouse gas emissions drastically and to become climate neutral by 2050 (European Commission, 2023a). However, public sector investments alone are insufficient to reach this target. The sustainable transition investment gap, in Europe alone, is estimated to be up to €290 billion annually (European Commission, 2019).

Consequently, the EU introduced the Action Plan on Sustainable Finance Growth (European Commission, 2020a), which incorporates three extensive legislations regarding the classification of sustainable activities, as well as transparent sustainability reporting and benchmarks. These regulatory requirements increase the pressure on the private sector to transition towards sustainable economic activities, thereby acquiring the necessary investments for a successful sustainability transition. The financial sector plays a key role in the implementation of these regulations. It has, on the one hand, started to incorporate sustainability criteria into investment and credit assessments to push investments towards sustainable activities and, on the other hand, developed specific financial instruments to finance particularly the sustainability transition.

Transition financing can be divided into two main groups, use-of-proceeds and sustainability-linked instruments. Use-of-proceeds instruments are restricted to financing or refinancing a classified sustainable project and can be issued independently of the issuer's sustainability (International Capital Market Association (ICMA), 2021). One of the most commonly used instruments is a green bond, which assigns the proceeds to a green investment project. In contrast, sustainability-linked instruments take a company-level sustainability perspective and allow for proceeds to be used flexibly according to a company's investment strategy (ICMA, 2023). Moreover, the company needs to set overall sustainability targets in line with their economic activities and pays a financial penalty in the case of failure to achieve these targets, for instance in the form of a coupon step-up.

So far, research has focused on the pricing and credibility of sustainability-linked instruments. The sustainability-linked bond (SLB) is an attractive instrument for issuers to communicate their transition strategy. It might even present an opportunity for issuers to receive a lower yield, a so-called premium, than they would have received for a comparable conventional bond (Berrada et al., 2022; Kölbel & Lambillon, 2022). Consequently, the SLB market has been growing rapidly in the last few years. Nevertheless, investors also show concern regarding the credibility and greenwashing potential of SLBs, especially in regard to the ambitiousness and materiality of sustainability targets and transition pathways (Vulturius et al., 2022; Liberadzki et al., 2021). However, the existing literature has not yet considered the efficiency of the SLB market in attracting those companies that are most crucial for a successful sustainability transition.

For a successful sustainability transition, carbon-intensive industries are imperative, as they promise the potential of high overall carbon emission reductions. Moreover, within the carbon-intensive industries, companies vary greatly in their progress to decarbonize and to transition their economic activities towards sustainability. Refinitiv sustainability ratings represent a company's relative sustainability performance respective to the industry level and thereby allow to differentiate between ESG leaders and ESG laggards, the latter defining companies which are lagging behind in their sustainability transition. Consequently, in order to ensure an economy-wide successful sustainability transition, the SLB market should attract particularly carbon-intensive industries and ESG laggards. But does the SLB market efficiently attract this target group?

This paper answers the question by developing a conceptual framework of the SLB market and subsequently testing the SLB market structures and accessibility to the relevant target groups. Based on the increasing pressure for transformation due to the implementation of sustainable finance regulations and the assumption of an efficient SLB market, carbon-intensive industries and ESG laggards should have a higher probability to issue a SLB. Moreover, the framework defines eight market, company and financial characteristics that could potentially influence a company's probability to issue a SLB through the established SLB market structures. One criterion is the issuer home market, which could influence the probability to issue a SLB apart from a company's industry and relative sustainability performance. The level of sustainability regulations adaptation differs even between EU countries and consequently leads to varying supportive environments, which could affect the attractiveness of the SLB market for issuers. Moreover, any potential effects of the issuer market are likely to become stronger for a more mature market, defining the second criterion, market maturity. Furthermore, the regulatory pressure of the sustainable finance regulations can vary depending on a company's size and can thereby affect its probability to issue a SLB. Additional company characteristics, which could also have an influence on the probability to issue a SLB, are a company's credit rating and sustainable finance experience. Lastly, financial characteristics could also play an influential role, namely the financial instrument's issue size, maturity and currency, defining the sixth, seventh and eighth criterion.

Based on the conceptual framework, the paper estimates the significance of the different influential variables on the probability to issue a SLB, using a probit choice model. Moreover, the estimations' robustness is tested using a logit choice model and the risk ratios for the respective significant variables are calculated. The regression analysis is run on a data sample that focuses on the European bond market and the sustainability transition of the real economy, thus omitting bond issues by financial and governmental institutions. The probit regression is run for a final sample consisting of 2,138 bonds, including normal, green, sustainability, social and (green) sustainability-linked bonds, which were issued by a total of 823 companies in the period September 2019 to November 2022.

The results show that the SLB market does indeed efficiently attract carbon-intensive industries. Being a company from the carbon-intensive materials or utilities sector more than triples the probability to issue a SLB. However, the SLB market does not efficiently attract ESG laggards. In fact, companies that have a below-average sustainability performance within their respective industry, and are thus considered ESG laggards, have an 80 % decrease in the probability to issue a SLB.

Regarding the eight estimated market, company and financial characteristic effects, the results show that the first criterion, the issuer market, has a significant effect on the probability to issue a SLB, with a similar magnitude for the included EU countries. This indicates that the EU regulations create a comparable conducive sustainable investment environment. Secondly, the probability to issue a SLB increases with market maturity, implying further growth potential. Thirdly, the analysis shows that a company's size, measured in terms of both revenue and employee size, does not have a significant effect. Moreover, a company's sustainable finance experience, the fourth criterion, is insignificant. However, a company's credit rating at the time of the bond issuance, the fifth criterion, is significant, as companies with a lower credit rating a more likely to issue a SLB than companies with an upper investment grade credit rating. Regarding the financial characteristics, a bond's currency, the sixth criterion, does not have a significant effect. But, the estimation results demonstrate a significant impact for bond issue size, the seventh criterion, as having a bond issue size larger than $1,250 million almost triples the probability to issue a SLB. Finally, for the eight criterion, a bond's maturity, the analysis finds that a bond issuance with a maturity of five to ten years increases the probability to issue a SLB by 45 %.

The paper contributes to the existing literature by analyzing the efficiency of the SLB market and by identifying four success factors for the SLB market to improve its accessibility for potential SLB issuers and credibility amongst sustainable investors. For a successful sustainability transition, the SLB market needs to attract those companies that are most crucial for advancing the economy's transition. This means that the SLB market needs to ensure the accessibility and market structures to particularly attract carbon-intensive industries and ESG laggards. This research paper shows that the SLB market efficiently attracts carbon-intensive companies, but fails to engage companies that are lagging behind in their sustainability transformation. These ESG laggards need to be particularly targeted, as they should have a substantially high incentive to transition their economic activities, based on the pressure for transformation through sustainable finance regulations. Consequently, the findings of this paper imply the need for sustainability policies, market structures and instruments that are especially adapted for ESG laggards.

The paper is structured as follows: section 2 gives an introduction to transformation policy measures and financing instruments, as well as the sustainability-linked bond market, and relates it to the relevant literature on sustainability-linked bonds. Section 3 develops the conceptual framework for the SLB market structures and potentially influential factors. Based on this framework, Section 4 first defines and subsequently gives a summary of the chosen data sample. Moreover, the empirical methodology is explained and the regression estimations and variables are outlined. Section 5 presents the findings of the regression analysis in regard to the SLB market's efficiency, as well as the impact of the market, company and financial characteristics. Finally, section 6 identifies four success factors for a further improvement of the SLB market and concludes by suggesting areas for future SLB market research.

1.2 Literature Review

1.2.1 The Action Plan on Sustainable Finance Growth

In December 2019, the European Commission presented the European Green Deal, with the aim to transform the European Union (EU) into a modern, resource-efficient and competitive economy (European Commission, 2023a). One of the biggest goals is to reduce greenhouse gas emissions by at least 55 % by 2030 and to be climate-neutral by 2050. In order to achieve these targets, Europe requires between €175 and €290 billion in annual sustainability transition investments for the upcoming decades (European Commission, 2019). As part of the European Green Deal Investment Plan (2020b), which aims to mobilize at least €1 trillion of sustainable investments over the next decade, the EU has committed to contribute €600 billion for the sustainability transition through the EU budget and the Next Generation EU Recovery Plan (European Commission, 2023a). However, these public sector contributions are far from closing the green finance gap. Consequently, the EU additionally developed the Action Plan on Sustainable Finance Growth (European Commission, 2020a), which entails three main legislations that are supposed to incentivize and channel private sector investments into a green and sustainable transformation.

The first key legislation is the EU Taxonomy, which is a unified classification of economic activities in regard to their sustainability contributions (European Commission, 2021). This is supplemented by several disclosure legislations, such as the Sustainable Finance Disclosure Regulation (SFDR) and the Non-Financial Reporting Directive (NFRD), which will soon be replaced by the Corporate Sustainability Reporting Directive (CSRD)[1]. These legislations ensure improved

1 The SFDR defines sustainability disclosure obligations for financial institutions and financial advisors. The NFRD requires companies to report on both, how climate change affects their business and how their business impacts the climate. On January 5th 2023, the NFRD was replaced by the CSRD, strengthening the reporting rules and expanding the mandatory corporate sustainability reporting to a larger set of companies (European Commission, 2023b; European Commission 2023c).

transparency concerning non-financial information, which is necessary for investors to make informed sustainable investment decisions (European Commission, 2021). Finally, the EU has developed several tools to aid companies and financial intermediaries in setting ambitious sustainability goals and preventing greenwashing. This includes the EU Climate Benchmark Regulation, which consists of the EU climate transition and Paris-aligned benchmarks[2].

1.2.2 Transition Financing

Through the three key legislations, the EU Green Deal Investment Plan increases transparency and improves the disclosure of non-financial information, thereby pushing the private sector towards more sustainable economic activities (Schütze & Stede, 2021). For the successful implementation of these legislations, the financial sector is being actively involved to adopt the regulatory requirements in the form of adjusted financing instruments and revised risk assessment methods that incorporate sustainability criteria, among others. Moreover, financial institutions are expected to ensure the climate-alignment[3] of their portfolios and are thereby driven to increase low-carbon investments and to support the transition of carbon-intensive sectors (Platform on Sustainable Finance, 2021). Among the most prominent tools to advance the economy's sustainability transition are sustainable finance instruments. In order to ensure a real economic impact, the instruments need to encourage Paris-aligned economic activities, which means activities in line with the goals of the Paris Agreement, such as limiting global warming to well-below 2°C, and to enable issuers to manage their climate-related risks (Caldecott, 2020). For instance, sustainable finance instruments can incentivize companies to align their practices to a ze-

2 The EU climate transition benchmark (EU CTB) and the EU Paris-aligned benchmark (EU PAB) aim to improve ESG transparency and comparability among benchmarks, as well as to provide minimum technical requirements to avoid greenwashing (European Commission, 2023d).

3 A climate-aligned portfolio takes into account the necessary emission reductions to reach the 1.5°C target (Platform on Sustainable Finance, 2021).

ro-emission future by reducing the cost of capital for Paris-compatible activities (Caldecott, 2020).

One of the most influential levers for a company's sustainability transition is debt financing, which led to the growing market of transition financing. Transition financing can be divided into two major categories, use of proceeds instruments and sustainability-linked instruments[4]. Use of proceeds instruments are characterized by the restrictive allocation of proceeds to classified environmental or socially beneficial projects (Climate Bonds Initiative (CBI), 2022a). The most common use of proceeds instrument is a green bond, which allocates all proceeds to a predetermined climate or environmentally valuable project (Hinsche, 2021). In contrast, sustainability-linked instruments allow for proceeds to be used for general purposes, thereby taking a company-level sustainability perspective, rather than a project focus (ICMA, 2023). One prominent example of this category is the sustainability-linked bond.

1.2.3 Sustainability-Linked Bonds

According to the Sustainability-Linked Bond Principles (SLBP), a SLB is a financial instrument, which defines company-level sustainability targets and demands a penalty, for example in form of a coupon step-up, if the company should fail to meet its targets (ICMA, 2023). In advance of the issuance, the company defines Key Performance Indicators (KPIs) that measure the respective sustainability targets, as well as Sustainability Performance Indicators (SPTs), which indicate the desired level of the KPIs[5]. Both, KPIs and SPTs, are reported in the SLB Framework, as well as the timeline for the achievement of the KPIs.

4 In some cases, the two instruments are combined, leading to a green sustainability-linked bond, for example.

5 KPIs can consist of environmental, social, as well as governance criteria and can either be measured by an external ESG rating or predefined metrics, for example greenhouse gas (GHG) emission intensity. SPTs set the desired level of achievement, which in the case of a greenhouse gas emission (GHG) intensity metric would be measured in gCO2/kWh.

Moreover, the issuer decides which bond characteristic they would like to tie to the fulfillment of the KPIs and what the penalty scenario should be. The most commonly used bond adjustment in case of failure to reach the sustainability targets is a coupon step-up (Vulturius et al., 2022). The International Capital Markets Association (ICMA, 2023) recommends that the SLB Framework is verified through an external and independent party in form of a Second Party Opinion, certifying that the SLB issuance is in line with the SLBP.

1.2.4 Sustainability-Linked Bond Market

Sustainability-linked instrument issuances have increased rapidly in the last three years, with sustainability-linked bonds being the fastest-growing segment of the sustainability bond market (Vulturius et al., 2022). SLBs make up 11 % of total sustainable finance debt issuances in the first half of 2022, even though the first SLB was issued only in December 2018 (CBI, 2022a). The growth is likely driven by the fact that SLBs can be used by a broader range of issuers compared to green bonds. For instance, companies that would not be able to issue a green bond, due to insufficiently large capital expenditures connected to a potential sustainability project, can issue a SLB (CBI, 2022a). Moreover, companies can use existing company-level sustainability performance indicators and reporting structures to set KPIs and SPTs, instead of setting up project-level tracking and reporting practices. This is especially attractive for smaller issuers, as it lowers issuance costs. Furthermore, SLBs offer companies the opportunity to signal their sustainability strategy and give them more flexibility in how to use the proceeds to achieve their successful sustainability transition (Liberadzki et al., 2021). This is crucial, especially for carbon-intensive industries, because financial institutions are increasingly incorporating sustainability indicators in their risk assessments and credit analysis (Bundesanstalt für Finanzdienstleistungen (BaFin), 2019). Consequently, companies have to be able to either already perform well in regard to their sustainability or to provide a credible transition plan to improve their sustainability.

The increased demand for SLBs has fueled a discussion about the pricing mechanisms and the existence of a potential premium for issuers, similar to the so-called Greenium in the green bond market. Even though the existence of a Greenium in the green bond market is still being debated (Hinsche, 2021) and the SLB market is still very young, there are two research papers which try to detect a potential premium for SLB issuers. Kölbel and Lambillon (2022) apply a matching method in their research, which has also been used in a similar manner to calculate a potential green bond premium (Zerbib, 2019; Larcker & Watts, 2020; Flammer 2020). They find a statistically significant average sustainability premium of -29.2 bps, indicating that issuers can benefit from a SLB issuance. Employing a similar method, an analysis by the Climate Bonds Initiative (2022b) supports these results, as they find 14 SLBs in the years 2021 and 2022 that were priced with a significant premium, ranging from -4 bps to -34 bps.

Moreover, Kölbel and Lambillon (2022) show that the average penalty coupon step-up is lower than the average sustainability premium, indicating that companies could benefit from lower costs of capital even in the scenario that they fail to achieve their sustainability performance targets. These results suggest that there could be a "free lunch" for SLB issuers. However, the authors also point out that one-third of SLB issuers do not benefit from a premium at all, showing that the SLB market is still very young and that pricing mechanisms are very volatile. The second paper searching for a potential SLB premium, by Berrada et al. (2022), makes use of a one-period SLB pricing model to measure and analyze the potential mispricing of SLBs. The authors demonstrate that one-quarter of SLBs is overpriced at issuance and will experience a following price drop in the secondary market. This indicates that the industry overestimates SLB issuance benefits, which leads to a price premium for issuers (Berrada et al., 2022).

1.2.5 Risks and Challenges for Sustainability-Linked Bonds

As explained above, SLBs offer a great opportunity for companies to finance their sustainability transition. However, researchers and financial market participants are also pointing out potential problems in regard to a SLB's credibility and effectiveness. For instance, the ICMA (2023) recommends using science-based emission targets to ensure that a company's sustainability transition is Paris aligned. However, it does not define how to evaluate a KPI's and SPT's ambitiousness in relation to different sectors and how to assess the target's materiality regarding the company's sustainability transition (Vulturius et al., 2022). Consequently, companies might choose more feasible SPTs, thereby decreasing a SLB's transition effectiveness. Moreover, as SLBs are general-purpose instruments, investors are skeptical about the lack of transparency regarding the use of proceeds and their contribution to the issuer's sustainability transition (Ul Haq & Doumbia, 2022).

Furthermore, investors are skeptical about whether the penalty coupon step-up is high enough in most cases, to ensure sufficient incentivization for companies to prioritize their sustainability transition. In fact, Kölbel and Lambillon (2022) show that companies might benefit from a "free lunch", suggesting that SLB penalty coupon step-ups are not high enough. Finally, SLB investors are concerned about the potential reputational harm of profiting from a margin adjustment in case the SLB issuer should fail to reach their targets (UniCredit, 2022). Overall, there is substantial greenwashing concern from both, the issuer side in regard to choosing the right KPIs and SPTs, as well as the investor side (Natixis, 2021).

So far, research has focused on the functionality of a SLB's incentive characteristics and the pricing mechanisms in the market. However, in order to ensure a successful transition towards a zero-emission economy, the type of SLB issuer is crucial as well. In fact, high-emitting sectors are imperative for an economy-wide transition (CBI, 2022a). Moreover, within these high-emitting sectors, companies differ vastly in their progress with regard to decarbonization and their sustainability transition. Refinitiv (2022) calculates ESG[6] ratings that evaluate a company's sustainability level relative to the respective industry level. For instance, Shell PLC, one of the biggest oil and gas companies worldwide, has a Refinitiv ESG Rating of A+, which marks it as an ESG leader (Refinitiv, 2023). Even though the industry itself is very carbon-intensive, Shell PLC has the best sustainability performance relative to all 404 rated companies in the oil and gas industry. Taking this into consideration, a successful transition not only includes carbon-intensive industries but especially needs to target companies that are falling behind in terms of their sustainability transition, subsequently termed as ESG laggards. Consequently, an efficient SLB market with the goal of a successful economy-wide sustainability transformation requires accessibility and market structures that particularly attract carbon-intensive industries and ESG laggards.

1.3 Conceptual Framework

The following section develops a conceptual framework to assess the efficiency of the regulatory pressure for transformation and the SLB market in attracting those companies that are crucial for a successful sustainability transition. With the overarching goal to achieve the 2°C Paris target, the sustainability legislations should create pressure particularly for carbon-intensive industries and ESG laggards to transform their economic activities, as explained above. Complementary, the SLB market should offer an attractive environment for these companies to finance their sustainability transition. The efficiency of the sustainability legislations and the SLB market in attracting carbon-intensive industries and ESG laggards is measured through the probability to issue a SLB. Based on the pressure for transformation through regulatory requirements and the assumption of an efficient SLB market, carbon-intensive industries and ESG laggards should have a higher probability to issue a SLB compared to low-carbon industries and ESG leaders. The

6 ESG ratings contain ecological, social and governance criteria to assess a company's sustainability level.

subsequent analysis tests this hypothesis by estimating the probability to issue a SLB based on a company's industry and sustainability performance, whilst controlling for influential market, company and financial characteristics. The following framework defines the potential criteria which could represent either possible barriers to entering the SLB market or opportunities to more precisely address carbon-intensive ESG laggards. As seen in Figure 1, the framework divides the potentially influential factors into five broad categories, including a company's industry and relative sustainability performance, as well as market, company and financial characteristics.

1.3.1 Sustainability Transformation Target Groups

Due to the fact that companies from carbon-intensive industries have a higher pressure to implement their sustainability transformation, as explained above, they should have a higher probability to issue a SLB to obtain debt financing and to communicate their transition strategy. As of January 27th 2023, there are 773 SLBs outstanding, with the majority of issuers coming from the industrials (19 %), materials (17 %) and utilities (15 %) sectors (see Appendix B, Figure 2). This indicates that companies from carbon-intensive sectors are already present in the SLB market. Nevertheless, the SLB market might be less receptive to carbon-intensive companies, due to investor concern regarding greenwashing and transition credibility, as explained above. Consequently, companies from carbon-intensive industries would have to overcome a higher entry barrier to the SLB market than low-emission companies, making them more hesitant to choose a sustainability-linked structure for their financing instrument.

Figure 1. SLB Market Structure

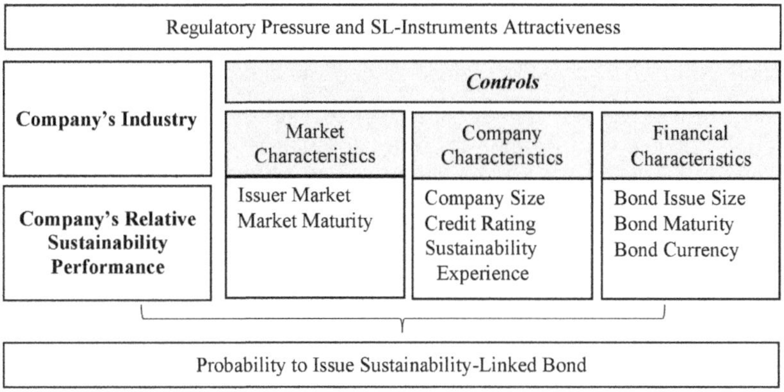

Source: Dr. Isabelle Hinsche

Moreover, companies that are lagging behind in terms of their sustainability performance and transition should have a higher incentive and consequently a higher probability to issue a SLB. However, in order to issue a SLB, companies have to choose appropriate KPIs and SPTs. This process is likely easier for companies that already have an existing sustainability strategy or are at least aware of their own sustainability performance, for instance in the form of an ESG rating. Moreover, an ESG rating might also improve a company's transition credibility amongst sustainability investors. The influence of sustainability knowledge and credibility in the sustainable finance market would suggest that companies which lack an ESG rating might have to overcome a higher barrier to enter the SLB market.

1.3.2 Market Characteristics

Market characteristics might influence the probability to issue a sustainability-linked instrument through several channels. First, the level of adaptation of sustainability regulations can differ between countries and consequently lead to varying supportive environments. For instance, Steffen (2021) shows that even though a lot of green financial policies are decided on the EU level, adaptations on a country level can diverge. By conducting a comparative analysis of green financial policy output among OECD countries, he shows that France, UK and the Netherlands have the highest green financial policy density among European countries. This is supported by findings from D'Orazio and Thole (2022), who develop an index to analyze country-level engagement in climate-related policies. According to their results, France and the Netherlands have the highest climate-related financial policy index (CRFPI) followed by Germany, UK and Sweden. Moreover, not only do countries differ in regard to the number of sustainability regulations but D'Orazio and Thole (2022) also find that a higher density of regulations has a significant impact on climate change mitigation. D'Orazio and Dirks (2022) demonstrate that both, short-term and long-term climate-related financial policies have a negative effect on a country's carbon emissions. This shows that the density and the type of country-level regulations create differing market environments that ultimately affect an economy's transition outcome. Consequently, the issuer market could likely influence the probability to issue a SLB. Furthermore, a more mature SLB market, with a higher number of established issuers and lower pricing volatility, is likely to attract more companies. Overall, the issuer market and the SLB market's maturity could potentially influence the probability to issue a SLB.

1.3.3 Company Characteristics

Regarding the potential influence of company characteristics, the first aspect is a company's size. As EU sustainability disclosure regulations apply to companies based on their size, for instance the NFRD[7] is based on employee count, smaller companies might not need to adhere to these requirements yet and are therefore exposed to a lower regulatory pressure than larger companies. Moreover, issuing a financing instrument with a sustainability structure involves additional costs in

7 The NFRD currently applies to public-interest companies with an employee count larger than 500 (European Commission, 2023b).

terms of both, financial and administrative costs (Gianfrate & Peri, 2019). These costs are relatively lower for larger companies, as they primarily consist of a fixed component, and could thereby influence a company's probability to issue a SLB. Secondly, the company's financial background, measured in terms of its credit rating, could also have an effect on a potential SLB issuance. On the one hand, if a company has a lower credit rating than competitors, it could aim to improve the attractiveness of its financing instrument by choosing a sustainable structure. On the other hand, the SLB market could be less receptive to issuers with a low credit rating, creating a market barrier. Finally, a company's experience with sustainable financing instruments might have an influence on the probability to issue a SLB as well. For instance, if a company has already issued another type of sustainable finance instrument, such as a green bond, they might profit from an existing sustainability reporting structure, as well as an established credibility amongst investors and resulting confidence regarding the use of sustainable financing instruments.

1.3.4 Financial Characteristics

The last category of potentially influential factors are financial characteristics, representing the company's financing needs. First, the company's desired issue size for the financing instrument could play a role in the decision regarding a sustainability-linked structure. Because the issuance of a sustainability-linked instrument is relatively more costly, as explained above, a company might be more likely to choose a sustainability-linked structure for a larger issuance size, especially if they hope to profit from a pricing premium compared to a conventional bond structure. Moreover, also the desired financing length and currency could potentially influence the decision for a SLB issuance. Overall, the conceptual framework has identified eight different market, company and financial characteristic channels, as seen in Figure 1, that could influence the probability of a SLB issuance, apart from a company's industry and sustainability performance. Based on this framework, their respective significance and effect will be assessed in the next section.

1.4 Methodology

1.4.1 Probit Choice Model

Based on the developed conceptual framework for the SLB market in section 3, the following analysis uses a probit choice regression model to assess whether the current regulatory pressure for transformation and the SLB market structures successfully attract carbon-intensive industries and ESG laggards. For this purpose, the regression estimates a company's probability to issue a SLB based on its industry and relative sustainability performance. The binary outcome variable is the observation that the bond has a sustainability-linked structure or not. The independent variables are chosen according to the influential factors determined in the conceptual framework. The subsequent regression analysis determines the significance of the respective independent variables and the likelihood of a sustainability-linked structure based on the assessed significant factors, using a standard normal cumulative distribution function. The robustness of the analysis will be tested by additionally running the regression using a logit choice model, based on a logistic cumulative distribution function. Finally, the respective risk ratios of the significant influential factors will be calculated based on the logit regression coefficients, in order to obtain a comparable measure of influence.

1.4.2 Data and Sample Selection

The analysis focuses on the European SLB market, more precisely on countries for which the European sustainable finance legislations, such as the EU Taxonomy and NFRD, apply and for which issuers are thus embedded in a common regulatory environment with a unified understanding of sustainability. Consequently, it only includes issuer entities that are part of the European Union. The first SLB in the European market was issued by Enel S.p.A. on 10.09.2019. Therefore, the database includes all public bond issuances from 01.09.2019 until 02.11.2022. Moreover, as the analysis wants to evaluate the efficiency of the SLB market structures, the market itself should have reached a certain level of maturity, in order to reduce potential effects due to the infancy and volatility of the market. Therefore, the sample only includes SLB markets that have at least five different SLB issuers on a country level. Finally, this paper focuses on the SLB market mechanisms and the sustainability transition of the real economy. Therefore, the sample excludes financial and governmental institutions as bond issuers. Applying these rules to the database, the final sample consists of 2,138 bonds, including normal, green, sustainability, social and (green) sustainability-linked bonds. The primary data source for the identification of the bond sample and the subsequent analysis is Bloomberg, as well as Refinitiv for the companies' ESG and environmental rating data. The respective Bloomberg and Refinitiv data points are matched based on the individual bond's International Securities Identification Number (ISIN).

1.4.3 Data Summary

The sample includes 823 companies that have issued at least one bond in the time from 01.09.2019 until 02.11.2022, out of which 85 companies have issued at least one SLB. As seen in Table 1a, France has the highest number of companies that have issued at least one SLB, in the following denoted as SLB companies, followed by Luxembourg and the Netherlands. Austria and Germany only have six SLB issuers each, but Austria has the highest density of SLB issuers. In fact, more than a quarter (27 %) of the companies that were active in the debt financing market from 2019 until 2022 have issued a SLB. The majority of SLB companies come from the materials (21 %), industrials (16 %) and consumer discretionary (16 %) sector, as seen in Table 1b. This is in line with the observation by CBI (2022a) that the worldwide

SLB market already includes a significant number of issuances from carbon-intensive sectors.

Table 1. Company and Bond Level Summary Statistics

a. Company's Country of Domicile

Country	Has Issued SLB Indicator		
	0	1	Total
Austria	16	6	22
Germany	102	6	108
France	136	23	159
Italy	95	12	107
Luxembourg	116	14	130
Netherlands	171	13	184
Sweden	102	11	113
Total	738	85	823

Source: Bloomberg as of 02.11.2022.

b. Company's Industry

Industry	Has Issued SLB Indicator		
	0	1	Total
Communications	61	4	65
Consumer Discretionary	175	14	189
Consumer Staples	54	11	65
Energy	43	4	47
Health Care	73	6	79
Industrials	133	14	147
Materials	89	18	107
Technology	54	3	57
Utilities	56	11	67
Total	738	85	823

Source: Bloomberg as of 02.11.2022.

c. Company's ESG Rating

ESG Rating	Has Issued SLB Indicator		
	0	1	Total
A+	53	14	67
A	291	21	312
A-	200	29	229
B+	253	10	263
B	63	7	70
B-	58	4	62
C+	34	1	35
C	52	1	53
C-	8	0	8
D+	4	0	4
D	2	0	2
D-	22	0	22
NR	956	55	1011
Total	1996	142	2138

Source: Refinitiv as of 02.11.2022. Company's ESG rating at the time of issuance. "NR" denotes no rating.

Looking at companies' sustainability performance, 14 % of currently ESG-rated companies have issued a SLB, compared to only 8 % of non-ESG-rated companies (see Appendix A, Table 2a). This could indicate that an ESG rating increases the probability to enter the SLB market. However, the biggest group of sustainability-linked issuers (38 %) does not have an ESG rating, indicating that an ESG rating might not necessarily be an entry barrier to the market. Taking a closer look in Table 1c, the majority of companies that have an ESG rating at the time of issuance either have an A+, A or A- rating. In fact, 26 % of companies with an A+ ESG rating, which thereby belong to the top sustainability performers within their respective industries, have issued a SLB. This suggests that the majority of SLB issuers already have an above-average sustainability performance and that the SLB market includes almost no sustainability laggards. The same holds true for companies' environmental performance at the time of the bond issuance (see Appendix A, Table 2b).

Taking a bond-level view at the sample data, the majority of SLBs was issued in Euro (68 %), followed by US dollars (20 %), and are either callable (82 %) or at maturity (15 %) bonds, thereby mirroring the conventional bond market (see Appendix A, Table 2c and 2d). This is also the case for payment rank distributions, with the majority of SLBs being either senior unsecured (84 %) or secured (14 %), as well as for issue size and time to maturity (see Appendix A, Table 2f and 2g). Moreover, in terms of fiscal year revenue and employee count, sustainability-linked bond issuers have a slightly lower average revenue and employee count (Table 2g, appendix). Interestingly, the majority of sustainability-linked bond issuers have a credit rating at the time of issuance in the range of B to BBB+ (see Appendix A, Table 2e). This could indicate that companies choose a sustainability-linked structure in order to increase attractiveness in contrast to companies with an A- credit rating. The highest density of sustainability-linked issuers can be found for BBB+ rated issuers, supporting this hypothesis (see Appendix A, Table 2e).

1.4.4 Empirical Methodology

As explained above, the following analysis uses a probit choice regression model to estimate a company's probability to issue a SLB based on potentially influential factors. The base regression model for studying the effect of a company's industry and controlling for market, company and financial characteristics can be seen in Equation 1, with further variables for the issuer's sustainability performance being added in the subsequent analysis.

(1) $Pr(SLB = 1) = \Phi\,(\beta_0 + \beta_1{*}Industry + \beta_2{*}Control\ Variables)$

The term Φ defines the standard normal cumulative distribution. *SLB* is a binary dependent variable that denotes whether a bond has a sustainability-linked structure (*SLB*=1) or not (*SLB*=0). The independent categorical variable *Industry* captures the company's sector according to Bloomberg's BICS classification system. A company's relative sustainability performance is measured using the company's Refinitiv ESG rating, which represents a company's ESG performance relative to its respective industry level. The variable *ESGRating* defines the companies' relative sustainability performance based on their respective Refinitiv ESG ratings, namely being a sustainability leader (A+ to B-), a sustainability laggard (C+ to D-) or having no ESG rating. The classification as a sustainability leader or laggard is based on the definition by Refinitiv (2022) that companies with an ESG rating of A+ to B- have a sustainability performance higher than 50 % of sustainability ratings within the same industry, whilst companies with a rating of C+ to D- have a sustainability performance lower or equal to 50 %. The same method is used for developing the variable *EnvRating*, which is based on the Refinitiv environmental rating. The environmental rating only considers the environmental criteria resource use, emissions and innovation, whilst excluding social and governance criteria.

The market controls include *Country* and *IssueDate*, to capture the potential effect of the issuer market, as well as the maturity of the market. An alternative robustness measure for *IssueDate* is *NSLBIssuers*, which measures the number of existing SLB issuers in the market at the time of the bond issuance. Furthermore, the company controls include *Revenue* and *EmployeeCount* as measures for the company's size, as well as an alternative robustness measure called *RevenueGroup*, based on the fiscal year 2021 revenue, which includes more data points and allows to test for significant effects on the respective group size levels. Moreover, the analysis includes the company's *CreditRating* at the time of the bond issuance. For the variable *CreditRating*, the sample is divided into four credit rating groups, differentiating between Upper Investment Grade (AA to A-), Lower Investment Grade (BBB+ to BBB-), Speculative Grade (BB+ to CCC) and having no credit rating. Additionally, a company's sustainability experience in the form of earlier sustainable finance issuances, such as a green bond, is controlled for with the dummy variable *SFExperience*.

Table 3. Overview of Variables

Variable	Description	Type	Unit
SLB	The issued bond has a SLB structure.	Quantitative	Binary (0 or 1)
Industry	An issuer's industry (BICS Level 1).	Qualitative	Categorical
ESGRating	The issuer's Refinitiv ESG rating group: Leader (A+ to B-); Laggard (C+ to D-); No Rating. The ESG rating at the time of the bond issuance is used for the variable.	Quantitative	Group (1–3)
EnvRating	The issuer's Refinitiv Environmental rating group: Leader (A+ to B-); Laggard (C+ to D-); No Rating. The Environmental rating at the time of the bond issuance is used for the variable.	Quantitative	Group (1–3)
Market Characteristics			
Country	An issuer's country of domicil (ISO Code).	Qualitative	Categorical
IssueDate	The bond's issuance quarter calculated based on the issuance date.	Quantitative	Quarters
NSLBIssuers	Number of SLB Issuers in the market at time of the bond issuance.	Quantitative	N. Issuers
Company Characteristics			
Revenue	The issuer's revenue during the fiscal year of the bond issuance.	Quantitative	USD millions
Revenue Group	The issuer's revenue during the fiscal year 2021 grouped according to size, revenues in USD millions (**1** ≤ 500 < **2** ≤ 1,000 < **3** ≤ 5,000 < **4** ≤ 10,000 < **5** ≤ 25,000 < **6** ≤ 50,000 < **7**)).	Quantitative	Group (1–7)
EmployeeCount	The issuer's employee count during the fiscal year of the bond issuance.	Quantiative	N. Employees
CreditRating	The issuer's credit rating group: Upper Investment Grade (AAA-A); Lower Investment Grade (BBB); Speculative Grade (BB-D); NR. The issuer's BB composite credit rating at the time of the bond issuance is used for the variable.	Quantitative	Group (1–4)
SFExperience	The issuer has issued a sustainable finance instrument before (dummy=1).	Quantitative	Binary (0 or 1)
Financial Characteristics			
IssueSize	The bond's issuance size.	Quantitative	USD millions
IssueSize Group	The bond's issue size group, issue sizes in USD millions (**1** ≤ 250 < **2** ≤ 500 < **3** ≤ 750 < **4** ≤ 1,000 < **5** ≤ 1,250 < **6**).	Quantitative	Group (1–6)
Currency	Bond issuance currency.	Qualitative	Categorical
Maturity	The bond's maturity size group, maturity in years (**1** ≤ 5Y < **2** ≤ 10Y < **3** ≤ 15Y < **4** ≤ 20Y < **5**; Perp.=**6**).	Quantitative	Group (1–6)

Note. BICS denotes Bloomberg Industry Classification Standard.

Finally, for the financial controls, the independent variables are the bond's *IssueSize, Maturity* and *Currency.* Moreover, the analysis additionally includes an alternative measure for issue size, with the variable *IssueSize Group* sorting the bond issuances into six different issuance groups with an increasing issuance volume. A detailed description of all independent variables can be found in Table 3. The subsequent analysis incorporates a company's industry and sustainability performance, as well as the eight defined market, company and financial criteria, which were outlined in section 3.2, 3.3 and 3.4. The ensuing probit regression analysis estimates whether the above defined independent variables have a significant effect on the probability to issue a SLB.

1.5 Results

1.5.1 SLB Market Attracts Carbon-Intensive Industries – But Not ESG Laggards

The first probit regression estimation (1) focuses on the companies' industry effect on the probability to issue a SLB, including the *Industry* variable with the low-carbon communication sector as a base level, as well as the respective market, company and financial characteristic controls. The results in Table 4 show that the carbon-intensive sectors materials and utilities have a significant positive effect on the probability to issue a SLB, as well as the consumer staples sector. The industry effect stays significant when adding companies' relative sustainability performance to the regression in Column (2) and (3), including the *ESGRating* variable with ESG leaders as the base group, whilst dropping in column 2 the insignificant control variable *Revenue* and in column 3 the insignificant control variable *Currency.* Moreover, the results show that being an ESG laggard, as well as having no ESG rating, has a significant negative impact on the probability to issue a SLB. The same holds true when including the *EnvRating* instead, as seen in Figure 4, Column (4).

Running the final two regression models from Table 4, Column (3) and (4), using a logit choice model to ensure the robustness of the test results confirms that both, industry and sustainability performance, have a significant effect on the probability to issue a SLB (see Appendix A, Table 5). Moreover, the Pearson goodness-of-fit test and a model specification test are both insignificant, supporting the chosen regression model (see Appendix A, Table 12).

Table 4. Probit Regression Results – Industry and Sustainability Performance

	(1)	(2)	(3)	(4)
	SLB	SLB	SLB	SLB
Industry Base: Communications				
Consumer Discretionary	.196	.081	.075	.065
	(.367)	(.332)	(.31)	(.314)
Consumer Staples	.68*	.715**	.714**	.656**
	(.389)	(.335)	(.328)	(.33)
Energy	.62	.51	.499	.465
	(.484)	(.401)	(.389)	(.389)
Health Care	.353	.218	.198	.191
	(.407)	(.361)	(.356)	(.354)
Industrials	.289	.336	.327	.279
	(.375)	(.339)	(.332)	(.332)
Materials	.662*	.798**	.789**	.767**
	(.369)	(.319)	(.312)	(.314)
Technology	-.171	.071	.038	-.013
	(.492)	(.411)	(.406)	(.406)
Utilities	.468	.88*	.875*	.843*
	(.432)	(.476)	(.473)	(.472)
ESGRating Base: ESG Leader				
ESG Laggard		-.822**	-.82**	
		(.375)	(.372)	
No ESG Rating		-.443***	-.444***	
		(.166)	(.169)	

	(1)	(2)	(3)	(4)
	SLB	SLB	SLB	SLB
Env.Rating Base: Env. Leader				
Env. Laggard				-.66**
				(.312)
No Env. Rating				-.456***
				(.169)
Country Control	Y***	Y***	Y***	Y***
IssueDate Control	Y***	Y***	Y***	Y***
Revenue Control	Y			
CreditRating Control	Y***	Y***	Y***	Y***
SFExperience Control	Y			
Currency Control	Y**	Y		
IssueSize Control	Y**	Y**	Y**	Y**
Maturity Control	Y***	Y**	Y*	Y**
Constant	-35.789***	-35.103***	-34.799***	-34.814***
	(8.475)	(4.335)	(4.217)	(4.22)
Clustered SE	Y	Y	Y	Y
Observations	1622	2122	2122	2122
Pseudo R^2	.221	.237	.23	.229
Log-Likelihood	-283.898	-397.403	-401.279	-401.905
Chi^2	116.133	177.048	167.078	167.608

Note. Standard errors (SE) are in parentheses *** p<.01, ** p<.05, * p<.1. The regression estimations only include 1,622 observations in column 1, as 448 bond issuances do not have a reported company revenue during the bond issuance year and some observations are omitted due to perfect prediction. The regression estimations in column 2, 3 and 4 include 2,122 observations, because 16 conventional bond issuances do not report their issuance volume. Standard errors are clustered at the issuer level, as some companies have issued more than one SLB.

Calculating the individual risk ratios based on the logistic regression coefficients, the results in Table 6 show that being a company from the carbon-intensive sectors materials (ß= 3.612) or utilities (ß=3.885) more than triples the probability to issue a SLB compared to a company from the low-carbon communication sector. Moreover, companies that do not have an ESG rating have a 52 % decrease in the probability to issue a SLB, whilst companies considered as ESG laggards even have an 80 % decrease (see Table 6, Column 1). The effect is only slightly smaller when using the Refinitiv environmental rating, which focuses on a company's environmental performance, excluding social and governance criteria. The results in Table 6, Column 2 show that environmental laggards have a decrease of 75 % in the probability to issue a SLB. This emphasizes that the environmental criteria are in fact the driving force behind the ESG rating effect on the probability to issue a SLB.

Based on these findings, it can be said that the probability to issue a SLB is higher for some carbon-intensive industries. This is in line with the observation by the Climate Bonds Initiative (2022a) that the SLB market includes a significant number of SLB issuances by carbon-intensive industries.

The insignificant effect for the carbon-intensive energy and industrial sector (see Tables 4, 5 and 6) could be due to the fact that these sectors generally have a better availability of eligible green bond projects both in size and sustainability measures compared to other sectors. This is supported by the fact that renewable energy is the largest (35 %) use of proceeds category as of 2022 (CBI, 2022a), followed by buildings (27.1 %) and transport (18.1 %), which is the biggest industry group of the industrial sector according to the used BICS classification system. Consequently, the energy and industrial sectors are likely more indifferent between issuing a green bond or SLB compared to other industries, leading to an insignificant effect.

Table 6. Estimated Risk Ratios – Industry and Sustainability Performance

	(1) SLB	(2) SLB
Industry Base: Communications		
Consumer Discretionary	1.095	1.056
	(.677)	(.657)
Consumer Staples	3.271*	2.939*
	(2.004)	(1.810)
Energy	2.460	2.299
	(1.761)	(1.639)
Health Care	1.363	1.365
	(.954)	(.951)
Industrials	1.770	1.614
	(1.166)	(1.064)
Materials	3.612**	3.453**
	(2.125)	(2.035)
Technology	1.135	1.035
	(.90)	(.818)
Utilities	3.885*	3.653*
	(2.936)	(2.756)
ESGRating Base: ESG Leader		
ESG Laggard	.197**	
	(.153)	
No ESG Rating	.476***	
	(.122)	
Env.Rating Base: Env. Leader		
Env. Laggard		.254**
		(.164)
No Env. Rating		.463***
		(.120)
Constant	4.20e-25***	3.52e-25***
	(4.34e-24)	(3.65e-24)
Clustered SE	Y	Y
Observations	2122	2122
Log-Likelihood	-421.237	-421.497

Note. Standard errors (SE) are in parentheses *** p<.01, ** p<.05, * p<.1. Standard errors are clustered at the issuer level, as some companies have issued more than one SLB. The two equations include the industry, market and financial characteristics variables, as well as the *ESGRating* (1) and *EnvRating* (2) variables respectively. This is an excerpt of the full regression results, which can be found in Table 11 in the appendix.

Regarding companies' sustainability performance, ESG laggards and non-ESG-rated companies have a significantly lower probability to issue a SLB. The lower probability for non-ESG rated companies suggests that not having an ESG rating represents a barrier to the SLB market, even though the SLB instrument was designed in a way that companies can choose KPIs and SPTs independently of an ESG rating. One explanation could be that the SLB market values a company's sustainability awareness and experience, represented in the form of an existing ESG rating. In order to test for the potential effect of a company's sustainability experience and knowledge, the dummy variable *SFExperience* is included in the regression (see Table 4). As explained in section 4.4, the dummy variable represents whether a company has used any type of sustainable finance instrument before and has consequently acquired a certain level of sustainability experience and knowledge. However, the dummy variable is insignificant, indicating that a lack of sustainable finance experience does not constitute a barrier to enter the SLB market.

An alternative explanation could be that the SLB market interprets an ESG rating as a sustainability credibility tool and is thus leaning more towards companies that have an existing ESG rating. Furthermore, the results point out that the SLB market does not particularly attract ESG laggards, but rather that they have a very low probability to issue a SLB. This could be due to investors' greenwashing concerns and skepticism regarding SLB's transition effectiveness and credibility, which in turn leads to higher reservations towards companies that are lagging behind in their sustainability transition, the ESG laggards. Overall, the SLB market efficiently attracts carbon-intensive industries, but not ESG laggards. This observed market barrier is a clear area of concern and needs to be addressed with appropriate policies to ensure an efficient SLB market and thereby a successful sustainability transition of the real economy.

1.5.2 Influential Market, Company and Financial Characteristics

Taking a closer look at the variables for the market, company and financial characteristics in Table 8, the issuer market and maturity of the SLB market both have a significant effect on the probability to issue a SLB. Firstly, the *Country* variable results show that Germany, France, Italy, Luxembourg, the Netherlands and Sweden have a significant negative impact on the probability to issue a SLB, compared to Austria. Secondly, the variable *IssueDate* has a significant positive effect on the probability to issue a SLB, emphasizing that as the SLB market becomes more mature, the probability to issue a SLB increases. Using an alternative measure for the SLB market maturity in the form of the variable *NSLBIssuers* supports this result (see Appendix A, Table 7).

In regard to the analyzed company characteristics, a company's revenue and sustainable finance experience both do not have a significant effect and are thus only included in the first regression, as seen in Table 8, Column 1. Moreover, using the variable *EmployeeCount* as an alternative measure for a company's size does not find a significant effect on the probability to issue a SLB (see Appendix A, Table 7). As the data availability for a company's revenue and employee count for the issuance year 2022 is still limited at the time of this research, an additional variable called *Revenue Group* is included to test for a company's size effect. This variable uses companies' fiscal year 2021 revenue, which allows for more data points to be included. However, the company size effect on the probability to issue a SLB stays insignificant as seen in Appendix A, Table 7. In contrast, the issuer's credit rating at the time of the bond issuance has a significant positive impact on the probability to issue a SLB, as seen in Table 8.

Regarding the three inspected financial characteristics, the bond's currency has a significant impact on the probability to issue a SLB in the first regression, but the effect turns insignificant in the second regression and the variable is thus subsequently excluded (see Table 8, Column 1 and 2). Moreover, the bond's issue size coefficient is significant but indicates a very small positive effect, as seen in Table 8. Finally, the bond's maturity has a significant positive impact on the probability to issue a SLB. The significance of the market, company and financial characteristics is tested by running the regressions using a logit choice model (see Appendix A, Table 9). The significance of the market, company and financial characteristics variables is confirmed. Subsequently, the respective risk ratios are estimated based on the logit regression coefficients and reported in Table 10.

Table 8. Probit Regression Results – Market and Financial Characteristics

Variable	Description	Type	Unit
SLB	The issued bond has a SLB structure.	Quantitative	Binary (0 or 1)
Industry	An issuer's industry (BICS Level 1).	Qualitative	Categorical
ESGRating	The issuer's Refinitiv ESG rating group: Leader (A+ to B-); Laggard (C+ to D-); No Rating. The ESG rating at the time of the bond issuance is used for the variable.	Quantitative	Group (1–3)
EnvRating	The issuer's Refinitiv Environmental rating group: Leader (A+ to B-); Laggard (C+ to D-); No Rating. The Environmental rating at the time of the bond issuance is used for the variable.	Quantitative	Group (1–3)
Market Characteristics			
Country	An issuer's country of domicil (ISO Code).	Qualitative	Categorical
IssueDate	The bond's issuance quarter calculated based on the issuance date.	Quantitative	Quarters
NSLBIssuers	Number of SLB Issuers in the market at time of the bond issuance.	Quantitative	N. Issuers
Company Characteristics			
Revenue	The issuer's revenue during the fiscal year of the bond issuance.	Quantitative	USD millions
Revenue Group	The issuer's revenue during the fiscal year 2021 grouped according to size, revenues in USD millions (**1** ≤ 500 < **2** ≤ 1,000 < **3** ≤ 5,000 < **4** ≤ 10,000 < **5** ≤ 25,000 < **6** ≤ 50,000 < **7**)).	Quantitative	Group (1–7)
EmployeeCount	The issuer's employee count during the fiscal year of the bond issuance.	Quantiative	N. Employees

Variable	Description	Type	Unit
CreditRating	The issuer's credit rating group: Upper Investment Grade (AAA-A); Lower Investment Grade (BBB); Speculative Grade (BB-D); NR. The issuer's BB composite credit rating at the time of the bond issuance is used for the variable.	Quantitative	Group (1–4)
SFExperience	The issuer has issued a sustainable finance instrument before (dummy=1).	Quantitative	Binary (0 or 1)
<u>Financial Characteristics</u>			
IssueSize	The bond's issuance size.	Quantitative	USD millions
IssueSize Group	The bond's issue size group, issue sizes in USD millions (**1** ≤ 250 < **2** ≤ 500 < **3** ≤ 750 < **4** ≤ 1,000 < **5** ≤ 1,250 < **6**).	Quantitative	Group (1–6)
Currency	Bond issuance currency.	Qualitative	Categorical
Maturity	The bond's maturity size group, maturity in years (**1** ≤ 5Y < **2** ≤ 10Y < **3** ≤ 15Y < **4** ≤ 20Y < **5**; Perp.=**6**).	Quantitative	Group (1–6)

Note. Standard errors (SE) are in parentheses *** p<.01, ** p<.05, * p<.1. The regression estimations only include 2,122 observations when adding the market and financial controls, because 16 conventional bond issuances do not report their issuance volume. Standard errors are clustered at the issuer level, as some companies have issued more than one SLB.

Firstly, looking at the issuer market in Table 10, companies from all included countries are less likely to issue a SLB compared to the base country Austria. The highest decrease (92 %) in the probability to issue a SLB is found for companies that are domiciled in Germany, as seen in Table 10. A possible explanation could be the density of sustainable finance policies in the respective countries. However, Steffen (2021) shows that France has the highest number of green financial policies, followed with a wide gap by Germany, the Netherlands and Italy. A potential explanation for the high density of SLBs in Austria, which were all issued starting September 2020, could be the political announcement, as part of Austria's government program for 2020–2024, to exempt sustainable investments from the capital gains tax (Bundeskanzleramt, 2020). In anticipation of a subsequently higher investor demand for sustainable investments, companies had a higher incentive to issue a SLB. Nevertheless, all countries demonstrate a similar probability to issue a SLB compared to Austria. This indicates that, even though regional sustainable finance policy density might differ, European regulations are the higher-level policies and successfully set a uniform environment for sustainable finance to thrive.

Secondly, the market maturity results in Table 10 demonstrate that with every quarter that the SLB market grows and matures, the probability to issue a SLB increases by 24 %. This can be seen as an opportunity, because with a more mature SLB market, transparency and SLB mechanisms should improve, thereby decreasing greenwashing as well as credibility concerns and as a result attracting more SLB issuers.

Thirdly, in order to take a closer look at a bond's issue size effect on the probability to issue a SLB, the categorical variable *IssueSize Group* is used (see Appendix A, Table 7). The probit regression results show a significant positive impact for bonds with an issue size larger than $1,250 million. Calculating the risk ratios accordingly, the probability to issue a SLB almost triples (ß=2.972, SE=1.428) if the bond has an issue size larger than $1,250 million, compared to the base issue size smaller than $250 million. This finding implies that the SLB market currently attracts primarily issuers with larger financing needs.

Table 10. Risk Ratios – Market and Financial Characteristics

	(1) SLB	(2) SLB
Country Base: Austria		
Germany	.081***	.083***
	(.052)	(.052)
France	.150***	.150***
	(.068)	(.068)
Italy	.162***	.164***
	(.082)	(.083)
Luxembourg	.191***	.197***
	(.088)	(.090)
Netherlands	.170***	.172***
	(.087)	(.089)

	(1)	(2)
	SLB	SLB
Sweden	.128***	.131***
	(.067)	(.068)
IssueDate	1.237***	1.238***
	(.052)	(.053)
IssueSize	1.001**	1.001**
	(.000)	(.000)
Maturity Base: <5Years		
5Y < M < 10Y	1.448*	1.477**
	(.326)	(.329)
10Y< M < 15Y	1.260	1.276
	(.424)	(.426)
15Y < M < 20Y	1.277	1.289
	(.640)	(.644)
20Y < M	.60	.612
	(.238)	(.251)
Perpetual	.277	.300
	(.225)	(.246)
CreditRating Base: Upper Investment Grade		
Lower Investment Grade	8.698***	8.445***
	(5.821)	(5.634)
Speculative Grade	16.732***	16.593***
	(10.655)	(10.539)
No Rating	11.106***	11.322***
	(6.760)	(6.877)
Constant	4.20e-25***	3.52e-25***
	(4.34e-24)	(3.65e-24)
Clustered SE	Y	Y
Observations	2122	2122
Log-Likelihood	-421.237	-421.497

Note. Standard errors (SE) are in parentheses *** p<.01, ** p<.05, * p<.1. Standard errors are clustered at the issuer level, as some companies have issued more than one SLB. The two equations include the industry, market and financial characteristics variables, as well as the *ESGRating* (1) and *EnvRating* (2) variables respectively. This is an excerpt of the full regression results, which can be found in Table 11 in the appendix.

Fourthly, the estimated risk ratio results for a bond's maturity show that bond issuances with a maturity between five to ten years increase the probability to issue a SLB by 45 %, as seen in Table 10. A possible explanation could be that the time frame for the first SPT assessments tends to be around five to ten years, often 2025 and 2030. Only on rare occasions do companies already set SPTs to, for example, be climate neutral by 2050. This result implies that the SLB market favors short-term targets, which promise short-term transition results, and is likely driven by investors' concern regarding the materiality and ambitiousness of the SLB's sustainability targets. A short-term target allows for a better assessment of whether the chosen KPI's are material to a company's current economic activities and whether the set SPTs are ambitious enough to ensure a real transition impact. This finding does not necessarily have to be a barrier, but it is an important realization, especially for ESG laggards, which initially might consider setting long-term targets for their transition. Instead, the SLB market analysis suggests that they should set credible and ambitious short-term targets in line with a long-term transition path.

Finally, as seen in Table 10, a company's credit rating at the time of issuance also has a highly significant effect. Companies with a lower investment grade (ß=8.698) are more likely to issue a SLB than companies with an upper investment grade. The effect is similar in size for companies with no credit rating (ß=11.106) and more than twice as big for companies with a speculative credit rating grade (ß=16.732). These findings demonstrate that the SLB market does not consider a lower credit rating as a hindrance. Instead, companies might use a sustainability-linked structure to increase the attractiveness of their financing instrument, compared to competitors with a better credit rating and a conventional bond issuance. This could be a convincing argument and opportunity for the SLB market to attract more companies to issue a SLB.

1.6 Discussion and Conclusion

In order to ensure a successful sustainability transition of our real economy and thereby achieve our climate goals, the European Green Deal Investment Plan has introduced several extensive sustainability legislations. The financial sector is a key channel to implement these regulatory requirements with the aim to push companies towards transitioning and to advance the economy's overall sustainability transition. Consequently, the capital market has developed an instrument to incentivize companies to align their activities with the two-degree climate path and to actively manage their climate risks: the sustainability-linked bond. The SLB incorporates a company-level sustainability perspective, encourages the issuer to set ambitious sustainability targets and incentivizes their achievement by demanding a payment in the case of failure to reach these goals. With the opportunity to communicate their transition strategy and a potential premium for SLB issuers, the instrument has gained a lot of attention leading to a rapidly increasing SLB market. But does the SLB market efficiently attract those companies that are most crucial for a successful sustainability transition?

This paper developed a conceptual framework to assess whether the SLB market works efficiently by ensuring accessibility and attractive market structures for potential SLB issuers, with a particular consideration of carbon-intensive industries and ESG laggards. The analysis is conducted by running a probit and logit choice model to estimate a company's probability to issue a SLB and subsequently calculating the respective risk ratios for the significant influential factors. The results show that the SLB market efficiently attracts carbon-intensive industries. In fact, being a company from the carbon-intensive sectors materials and utilities more than triples the probability to issue a SLB. Thus, for carbon-intensive ESG leaders, SLBs are an attractive instrument to finance and transparently communicate their sustainability transition.

However, the SLB market does not efficiently attract ESG laggards. The results demonstrate that companies considered as ESG laggards have an 80 % decrease in the probability to issue a SLB, compared to an ESG leader. Moreover, companies with no ESG rating are also less likely to issue a SLB compared to ESG leaders, with a decrease of 52 % in the probability to issue a SLB. These findings point out that the SLB market leans towards companies with an existing ESG rating and that the market demonstrates a reservation towards companies that are lagging behind in their sustainability transformation.

Additionally, the paper analyzed eight market, company and financial characteristics that could potentially influence the probability to issue a SLB. Firstly, the results show that the issuer market has a significant effect on the probability to issue a SLB, with all countries, apart from Austria, having a similar probability to issue a SLB. This implies that the European sustainability legislations are successful in establishing a comparable sustainable investment environment. Secondly, the probability to issue a SLB increases with the SLB market's maturity, pointing out the growth potential of the SLB market. Both findings can be seen as an opportunity for the SLB market to adapt current policies and adjust market structures to better attract ESG laggards, whilst the market is still developing.

Regarding the analyzed company characteristics, the results show that a company's size and sustainable finance experience do not have a significant effect on the probability to issue a SLB. However, the regression results and risk ratio estimations show that the fifth criterion, a company's credit rating at the time of the bond issuance, has a significant impact on the probability to issue a SLB. Companies with a lower investment grade, speculative grade or without a credit rating are more likely to issue a SLB, compared to a company with an upper investment grade credit rating. The increase in the probability to issue a SLB is particularly high for companies with a speculative grade rating. These findings imply that a low credit rating does not represent a barrier to entering the SLB market. On the contrary, companies with a lower credit rating might use a sustainability-linked structure to increase the attractiveness of their financing instrument, compared to competitors with a higher credit rating, that use a conventional financing instrument. This can be seen as an opportunity for the SLB market to attract more issuers.

For the financial characteristic, the regression results indicate that a bond's currency does not significantly affect the probability to issue a SLB. However, having a bond issue size larger than $1,250 million almost triples the probability to issue a SLB, demonstrating that the bond's issue size has a significant impact. Finally, the eighth defined criterion is a bond's maturity, for which the analysis finds that a bond issuance with a maturity of five to ten years increases the probability to issue a SLB by 45 %. This is in line with the commonly used time frame for SPTs being 2025 or 2030, rather than a long-term goal of for instance zero emissions by 2050. This finding implies that the SLB market favors short-term targets with the promise of short-term results and is likely driven by investors' concern regarding the materiality and ambitiousness of SLB sustainability targets. A closer time frame allows for a better comparability and assessment of whether the chosen KPIs are material to a company's economic activity and whether the respective SPTs are ambitious enough. Nevertheless, the practice to use climate-aligned transition pathways in order to set appropriate KPIs and SPTs is starting to become more prominent and could lead to a higher credibility for long-term targets as well. This finding is particularly interesting for ESG laggards, which might be more prone to choose long-term targets, due to the challenge of their sustainability transition. The results suggest that they should rather set an ambitious short-term target that is aligned with a long-term transition path instead.

To conclude, the paper makes two important contributions to the existing SLB literature, which has so far been mainly focused on the functionality and pricing of sustainability-linked instruments (Berrada et al., 2022, Kölbel & Lambillon, 2022; Vulturius et al., 2022; Liberadzki et al., 2021), by analyzing the efficiency of the SLB market in ensuring the accessibility and market structures for potential SLB issuers, with a particular consideration of carbon-intensive ESG laggards. In order to ensure a successful sustainability transition of the real economy, the SLB market needs to address those companies that are most crucial for advancing the economy's transition, namely carbon-intensive industries and ESG laggards.

Firstly, this paper shows that the SLB market does efficiently attract companies from carbon-intensive industries, but that those companies are predominantly ESG leaders. Companies without an ESG rating and ESG laggards have a significantly lower probability to issue a SLB, demonstrating a SLB market entry barrier for companies with a lower or nonexistent ESG rating. Consequently, the SLB market so far fails to attract a significant fraction of companies that are crucial for a successful sustainability transition. This result points out the need for sustainability policies, as well as sustainable finance market structures and instruments that are better adapted for ESG laggards.

Secondly, the paper identifies four success factors for the SLB market to improve the accessibility and credibility of the SLB market:

1) Any regulatory adaptations to better attract ESG laggards should be implemented through European policy adjustments rather than singular local customizations, as the European sustainability legislations have been successful in establishing a common sustainable finance investment environment among the different EU countries.

2) The findings demonstrate that with growing maturity, more companies will consider entering the SLB market. This potential needs to be seized by providing appropriate market structures that satisfy investors' expectations regarding transparency and credibility standards. Through improving transparency and market mechanism whilst growing, the SLB market can work on diminishing credibility and greenwashing concerns, thereby also creating a better environment for ESG laggards.

3) The SLB market's preference for short-term sustainability targets should encourage ESG laggards to focus on credible and ambitious short-term targets that are in line with a long-term transition pathway. Using a climate-aligned transition pathway when setting KPIs and SPTs is becoming more prominent and can assist in setting credible and ambitious sustainability targets.

4) A company's lower credit rating is not a hindrance, but rather an opportunity for the SLB market to address a large target group. Companies with a lower credit rating can use a sustainability-linked structure not only to finance and communicate their transition strategy, but also to increase the attractiveness of their financing instrument compared to competitors with a better credit rating, yet conventional financing instrument.

This paper focuses its analysis on the efficiency of the SLB market from a market perspective. Further research could extend the analysis to incorporate company and investor perspectives on the SLB market structures, to gain a better understanding of the market barriers and incentives from a potential SLB issuer and investor point of view. Moreover, the market mechanisms are continuously developing, as the SLB market is still very young, with the first European SLB issuance in 2019. As transparency and reporting legislations are slowly being put into action, the pressure for companies to transition will increase in the upcoming years and will thereby affect the market dynamics as well. Any policy and market behavior adjustments should be evaluated and implemented with these developments in mind.

References

Berrada, T., Engelhardt, L., Gibson, R., & Krueger, P. (2022). The economics of sustainability linked bonds. *Swiss Finance Institute Research Paper No. 22–26.* https://dx.doi.org/10.2139/ssrn.4059299

Bundesanstalt für Finanzdienstleistungsaufsicht. (2019). *Merkblatt zum Umgang mit Nachhaltigkeitsrisiken.* https://www.bafin.de/SharedDocs/Downloads/DE/Merkblatt/dl_mb_Nachhaltigkeitsrisiken.html

Bundeskanzleramt (2020). Aus Verantwortung für Österreich. Regierungsprogramm 2020–2024. Retrieved May 20, 2023, from https://www.bundeskanzleramt.gv.at/bundeskanzleramt/die-bundesregierung/regierungsdokumente.html

Caldecott, B. (2020). Achieving alignment in finance. In EIT Climate-KIC, *Aligning finance for the net zero economy: new ideas from leading thinkers.* https://www.climate-kic.org/wp-content/uploads/2020/09/200902_J932-CKIC-UNEP-ThoughtLeadershipSeries-DrBenCaldecott-1.pdf

Climate Bonds Initiative. (2022a). *Transition finance for transforming companies.* https://www.climatebonds.net/files/files/Transition%20Finance/Transition-Finance-for-Transforming-Companies-6-Sept-2022.pdf

Climate Bonds Initiative. (2022b). *Green bond pricing in the primary market January – June 2022.* https://www.climatebonds.net/files/reports/cbi_pricing_h1_2022_02g.pdf

D'Orazio, P., & Dirks, M. W. (2022). Exploring the effects of climate-related financial policies on carbon emissions in G20 countries: a panel quantile regression approach. *Environmental Science and Pollution Research, 29*(5), 7678–7702. https://doi.org/10.1007/s11356-021-15655-y

D'Orazio, P., & Thole, S. (2022). Climate-related financial policy index: a composite index to compare the engagement in green financial policymaking at the global level. *Ecological Indicators, 141.* https://doi.org/10.1016/j.ecolind.2022.109065

European Commission. (2019). *Financing sustainable growth.* https://finance.ec.europa.eu/system/files/2020-01/200108-financing-sustainable-growth-factsheet_en.pdf

European Commission. (2020a). *Renewed sustainable finance strategy and implementation of the action plan on financing sustainable growth.* https://finance.ec.europa.eu/publications/renewed-sustainable-finance-strategy-and-implementation-action-plan-financing-sustainable-growth_en

European Commission. (2020b). *Financing the green transition: The European Green Deal Investment Plan and the Just Transition Mechanism.* https://ec.europa.eu/commission/presscorner/detail/en/ip_20_17

European Commission. (2021). *EU sustainable finance strategy.* https://finance.ec.europa.eu/system/files/2021-07/210706-sustainable-finance-strategy-factsheet_en.pdf

European Commission. (2023a). *The European Green Deal.* Retrieved January 31, 2023, from https://commission.europa.eu/strategy-and-policy/priorities-2019-2024/european-green-deal_en

European Commission. (2023b). *Sustainability related disclosure in the financial service sector.* Retrieved 31 January 2023 from https://finance.ec.europa.eu/sustainable-finance/disclosures/sustainability-related-disclosure-financial-services-sector_en

European Commission. (2023c). *Corporate sustainability reporting.* Retrieved 31 January 2023 from https://finance.ec.europa.eu/capital-markets-union-and-financial-markets/company-reporting-and-auditing/company-reporting/corporate-sustainability-reporting_en

European Commission. (2023d). *EU labels for benchmarks (climate, ESG) and benchmarks' ESG disclosure.* Retrieved 31 January 2023 from https://finance.ec.europa.eu/sustainable-finance/disclosures/eu-labels-benchmarks-climate-esg-and-benchmarks-esg-disclosures_en

Flammer, C. (2020). Green bonds: effectiveness and implications for public policy. *Environmental and Energy Policy and the Economy,* 1(1), 95–128. https://doi.org/10.1086/706794

Gianfrate, G., & Peri, M. (2019). The green advantage: Exploring the convenience of issuing green bonds. *Journal of Cleaner Production, 219,* 127–135. https://doi.org/10.1016/j.jclepro.2019.02.022

Hinsche, I. C. (2021). A greenium for the next generation EU green bonds analysis of a potential green bond premium and its drivers. *Center for Financial Studies Working Paper No. 663, 20201.* https://dx.doi.org/10.2139/ssrn.3965664

International Capital Market Association. (2021). *Green Bond Principles.* https://www.icmagroup.org/assets/documents/Sustainable-finance/2022-updates/Green-Bond-Principles-June-2022-060623.pdf

International Capital Market Association. (2023). *Sustainability-Linked Bond Principles.* https://www.icmagroup.org/assets/documents/Sustainable-finance/2023-updates/Sustainability-Linked-Bond-Principles-June-2023-220623.pdf

Kölbel, J. F., & Lambillon, A. P. (2022). Who pays for sustainability? An analysis of sustainability-linked bonds. *Swiss Finance Institute Research Paper No. 23–07.* https://dx.doi.org/10.2139/ssrn.4007629

Larcker, D. F., & Watts, E. M. (2020). Where's the greenium?. *Journal of Accounting and Economics, 69*(2–3). https://dx.doi.org/10.2139/ssrn.3333847

Liberadzki, M., Jaworski, P., & Liberadzki, K. (2021). Spread analysis of the sustainability-linked bonds tied to an issuer's greenhouse gases emissions reduction target. *Energies,* 14(23), 7918. https://doi.org/10.3390/en14237918

Natixis. (2021). *Sustainability-linked bonds – investors views.* https://gsh.cib.natixis.com/api-website-feature/files/download/11818/SLB-Survey-Short-Results_2021-03-FinalVersion_LAST.pdf

Platform on Sustainable Finance. (2021). *Transition finance report.* https://finance.ec.europa.eu/system/files/2021-03/210319-eu-platform-transition-finance-report_en.pdf

Refinitiv. (2022). *Refinitiv ESG scores methodology.* Retrieved 31 January 2023 from https://www.refinitiv.com/content/dam/marketing/en_us/documents/methodology/refinitiv-esg-scores-methodology.pdf

Refinitiv. (2023). *ESG Scores – Shell PLC.* Retrieved 31 January 2023 from https://www.refinitiv.com/en/sustainable-finance/esg-scores

Schütze, F., & Stede, J. (2021). The EU sustainable finance taxonomy and its contribution to climate neutrality. *Journal of Sustainable Finance & Investment, 14*(1), 128–160. https://doi.org/10.1080/20430795.2021.2006129

Steffen, B. (2021). A comparative analysis of green financial policy output in OECD countries. *Environmental Research Letters, 16*(7). https://doi.org/10.1088/1748-9326/ac0c43

Ul Haq, I., Doumbia, D. (2022). Structural loopholes in sustainability-linked bonds. *World Bank Policy Research Workin Paper Series,* 10200. https://dx.doi.org/10.2139/ssrn.4099829

UniCredit. (2022). *Sustainability-linked corporate bonds: gauging ambition.* https://www.research.unicredit.eu/DocsKey/credit_docs_9999_182488.ashx?M=D&R=96313022

Vulturius, G., Maltais, A., & Forsbacka, K. (2022). Sustainability-linked bonds–their potential to promote issuers' transition to net-zero emissions and future research directions. *Journal of Sustainable Finance & Investment, 14*(1), 116–127. https://doi.org/10.1080/20430795.2022.2040943

Zerbib, O. D. (2019). The effect of pro-environmental preferences on bond prices: Evidence from green bonds. *Journal of Banking & Finance, 98,* 39–60. https://doi.org/10.1016/j.jbankfin.2018.10.012

Appendix A: Tables

Table 2. Additional Company and Bond Level Summary Statistics

a. Company ESG Rating in 2022

	SL Indicator	N	Min	Median	Mean	Max	SD	t-value
Issue Size (USD Millions)	N	1980	.156	551.008	554.264	4115.281	444.94	54.154
	Y	142	30.23	592.19	657.383	2161.041	412.908	19.119
Time to Maturity (Years)	N	1916	.499	6.003	7.743	63.041	7.269	46.314
	Y	140	3.003	7.005	7.952	30.022	4.158	22.628

Source: Refinitiv as of 02.11.2022

b. Issuer Env. Rating at Time of Bond Issuance

	SL Indicator	N	Min	Median	Mean	Max	SD	t-value
Issue Size (USD Millions)	N	1980	.156	551.008	554.264	4115.281	444.94	54.154
	Y	142	30.23	592.19	657.383	2161.041	412.908	19.119
Time to Maturity (Years)	N	1916	.499	6.003	7.743	63.041	7.269	46.314
	Y	140	3.003	7.005	7.952	30.022	4.158	22.628

Source: Refinitiv as of 02.11.2022

c. Bond Currency

Currency	Sustainability-Linked Indicator		
	0	1	Total
EUR	1475	97	1572
GBP	36	2	38
JPY	7	2	9
NOK	23	1	24
SEK	241	11	252
USD	214	29	243
Total	1996	142	2138

Source: Refinitiv as of 02.11.2022

d. Bond Maturity Type

Maturity Type	Sustainability-Linked Indicator		
	0	1	Total
AT MATURITY	569	22	591
CALL/PUT	3	0	3
CALL/SINK	30	0	30
CALLABLE	1199	116	1315
CONV/CALL	2	0	2
CONV/CALL/PERP	2	0	2
CONV/PUT	9	0	9
CONVERTIBLE	67	2	69
PERP/CALL	69	2	71
PERPETUAL	9	0	9
PUTABLE	5	0	5
SINKABLE	32	0	32
Total	1996	142	2138

Source: Refinitiv as of 02.11.2022

e. Issuer Credit Rating at Bond Issuance

Credit Rating	Sustainability-Linked Indicator		
	0	1	Total
AA	24	1	25
AA-	35	0	35
A+	88	1	89
A	61	0	61
A-	134	1	135
BBB+	127	26	153
BBB	126	16	142
BBB-	161	6	167
BB+	73	4	77
BB	43	5	48
BB-	49	10	59
B+	32	5	37
B	85	8	93
B-	24	0	24
CCC+	10	1	11
CCC	5	0	5
NR	919	58	977
Total	1996	142	2138

Source: Refinitiv as of 02.02.2023s

f. Bond Payment Rank

Payment Rank	Sustainability-Linked Indicator		
	0	1	Total
1st lien	68	0	68
2nd lien	6	0	6
Jr Subordinated	70	1	71
Secured	231	20	251
Sr Preferred	1	0	1
Sr Subordinated	5	0	5
Sr Unsecured	1541	119	1660
Subordinated	24	1	25
Unsecured	50	1	51
Total	1996	142	2138

Source: Refinitiv as of 02.11.2022

g. Revenue, Employee Count, Bond Issue Size and Time to Maturity

	SL Indicator	N	Min	Median	Mean	Max	SD	t-value
Issue Size (USD Millions)	N	1980	.156	551.008	554.264	4115.281	444.94	54.154
	Y	142	30.23	592.19	657.383	2161.041	412.908	19.119
Time to Maturity (Years)	N	1916	.499	6.003	7.743	63.041	7.269	46.314
	Y	140	3.003	7.005	7.952	30.022	4.158	22.628

Source: Refinitiv as of 02.11.2022

Table 5. Logit Regression Results – Industry and Sustainability Performance

	(1) SLB	(2) SLB
Industry Base: Communications		
Consumer Discretionary	.108	.069
	(.688)	(.698)
Consumer Staples	1.406**	1.275*
	(.706)	(.712)
Energy	1.013	.937
	(.836)	(.835)
Health Care	.348	.353
	(.787)	(.785)
Industrials	.673	.567
	(.748)	(.752)
Materials	1.509**	1.462**
	(.675)	(.681)
Technology	.162	.053
	(.886)	(.887)
Utilities	1.66*	1.59
	(.978)	(.979)
ESGRating Base: ESG Leader		
ESG Laggard	-1.834**	
	(.843)	
No ESG Rating	-.875***	
	(.337)	
Env.Rating Base: Env. Leader		
Env. Laggard		-1.539**
		(.705)
No Env. Rating		-.902***
		(.337)
Country Control	Y***	Y***
IssueDate Control	Y***	Y***
Revenue Control		
CreditRating Control	Y***	Y***

	(1)	(2)
	SLB	SLB
SFExperience Control		
Currency Control		
IssueSize Control	Y**	Y**
Maturity Control	Y*	Y*
Constant	-65.619***	-65.747***
	(10.019)	(10.074)
Clustered SE	Y	Y
Observations	2122	2122
Pseudo R^2	.226	.226
Log-Likelihood	-403.17	-403.579
Chi^2	176.727	175.309

Note. Standard errors (SE) are in parentheses *** p<.01, ** p<.05, * p<.1. Standard errors are clustered at the issuer level, as some companies have issued more than one SLB.

Table 7. Probit Regression Results – Additional Control Variables

	(1) SLB	(2) SLB	(3) SLB	(4) SLB
Industry Base: Communications				
Consumer Discretionary	.106	-.142	.089	.058
	(.303)	(.337)	(.353)	(.308)
Consumer Staples	.749**	.456	.614*	.712**
	(.321)	(.362)	(.368)	(.326)
Energy	.521	.385	.13	.518
	(.387)	(.413)	(.465)	(.383)
Health Care	.222	.111	.216	.161
	(.349)	(.38)	(.393)	(.354)
Industrials	.369	-.035	-.016	.33
	(.326)	(.34)	(.38)	(.331)
Materials	.802***	.475	.397	.793***
	(.304)	(.338)	(.365)	(.307)
Technology	.043	-.492	-.34	.054
	(.4)	(.451)	(.462)	(.407)
Utilities	.907**	-.236	.403	.878*
	(.459)	(.361)	(.458)	(.476)
ESGRating Base: ESG Leader				
ESG Laggard	-.799**	-.853**	-.647*	-.834**
	(.371)	(.375)	(.364)	(.368)
No ESG Rating	-.431**	-.357**	-.304*	-.46***
	(.168)	(.17)	(.182)	(.171)
NSLBIssuers	.013***			
	(.002)			
Revenue Group Base: ⇐250 M. USD				
⇐500 M. USD		-.266		
		(.577)		
⇐ 700 M. USD		-.07		
		(.502)		
⇐ 1000 M. USD		.408		
		(.502)		
⇐1250 M. USD		-.171		
		(.46)		
> 1250 M. USD		-.164		
		(.485)		

	(1) SLB	(2) SLB	(3) SLB	(4) SLB
Employee Count			0	
			(0)	
IsseSize Group Base: ⇐250 M. USD				
⇐500 M. USD				.012
				(.221)
⇐ 700 M. USD				.048
				(.204)
⇐ 1000 M. USD				.149
				(.226)
⇐1250 M. USD				.291
				(.262)
> 1250 M. USD				.662**
				(.286)
Country Control	Y***	Y***	Y***	Y***
IssueDate Control		Y***	Y***	Y***
Revenue Control				
CreditRating Control	Y***	Y***	Y***	Y***
SFExperience Control				
Currency Control				
IssueSize Control	Y**	Y	Y	
Maturity Control	Y**	Y***	Y***	Y**
Constant	-2.439***	-45.769***	-35.9***	-35.104***
	(.515)	(5.128)	(9.365)	(4)
Clustered SE	Y	Y	Y	Y
Observations	2122	1679	1331	2122
Pseudo R^2	.22	.266	.205	.232
Log-Likelihood	-406.434	-267.941	-244.847	-400.426
Chi^2	151.528	136.552	82.296	170.694

Note. Standard errors (SE) are in parentheses *** p<.01, ** p<.05, * p<.1. Standard errors are clustered at the issuer level, as some companies have issued more than one SLB.

Table 9. Logit Regression Results – Market and Financial Characteristics

	(1) SLB	(2) SLB
Industry Variable	Y	Y
ESGRating Variable	Y	
Env.Rating Variable		Y
Country Base: Austria		
Germany	-3.219***	-3.184***
	(.895)	(.885)
France	-2.455***	-2.439***
	(.694)	(.681)
Italy	-2.413***	-2.377***
	(.779)	(.766)
Luxembourg	-2.195***	-2.139***
	(.707)	(.7)
Netherlands	-2.333***	-2.303***
	(.735)	(.738)
Sweden	-2.666***	-2.621***
	(.744)	(.733)
IssueDate	.252***	.253***
	(.041)	(.041)
IssueSize	.001**	.001**
	0	0
Maturity Base: <5Years		
5Y < M < 10Y	.445*	.469*
	(.256)	(.252)
10Y< M < 15Y	.294	.31
	(.43)	(.424)
15Y < M < 20Y	.23	.246
	(.648)	(.644)
20Y < M	-.593	-.568
	(.415)	(.437)
Perpetual	-1.567*	-1.451
	(.947)	(.943)

	(1) SLB	(2) SLB
CreditRating Base: Upper Investment Grade		
Lower Investment Grade	2.411***	2.368***
	(.731)	(.726)
Speculative Grade	3.178***	3.16***
	(.686)	(.681)
No Rating	2.67***	2.689***
	(.644)	(.642)
Constant	-65.619***	-65.747***
	(10.019)	(10.074)
Clustered SE	Y	Y
Observations	2122	2122
Pseudo R^2	.226	.226
Log-Likelihood	-403.17	-403.579
Chi^2	176.727	175.309

Note. Standard errors (SE) are in parentheses *** p<.01, ** p<.05, * p<.1. Standard errors are clustered at the issuer level, as some companies have issued more than one SLB.

Table 11. Estimated Risk Ratios – Complete Results

	(1)	(2)
	SLB	SLB
Industry Base: Communications		
Consumer Discretionary	1.095	1.056
	(.677)	(.657)
Consumer Staples	3.271*	2.939*
	(2.004)	(1.810)
Energy	2.460	2.299
	(1.761)	(1.639)
Health Care	1.363	1.365
	(.954)	(.951)
Industrials	1.770	1.614
	(1.166)	(1.064)
Materials	3.612**	3.453**
	(2.125)	(2.035)
Technology	1.135	1.035
	(.90)	(.818)
Utilities	3.885*	3.653*
	(2.936)	(2.756)
ESGRating Base: ESG Leader		
ESG Laggard	.197**	
	(.153)	
No ESG Rating	.476***	
	(.122)	
Env.Rating Base: Env. Top Performer		
Env. Laggard		.254**
		(.164)
No Env. Rating		.463***
		(.120)
Country Base: Austria		
Germany	.081***	.083***
	(.052)	(.052)
France	.150***	.150***
	(.068)	(.068)
Italy	.162***	.164***
	(.082)	(.083)
Luxembourg	.191***	.197***
	(.088)	(.090)
Netherlands	.170***	.172***
	(.087)	(.089)

Appendix A: Tables

	(1)	(2)
	SLB	SLB
Sweden	.128***	.131***
	(.067)	(.068)
IssueDate	1.237***	1.238***
	(.052)	(.053)
IssueSize	1.001**	1.001**
	(.000)	(.000)
Maturity Base: <5Years		
5Y < M < 10Y	1.448*	1.477**
	(.326)	(.329)
10Y< M < 15Y	1.260	1.276
	(.424)	(.426)
15Y < M < 20Y	1.277	1.289
	(.640)	(.644)
20Y < M	.60	.612
	(.238)	(.251)
Perpetual	.277	.300
	(.225)	(.246)
CreditRating Base: Upper Investment Grade		
Lower Investment Grade	8.698***	8.445***
	(5.821)	(5.634)
Speculative Grade	16.732***	16.593***
	(10.655)	(10.539)
No Rating	11.106***	11.322***
	(6.760)	(6.877)
Constant	4.20e-25***	3.52e-25***
	(4.34e-24)	(3.65e-24)
Clustered SE	Y	Y
Observations	2122	2122
Log-Likelihood	-421.237	-421.497
AIC	.422	.423
BIC	-15489.47	-15488.95

Note. Standard errors (SE) are in parentheses *** p<.01, ** p<.05, * p<.1. Standard errors are clustered at the issuer level, as some companies have issued more than one SLB.

Table 12. Pearson Goodness-of-Fit and Model Specification Test

Pearson Goodness-of-Fit Test

Number of observations	2,122
Number of covariate patterns	2,077
Pearson chi2(2050)	2016.65
Prob > chi2	.696

Linktest

Number of observations	2,122
LR chi2(2)	241.10
Prob>chi2	.000
Pseudo R2	.231

SLB	Coefficient	Std. err.	z	P>|z|
_hat	.705	.269	2.63	.009
_hatsq	-.116	.103	-1.13	.259
_cons	-.143	.165	-.87	.385

Appendix B: Figures

Figure 2. Worldwide SLB Issuances by Industry

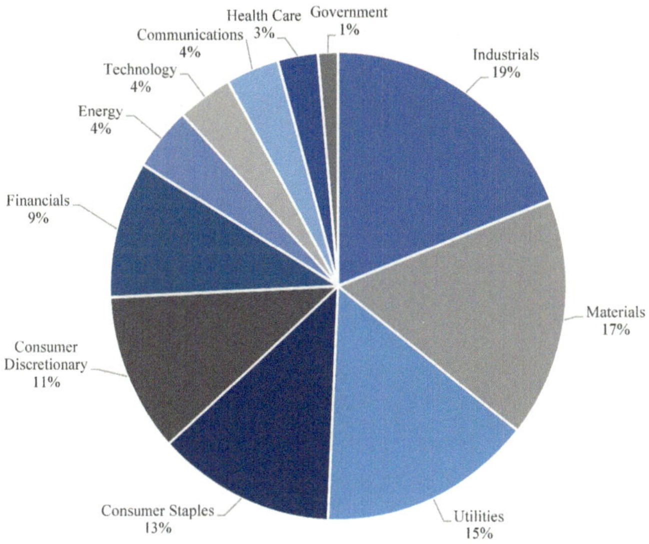

Source: Bloomberg Data as of 27.01.2023

Chapter 2 Sustainable Finance Instruments and Support – One Size Does Not Fit All –

Understanding Companies' Individual Sustainable Finance Needs and Providing Tailored Support

Isabelle Cathérine Hinsche[*]

Abstract

The financial sector is taking on a crucial role in advancing the transition towards a sustainable economy and society. In particular, banks advise companies and investors on sustainable finance and sustainable finance instruments. This study conducted an online survey with 700 invited companies to assess how companies differ in their sustainable finance interests and needs, using a mixed method approach, and to subsequently determine how banks can improve and tailor their sustainable finance support accordingly. The study analyzes market relevant factors and company characteristics that can drive and simplify sustainable finance instrument use. Moreover, it determines barriers and motivational factors regarding the implementation, as well as companies' evaluation of their banks' support. The survey results show that sustainable finance interests and needs differ particularly for company sizes and that companies view their banks as potential sparring partners who help them acquire the necessary financial resources for their sustainability transition. Based on these findings, the paper formulates three recommendations on how to improve the effectiveness of banks' sustainable finance support, including how banks can provide a tailored sustainable finance support to their customers.

JEL Classification: C83, G21, G23, G28, G32, G38, H23, Q01, Q58

Keywords: Sustainable Finance, Sustainable Finance Instruments, Sustainable Finance Support, Bank Advisory, Corporate Customers

---

* I would like to thank Rainer Klump, Tim Buchholz and Marcus Pratsch for intriguing discussions, valuable input and support. Furthermore, I thank DZ BANK Stiftung for providing the funds to implement the research project. The usual disclaimer applies.

2.1 Introduction

We are currently on a climate path that can lead to a temperature increase of as much as 4.4 °C by the end of the century and have missed the potential path of 1.5 °C global warming (Intergovernmental Panel on Climate Change (IPCC), 2021). To have a chance yet at achieving our climate targets and to limit global warming to at least 2°C, investments and economic activities urgently need to be directed towards a successful sustainability transformation. The financial sector is expected to contribute substantially by redirecting capital flows into sustainable activities. This process is termed sustainable finance and entails the inclusion of sustainability criteria in investment and credit decisions (European Commission, 2023a). To strengthen sustainable finance investments, the European Union (EU) adopted the European Green Deal Investment Plan, which is set to mobilize €1 trillion of public and private investments into sustainable activities (European Commission, 2020a), and developed the Action Plan on Sustainable Finance (European Commission, 2020b). The action plan includes several sustainability disclosure regulations with the aim to increase transparency in regard to companies' sustainability performance and to foster the integration of sustainability criteria into risk management. This regulatory background has fueled the development of sustainable finance instruments (SFIs), which can either be used to finance a classified sustainable project or can be linked to a company's sustainability targets.

Banks are taking on a crucial role in advancing the sustainability transition by advising companies on sustainable finance and SFIs. However, the aforementioned sustainability disclosure regulations do not apply to all companies equally and the increased transparency regarding their sustainability performance can affect companies differently. Therefore, companies' interest in sustainable finance and their needs regarding SFIs likely differ as well. Consequently, banks should provide a tailored sustainable finance support to their corporate customers, to foster an efficient use of sustainable finance. *But how do companies differ in their sustainable finance interests and needs, and how can banks provide a tailored sustainable finance (instrument) support to their credit customers accordingly?*

In order to answer this research question, this study implemented an online survey together with DZ BANK AG, Germany's second largest bank. In June 2023, 700 corporate customers of the bank were invited to an anonymous survey based on a mailing list that was generated by the bank's client supervisors. The survey consists of four parts. Firstly, respondents were introduced to the concept of sustainable finance instruments and were subsequently asked about their sustainable finance instrument use. Secondly, the survey questioned companies about their promotional loan use and their desired form of support through their financing partners. Thirdly, the survey included questions about the companies' perceived transformation risk, regulatory pressure, financing access and financing conditions. Finally, the survey concluded by collecting company characteristics and personal information. Of the 700 addressed companies, 123 responses were recorded, yielding a response rate of 17.6 %.

In order to assess companies' individual sustainable finance interests and needs, this study uses a mixed method research approach, including both quantitative and qualitative questions in the survey. The quantitative variables are analyzed using correlation and logistic regression analysis to test for the strength and direction of association between variables. The qualitative questions are evaluated using thematic content analysis based on Kuckartz (2014) and the final categorical system can be interpreted together with the quantitative results using quantification.

Furthermore, the study divides respondents into respective company size, company sector and company capital market groups. The defined company groups provide a foundation to analyze companies' sustainable finance instrument use and interest, as a company's size, sector and capital market activity influence whether and how sustainability transparency regulations affect a company's financing access and conditions. Indeed, survey results show that SFI use is particularly high for companies that have a large revenue and for companies that are active in capital markets.

Based on the survey questions, the study subsequently studies four push factors and three pull factors that could affect companies' sustainable finance instrument use and likely vary for the defined company size, sector and capital market groups respectively. The four defined push factors, which could drive companies to use SFIs, are a company's perceived regulatory pressure, transformation risk, risk to lose financing access and likelihood that sustainability criteria and credit conditions will be linked. The survey results demonstrate a higher share of SFI users for companies that perceive a strong regulatory pressure and a slightly higher share of SFI users for companies that perceive a strong transformation risk. Moreover, all four push factors vary among the different company group sizes. The three defined pull factors, which could make it easier for companies to use SFIs, are a company's sustainability awareness, action and knowledge. The survey results demonstrate a higher share of SFI users for all companies that have a high sustainability awareness, sustainability action or sustainability

knowledge. Furthermore, all three pull factors vary statistically significantly between the defined company group sizes, with smaller companies showing a lower level of sustainability awareness, action and knowledge.

To fully understand companies' individual sustainable finance needs and to provide tailored support, the survey continues by analyzing companies' barriers and motivational factors to use SFIs. Almost half of the respondents state that they perceive barriers to SFI use and this observation does not vary for the different company size groups. However, the type of barriers differ between the company size groups, as for instance only medium-sized and large medium-sized companies state applicability in terms of company characteristics and financing needs as a barrier. Furthermore, the ranking of barriers to SFI use do not differ for the defined company size groups. Ranked as the most influential reason for not using a SFI is an insufficient SFI knowledge, followed by insufficient sustainability data, additional costs of implementing a SFI and potential greenwashing accusations. In contrast, the ranking of motivational reasons for SFI use differs between company size groups, as large medium-sized and large companies rank a potential pricing advantage as the most influential reason, compared to multinational companies that rank communication of their sustainability strategy to investors as the most influential factor.

Based on these insights and additional survey results, the study proceeds by defining companies' desired role for banks in providing sustainable finance support. Half of the respondents believe that their bank can support them in their sustainability transition, but there is also a high share (32 %) of respondents that are unsure whether their bank can support them. Nevertheless, companies view their bank as a potential sparring partner and would like to see a clear commitment from their bank to sustainable finance. Furthermore, companies primarily would like to receive information on the sustainable finance market, sustainable finance mechanisms and sustainable finance use, as well as consultation regarding KPI choice, reporting, rating optimization and promotional loans. In regard to promotional loan programs, the survey results additionally show that whilst almost half of the respondents know programs connected to sustainable finance, only 9 % have used a promotional loan. However, the interest in these programs is very high for all company sizes and supports the potential of promotional loans to support investments in companies' sustainability transition.

The aim of this paper is to assess how companies differ in regard to their sustainable finance interests and needs, and to develop a recommendation on how banks can improve their tailored sustainable finance support accordingly. Based on the survey results, this paper formulates three recommendations that could improve banks' sustainable finance support. Firstly, the survey results indicate that companies are insufficiently aware of how sustainability disclosure regulations and the subsequent increase in transparency can impact their financing access and conditions, as well as that companies do not have sufficient knowledge on sustainable finance and how sustainable finance instruments work. Consequently, banks should improve companies' awareness and knowledge regarding the sustainable finance market and instruments. Secondly, the analysis results emphasize the need for banks to advance their support regarding the implementation of SFI, as companies are asking for best practice examples and more standardized processes. Moreover, banks should clearly communicate their expectations regarding the required sustainability measures for respective company industries and sizes. Thirdly, banks need to tailor their sustainable finance support to their corporate customers, particularly to a company's size. For instance, smaller companies tend to require a more fundamental consultation and benefit from cost-sensitive sustainability measures. Overall, there is a significant potential for banks to support their corporate customers in acquiring the necessary funds to invest in their sustainability transition and to thereby strengthen the impact of sustainable finance.

This study contributes to the existing literature by identifying companies' individual sustainable finance interests and needs, with a particular focus on company size differences. Small and medium-sized companies (SMEs) make up 99 % of Germany's companies (Bundesverband mittelständische Wirtschaft (BVMW), 2023) and need to invest in their sustainability transition in the same manner as large and multinational companies. However, their respective financing needs and regulatory environment differ and can lead to varying sustainable finance interests and needs. This study highlights how banks can tailor their sustainable finance support accordingly.

The paper is structured as follows: section 2 gives an overview of the current sustainability regulatory framework and how these regulations drive companies' and banks' interest in sustainable finance (instruments). Section 3 explains the survey design and methodology, presents the data summary and analyzes the representativeness of the data sample. Based on the survey results, section 4 divides respondents into respective company size, company sector and company capital market activity groups, and subsequently evaluates how SFI use differs within these groups. Section 5 depicts companies' individual sustainable finance interests and needs by defining the current push and pull factors in the sustainable finance market and how this might differ between the defined company groups. Moreover, the study analyzes whether these factors translate into different challenges and barriers for companies' sustainable finance use and how these vary for the different company groups. Based on these insights and on the survey results, section 6 identifies companies' desired role for banks in providing sustainable finance support, as well as companies' promotional loan interest and use. Finally, based on the findings, section 7 outlines three recommendations to provide an improved and tailored sustainable finance support for companies and section 8 concludes by summarizing the paper's results and by suggesting further sustainable finance research potentials.

2.2 Sustainable Finance: Regulatory Framework, Motivation and Instrument Use

Before explaining the survey design and analyzing the survey results, the following section gives an overview of the current regulatory framework and how these regulations fuel banks' and companies' interest in sustainable finance (instruments). Based on these insights, the research question is formulated.

2.2.1 Regulatory Framework

In order to achieve its Paris Agreement targets, the European Union needs additional yearly investments of up to €290 billion (European Commission, 2019). Estimated required global annual investments to limit global warming to below 2°C even reach up to $8.1 trillion (Buchner et al., 2023). The necessary investments cannot be delivered entirely by the public sector, but significantly rely on private sector investments (Georgieva & Adrian, 2022). Consequently, the European Green Deal, which was published in 2019, includes the European Green Deal Investment Plan, with the aim to mobilize €1 trillion of sustainable investments through both, public and private investments (European Commission, 2020a).

The process of incorporating sustainability criteria into investment decisions and thereby redirecting capital flows towards more sustainable economic activities is called sustainable finance (European Commission, 2023a). To facilitate sustainable finance growth, the European Commission has developed an action plan, with three main objectives (European Commission, 2020b). Firstly, the action plan aims to redirect capital flows towards a more sustainable economy, which includes a unified classification system for sustainability activities called EU Taxonomy, as well as green financial product labels and the inclusion of sustainability in financial advice (European Commission, 2020b). Secondly, it involves the integration of sustainability into risk management through establishing sustainability-related disclosures in the financial services sector, such as the sustainable finance disclosure regulation (SFDR[8]). Finally, the action plan fosters transparency by developing guidelines on climate-related information reporting. The most prominent example is the corporate sustainability reporting directive (CSRD[9]).

2.2.2 Why Do Companies and Banks Care About Sustainable Finance?

The sustainability disclosure regulations apply to both, companies and financial institutions, increasing the transparency regarding their sustainability performance and risk. This in turn leads to varying effects and motivations for companies and banks respectively. Financial institutions for instance need to adhere to the SFDR, as well as the CSRD,

8 The SFDR entered into force January 2021 and requires financial institutions to report on their products' sustainability risk, both in terms of how climate risk affects the product and how the product affects the climate (European Commission, 2023b).

9 The CSRD entered into force January 2023 and requires companies to report on how sustainability risk affects their company and how their company impacts society and the environment, starting for the financial year 2024 (European Commission, 2023c).

and new measures such as the green asset ratio[10] are introduced as a comparable sustainability measure among lenders. Currently, the increased transparency has no impact on banks' business operations (Deutsche Bank, 2022). However, banks are preparing for potential further regulations that, for example, link a bank's capital requirements to its green asset ratio or that introduce other forms of penalties for having a low green asset ratio.

Furthermore, financial supervisory institutions, such as the European Central Bank (ECB), have started to analyze and test banks' exposure and resilience to climate-related risks in the form of climate stress tests (ECB, 2022). So far, the assessment does not include any consequences for banks' capital requirements, but the ECB urges banks to comply with their supervisory expectations on climate and environmental risk by the end of 2024 (Walther, 2023). Finally, banks are interested in sustainable finance, as they can strengthen and expand their customer relations by providing guidance and helping their customers to seize the opportunities of sustainable finance (Coleton et al., 2020).

Companies also have to adhere to the CSRD and potentially further national sustainability disclosure regulations, such as the Supply Chain Act (LkSG) in Germany (Federal Ministry of Labour and Social Affairs (BMAS), 2023). The increased transparency on a company's sustainability performance can affect their financing access and conditions. Firstly, as investors are increasingly using exclusion criteria in their investment decisions, a company's sustainability performance can affect its financing access (Bogmans et al., 2023). Secondly, financial instruments are increasingly being linked to a company's sustainability performance or are restricted to financing a predetermined sustainable project, thereby affecting the issuer's financing conditions (Berrada et al., 2022; Kölbel & Lambillon, 2022; Kapraun et al., 2021).

10 The green asset ratio (GAR) measures the percentage of a lender's assets invested in sustainable activities. As small and medium-sized companies (SMEs) predominantly do not have to adhere to CSRD-level reporting yet, they cannot be included in the ratio. This prompted a second measure called banking book taxonomy alignment ratio (BTAR), which also includes SMEs through a bilateral data exchange (Deutsche Bank, 2022).

Financial instruments with a sustainable finance structure are called sustainable finance instruments (SFIs) and can either be use-of-proceeds or sustainability-linked instruments. Use-of-proceeds instruments restrict the allocation of their proceeds to a predetermined environmentally or socially beneficial project (International Capital Market Association (ICMA), 2021). The most commonly known use of proceeds instrument is a green bond, which allocates all proceeds to an environmentally focused investment project (Hinsche & Klump, 2023). In contrast, sustainability-linked instruments take a company-level view by allowing their proceeds to be used for general purposes. They are linked to company-level sustainability targets and require a penalty in case of failure to meet these targets, for instance in the form of a coupon step-up (ICMA, 2023). SFI structures can be applied to any form of credit instruments, such as for example a bond, schuldscheindarlehen (SSD) or loan.

Research on the pricing of SFIs suggest a pricing premium for SFIs compared to an equal conventional instrument. A potential pricing premium is most commonly known as a Greenium and indicates that investors are willing to accept a lower yield for a green instrument compared to an equivalent conventional instrument, which leads to a negative pricing premium and thus lower financing costs for the issuer (Hinsche, 2021). The estimations vary greatly, for instance in the green bond market from -2 basis points to -48 basis points (Gianfrate & Peri, 2019; Zerbib, 2019; Partridge & Medda, 2020; Kapraun et al., 2021; Climate Bonds Initiative (CBI), 2023), but in general imply that a company's sustainability performance and SFI use can affect its financing conditions. Beyond a company's financing, SFIs allow companies to communicate their sustainability transition strategy and can have effects, for example, on the stock market and employer attractiveness (Deschryver & De Mariz, 2020; Flammer, 2020; Maltais & Nykvist, 2020; Tang & Zhang, 2020).

Overall, looking at the company-bank relation from a sustainable finance point of view, companies are interested in sustainable finance, as well as SFIs, to receive attractive financing and banks are interested in sustainable finance to maintain their customer relations and to strengthen their business model by providing high-quality advisory services and support for companies. However, the regulatory framework differs for companies, creating varying environments for sustainable finance and SFI use. For instance, the CSRD, which entered into force January 2023, currently only applies to companies that fulfil two out of the following three criteria; the company must have a minimum of €20 million in total assets, €40 million in turnover or 250 employees (European Commission, 2023c). Furthermore, the CSRD applies to all listed SMEs. Consequently, SMEs that do not fulfil these criteria so far do not have to adhere to the CSRD, but might be affected by increased transparency requirements through the supply chain. Therefore, companies are facing different regulatory environments and can subsequently be expected to have varying sustainable finance interests and needs.

These differing regulatory environments can be narrowed down to three distinct company characteristics. Sustainability disclosure regulations apply to a company depending on its company size and whether it is listed. Furthermore, an increased transparency regarding a company's sustainability performance can affect its financing differently, depending on the company's industry, as for instance companies from the oil and gas industry are more often subject to exclusion criteria and subsequent divestment (Bogmans et al., 2023). Consequently, banks should recognize these potential differences and provide sustainable finance support tailored to companies' individual needs. ***But how do companies differ in their sustainable finance interests and needs, and how can banks provide a tailored sustainable finance (instrument) support to their credit customers accordingly?*** To answer this question, this research paper develops and conducts a survey with a large population of corporate customers from Germany's second largest bank, DZ BANK AG. Subsequently, the paper defines companies' individual sustainable finance interests and needs, and develops an action plan to customize sustainable finance (instrument) support for the identified company groups.

2.3 Sustainable Finance Survey

2.3.1 Survey Design

As explained above, this study aims to investigate companies' individual sustainable finance needs by conducting a survey. In June 2023, 700 corporate customers of DZ BANK AG were invited to participate in an online survey. The survey consists of four parts, an overview of the survey can be found in Appendix C. The first part shortly introduces and explains the concept of sustainable finance instruments and subsequently poses questions about companies' sustainable finance instrument use. The second part includes questions regarding companies' promotional loan use, as well as the desired advisory and support of their respective banks. The third part asks companies about their perceived transformation risk, regulatory pressure, as well as financing access and financing conditions. The survey concludes with questions concerning company characteristics and personal information. The survey was conducted anonymously, in order to enable a true assessment, particularly for questions that included the evaluation of their financing partners, as well as companies' sustainability knowledge and awareness. Consequently, self-reported answers could not be linked to publicly available administrative data. Companies were able to voluntarily state their company name, in order to receive the survey results, however, only 34 out of 93 companies chose to submit their company name.

2.3.2 Methodology

This study follows a mixed method approach using both quantitative and qualitative research methods. The survey predominantly consists of quantitative questions, with some qualitative open questions. This denotes a convergent parallel design, as both quantitative and qualitative methods are employed within the same survey and subsequent analysis (Creswell & Creswell, 2018). Moreover, the survey uses a concurrent embedded strategy (Creswell & Creswell, 2018), as qualitative questions are integrated to allow for a deeper complementary understanding of the quantitative results (Greene et al., 1989) and to generate additional knowledge (Morgan, 2014). The quantitative variables are studied using correlation analysis, applying Fisher's exact test to check the existence of an association and Cramér's V to test the strength of association. Additionally, a logistic regression for each association is run, to gain a deeper understanding of the direction of association based on the resulting odds ratios.

In regard to the qualitative analysis, a thematic content analysis is performed using the seven steps of Kuckartz (2014). Using this method, all qualitative answers are first translated, main thematic categories developed and all qualitative answers coded accordingly. Subsequently, using the existing material, subcategories for each main thematic category are developed inductively and all answers are coded in line with the advanced categorical system (Kuckartz, 2014). The final categorical system is interpreted together with the quantitative results using quantification (Fakis et al, 2014; Kuckartz, 2014), which enables the statistical analysis of qualitative data.

2.3.3 Data

The participants of the survey are corporate customers of DZ BANK AG, Germany's second largest bank, with total assets of €628 billion as of 31.12.2022 (DZ BANK, 2023a). Together with DZ BANK AG, a mailing list of corporate customers was developed and the survey link was sent out via the bank's mailing system, in order to avoid any data privacy concerns.[11] The mailing list was generated by contacting the bank's corporate client supervisors and asking them to take part in the survey project by providing their corporate customers' email addresses. The contact email emphasized that the provision is voluntary, as well as the anonymity of the survey, and highlighted the potential benefits for

11 At no point in time was the author of this paper provided with any contact details or personal information of corporate customers by DZ BANK AG.

an improved customer support. The company-wide collection yielded a final mailing list containing 700 direct corporate customers[12], which were subsequently invited by email to participate in the survey. Of the 700 addressed companies, 123 responses were recorded, resulting in a 17.6 % response rate, with 93 fully completed surveys. Table 1 and Table 2 present the summary statistics of the 93 companies that fully answered the survey.

First, looking at the company characteristics in Table 1, we find that the largest share of respondents is from the industrials sector (31.2 %), followed by the consumer discretionary (9.7 %), utilities (9.7 %), consumer staples (9.7 %) and materials (7.5 %) sector.[13] Companies from the financial, health care, information technology, communication services and real estate sector make up a share of less than 5 % respectively. Furthermore, 18 companies stated "no answer" for the company sector. Regarding companies' size, respondents were asked to state the company revenue. The data shows that the majority (50.5 %) has a company size of €50 million to €499 million in revenue, followed by 24.7 % that have a company size of €500 million to €5 billion, 10.8 % that have a company size larger than €5 billion and 9.7 % that have a company size of €10 million to €49 million. Only one respondent has a company size of up to €9 million and three companies stated "no answer" for their company size. Finally, the majority of respondents (62.4 %) are not active in capital markets[14].

12 The survey was only distributed to DZ BANK AG's direct corporate customers and not to corporate customers of the credit unions, which are also part of the DZ BANK GROUP and provide financial services to smaller companies and commercial customers.

13 The survey used the Global Industry Classification Standard (GICS) by MSCI (2023) and allowed respondents to select their industry. The responses were then aggregated to the respective sectors as defined by the GICS.

14 A company is defined as active in capital markets if it acquires financing through capital markets.

Table 1. Summary Statistics – Company Characteristics

	Survey Sample Characteristics		Population Characteristics	
	Observations	Percent of Data	Count	Percent of Data
Number of Companies	93	100 %	1,973	100 %
Company Sector				
Industrials	29	31.2 %	530	26.9 %
Consumer Discretionary	9	9.7 %	566	28.7 %
Utilities	9	9.7 %	212	10.8 %
Consumer Staples	9	9.7 %	119	6.0 %
Materials	7	7.5 %	133	6.7 %
Financials	4	4.3 %	55	2.8 %
Health Care	4	4.3 %	93	4.7 %
Information Technology	2	2.2 %	-	-
Communication Services	1	1.1 %	193	9.8 %
Real Estate	1	1.1 %	-	-
No Answer	18	19.4 %	-	-
Other	-	-	72	3.6 %
Company Size				
Up to €9 million	1	1.1 %	-	-
€10 mm to €49 million	9	9.7 %	786	39.8 %
€50 mm to €499 million	47	50.5 %	497	25.2 %
€500 mm to €5 billion	23	24.7 %	550	27.9 %
Bigger than €5 billion	10	10.8 %	140	7.1 %
No Answer	3	3.2 %	-	-
Company Capital Market Activity				
Yes	34	36.6 %	1,085	55 %
No	58	62.4 %	888	45 %
I don't know	1	1.1 %	-	-

Source: This table presents the company summary statistics of the 93 survey respondents, as well as the population characteristics of the 1,973 direct corporate customers of DZ BANK AG. The companies' sector is classified based on the Global Industry Classification Standard by MSCI and the companies' size in terms of revenue is rounded to millions and divided into five respective revenue groups.

Looking at the sustainability characteristics in Table 2, we find that slightly more than half of the respondents (55.9 %) have a carbon footprint, whilst only 22.6 % have an ESG rating. In fact, 9.7 % of all respondents are unfamiliar with the term ESG. Moreover, whilst a large share of respondents (69.9 %) has company-level sustainability targets, only 12.9 % have an additional commitment scheme, for instance in the form of board management compensation that is linked to sustainability criteria. Finally, 14 % of respondents have used a SFI and 6.5 % are currently underway to implement a SFI, whilst 12.9 % of companies were unfamiliar with SFIs before the survey, as seen in Appendix A, Table 6.

Table 2. Summary Statistics – Company Sustainability Characteristics

	Observations	Percent of Data
Number of Companies	93	100 %
Carbon Footprint		
Yes	52	55.9 %
No	33	35.5 %
I don't know	8	8.6 %
ESG Rating		
Yes	21	22.6 %
No	53	57.0 %
I don't know	10	10.8 %
Unfamiliar with ESG term	9	9.7 %
Company-Level Sustainability Targets		
Yes	65	69.9 %
No	25	26.9 %
I don't know	3	3.2 %
Sustainability Target Commitment Scheme		
Yes	12	12.9 %
No	65	69.9 %
I don't know	16	17.2 %

Source: This table presents companies' sustainability characteristics of the 93 survey respondents.

Lastly, looking at the recorded respondent information, we find that 94.5 % of respondents are working in the finance division, which was the intended target group of the survey (see Appendix A, Table 3). Furthermore, 87.9 % of respondents are male and the highest share of respondents are age 40 to 49 (30.8 %) and 50 to 59 (30.8 %) respectively, followed by 23.1 % that are age 30 to 39. Moreover, the majority of respondents (52.7 %) have neither study nor work experience in the field of sustainability, whilst 29.7 % have work experience and only 8.8 % have both, work and study experience in the field of sustainability.

2.3.4 Representativeness

In order to assess the sample's representativeness, the following section compares the survey sample characteristics to DZ BANK AG's total direct corporate customer population, as seen in Table 1.[15] DZ BANK AG has a total of 1,973 direct corporate customers, as of July 2023. The highest share of corporate customers are from the consumer discretionary (28.7 %) and industrials (26.9 %) sector. This also hold true for the survey sample, however, the share of respondents from the consumer discretionary sector is significantly smaller, as seen in Table 1. In regard to company size, the total corporate customer population has equal shares of companies with a revenue of €10 to €49 million, €50 to €499 million and €500 million to €5 billion respectively, but only 7.1 % have a revenue larger than €5 billion. The survey sample demonstrates a similar share for companies with a revenue of €500 million to €5 billion and a revenue larger than €5 billion, but a higher share of companies that have a revenue of €50 to €499 million and a lower share of companies that have a revenue of €10 to €49 million. Finally, whilst approximately 55 % of the total corporate customer population is active in capital markets, only 36.6 % of the survey sample are active in capital markets.

15 DZ BANK AG's population characteristics are based on administrative data, whilst the survey sample characteristics are based on self-reported data, because the survey cannot be linked to administrative data, as explained in section 3.1.

2.4 Realizing That One Size Does Not Fit All

As explained in section 2, sustainability-related disclosure regulations apply to companies depending on the company's size and whether the company is listed. Furthermore, the increased transparency regarding a company's sustainability performance leads to varying effects on a company's financing access and conditions, depending on a company's sector. Consequently, companies face very different regulatory and market environments that in turn can influence their sustainable finance needs, as well as SFI use, and are therefore divided into company size, company sector and capital market groups.

2.4.1 Identifying Company Groups

Firstly, respondents are split into four company size groups based on their respective revenue group, as reported in the survey. Companies with a revenue of €10 to €49 million are considered "medium-sized companies", companies with a revenue from €50 to €499 million are called "large medium-sized companies", companies with a revenue from €500 million to €5 billion are called "large companies" and companies with a revenue larger than €5 billion are called "multinationals". This division is based on the internal allocation used by DZ BANK AG, as it reflects the different financing needs in the conventional finance market and is therefore a good baseline to analyze how it translates to the sustainable finance market. The sample only includes one respondent with a revenue smaller or equal to €9 million, which is excluded as an outlier for the company size group division. The sample does not include more companies with such a small revenue, as the survey was only distributed to DZ BANK AG's direct corporate customers and not to corporate customers of the credit unions, which are also part of the DZ BANK GROUP and provide financial services to smaller companies and commercial customers.

Secondly, respondents are split into two capital market groups, differentiating between companies that are active in capital markets and companies that are not active in capital markets, as reported in the survey. A company is defined as active in capital markets if it acquires financing through capital markets. Finally, respondents are split into ten sector groups, based on companies' reported industries and in line with the Global Industry Classification Standard by MSCI (2023).

2.4.2 Sustainable Finance Instrument Use

Having defined the three respective company groups, the following section analyzes whether a difference in SFI use can be observed for the individual company groups. In general, 13 companies state that they have used a SFI before and 6 companies state that they are currently underway to implement a SFI. The reported SFIs used and being implemented are predominantly forms of loans and credits (69 %), followed by schuldscheindarlehen (27 %) and one bond.

Regarding SFI use among the respective company groups, the survey results show a significant difference between the four company size groups. As seen in Figure 1, SFI use increases with company size. This correlation is statistically significant at the 1 % level (see Appendix A, Table 4) and the positive association is confirmed by running a logistic regression, resulting in significant and larger than one odds ratios for large and multinational company groups compared to the baseline group of large medium-sized companies (see Appendix A, Table 5).

Figure 1. Sustainable Finance Instrument Use by Company Size

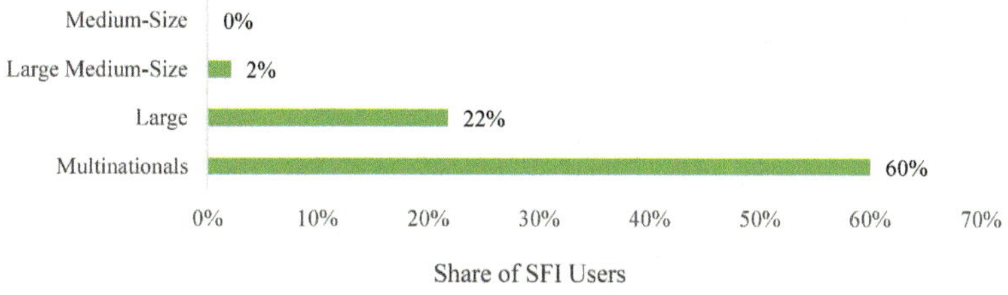

Source: This figure presents the share of SFI users for the four defined company size groups, based on the survey data reported in Appendix A, Table 6.

Whilst none of the medium-sized companies and only 2 % of large medium-sized companies have used a SFI, 22 % of large companies and 60 % of multinational companies have used a SFI. This is in line with a study by DZ BANK (2023b), which shows that companies' willingness to invest in sustainability increases with company size. Moreover, this pattern also holds when looking at the share of companies that have not used a SFI so far, but have considered it already. Whilst the share of companies is less than 50 % for medium-sized, large medium-sized and large companies, 75 % of multinational companies have considered using a SFIs (see Appendix A, Table 6). Overall, these results demonstrate that SFI use significantly differs between smaller and larger companies.

Secondly, a significant difference in SFI use can also be found looking at the two capital market groups. The percentage of companies which have used a SFI is more than three times as high (26 %) for companies which are active in capital markets, compared to companies which are not active in capital markets (7 %), as seen in Figure 2.

Figure 2. Sustainable Finance Instrument Use by Capital Market Activity

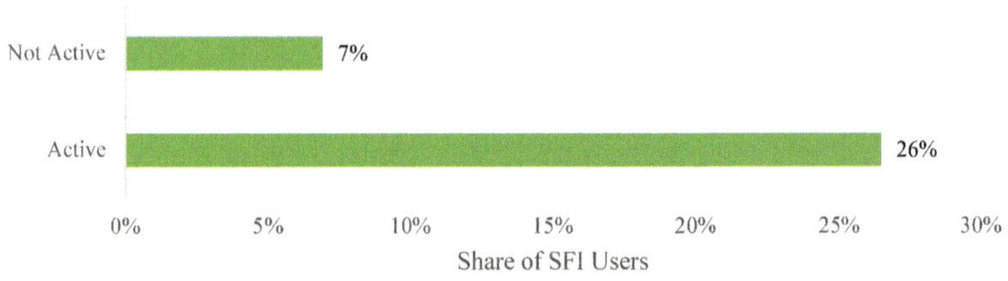

Source: This figure presents the share of SFI users for the two defined capital market activity groups, based on the survey data reported in Appendix A, Table 6.

This result shows that SFI use significantly differs with a company's capital market activity. The association between capital market activity and SFI use is statistically significant at the 5 % level (see Appendix A, Table 4). Moreover, the logistic regression results (see Appendix A, Table 5) confirm higher odds for companies active in capital markets to be SFI users compared to the baseline group of companies not active in capital markets.

Finally, the survey results demonstrate a difference in SFI use between the company sectors as well (see Appendix B, Figure 3), even though no statistically significant association between company sectors and SFI use can be found (see Appendix A, Table 4 and Table 5). The highest share of SFI users can be observed for the financials (25 %) and health care sector (25 %), followed by the consumer discretionary (22 %) and utilities (22 %) sector. In contrast, only 11 % of the consumer staples and 10 % of the industrials sector use SFIs and none of the companies from the communication services, information technology, materials and real estate sector. Interestingly, the results do not indicate a higher SFI use among more carbon-intensive sectors.

2.5 Companies' Individual Sustainable Finance Interests & Needs

The survey results suggest that companies' different regulatory and market environments indeed might lead to varying SFI use. The following section investigates how push and pull factors, as well as barriers, in regard to SFI use vary within the respective company groups. Moreover, the different desired roles for the financial sector and the use of alternative financial instruments in the form of promotional loans are discussed.

2.5.1 What Are Current Push and Pull Factors in the Sustainable Finance Market?

In the case at hand, push factors are aspects or circumstances that drive companies to use SFIs, whilst pull factors make it easier for companies to use SFIs. Based on the survey results, the following section studies four identified push and three identified pull factors that particularly capture how companies are affected by sustainability disclosure regulations, as well as companies' sustainability characteristics. The four push factors are perceived regulatory pressure, perceived transformation risk, perceived risk to lose financing access and perceived likelihood that sustainability criteria and credit conditions will be linked. The three pull factors are a company's sustainable awareness, sustainability action and sustainable finance knowledge. The individual push and pull factor's effect on SFI use is discussed, as well as how the push and pull factors vary with different company sizes, company sectors and with being active in capital markets.

2.5.1.1 Perceived Regulatory Pressure

The first push factor is a company's perceived regulatory pressure. As explained in section 2, a significant number of sustainability-related disclosure regulations have been introduced in recent years, increasing the transparency regarding a company's sustainability risk and performance. As sustainability criteria are progressively incorporated in investment and credit decisions, as well as risk management, the higher transparency increases a company's stake to communicate their sustainability transition strategy to investors and financing partners. Thus, a perceived strong regulatory pressure could drive companies towards an increased SFI use.

Indeed, the survey results show a higher share of SFI users among companies that also perceive a stronger regulatory pressure, as seen in Figure 4. The logistic regression results show, albeit not statistically significant, higher odds for companies with strong or very strong perceived regulatory pressure to be SFI users compared to the baseline of average perceived regulatory pressure (see Appendix A, Table 7a).

Figure 4. Sustainable Finance Instrument Use by Perceived Regulatory Pressure

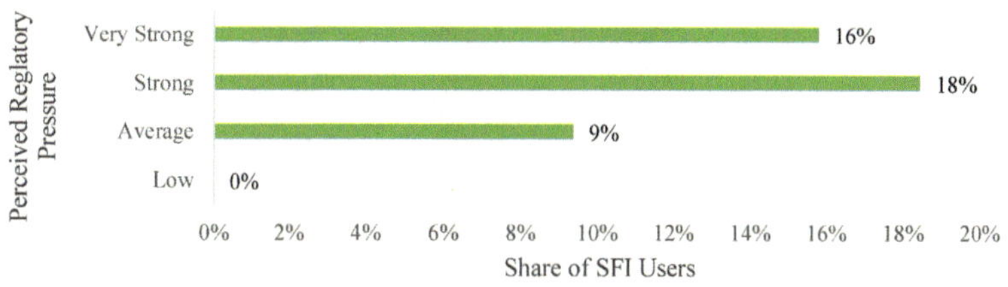

Source: This figure presents the share of SFI users for different levels of perceived regulatory pressure, based on the survey data reported in Appendix A, Table 8.

Of the companies which perceive regulatory pressure to be low, none have used a SFI. In contrast, of the companies which perceive regulatory pressure to be very strong, 16 % have used a SFI and the effect is strongest for companies which perceive strong regulatory pressure, of which 18 % have used a SFI. This observation suggests that the push factor of regulatory pressure mainly comes into action for companies with perceived strong or very strong regulatory pressure, compared to companies with perceived low or average regulatory pressure, and does not differentiate between varying levels of strong or very strong regulatory pressure.

Taking a closer look at perceived regulatory pressure by company size in Figure 5, it can be observed that perceived regulatory pressure on average increases with company size, albeit no statistically significant association is found (see Appendix A, Table 9). The share of companies which perceive a low regulatory pressure decreases from 11 % for medium-sized companies to none for multinational companies. In contrast, the share of companies which perceive a very strong regulatory pressure increases from 11 % for medium-sized companies to 40 % for multinational companies. In regard to capital market and company sector groups, no statistically significant relation with perceived regulatory pressure is found (see Appendix A, Table 9).

Figure 5. Perceived Regulatory Pressure by Company Size

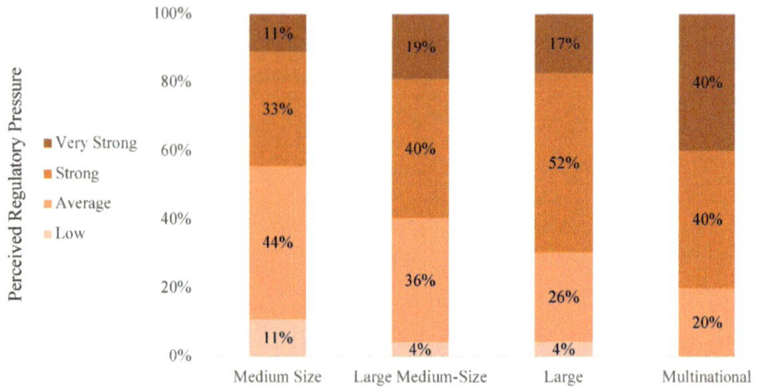

Source: This figure presents the respective share of different levels of perceived regulatory pressure by the four defined company size groups, based on the survey data reported in Appendix A, Table 10.

Based on Figure 5, the survey results suggest that larger companies perceive on average a stronger regulatory pressure than smaller companies. This difference in perception is expected, as a lot of sustainability regulations have so far been focused on large companies, such as the NFRD[16] and the Supply Chain Act[17]. However, sustainability regulations are evolving to apply to smaller and medium-sized companies as well, such as the CSRD, which replaced the NFRD in January 2023 and which will also apply to SMEs that are active in capital markets (European Commission, 2023c), as well as the Supply Chain Act which will be mandatory for a larger set of companies as of 2024 (BMAS, 2023). Therefore, regulatory pressure can be expected to be increasing for smaller companies in the future as well.

16 The Non-Financial Reporting Directive (NFRD) applied to public-interest companies with an employee count of more than 500 employees (European Commission, 2023c).

17 The Supply Chain Act is mandatory for companies with at least 3,000 employees as of 01.01.2023, but will be mandatory for companies with at least 1,000 employees starting 2024 (BMAS, 2023).

2.5.1.2 Perceived Transformation Risk

The second push factor is a company's perceived transformation risk. A company's line of business, sustainability performance, transformation strategy and financing likely affect how strongly a company perceives to be affected by the economy's overall sustainability transition. If a company perceives to be strongly affected by the economy's sustainability transition, the higher transformation risk could push a company to use SFIs to communicate and to finance its sustainability transition strategy.

The survey results indicate only a slightly higher share of SFI users for companies with a perceived stronger transformation risk, as seen in Figure 6. This is confirmed by the correlation and logistic regression analysis results (see Appendix A, Table 4 and 7a), which indicate higher odds for companies that perceive an average, strong or very strong transformation risk to be SFI users, compared to the baseline of companies that perceive a low transformation risk, but find no statistical significance. Of the companies which state that their business is only little affected by the economy's sustainability transition, 10 % have used a SFI, whilst of the companies which state that their business is very strongly affected, 13 % have used a SFI. The observed difference is strongest for companies which perceive to be strongly affected, of which 16 % have used a SFI.

Figure 6. Sustainable Finance Instrument Use by Perceived Transformation Risk

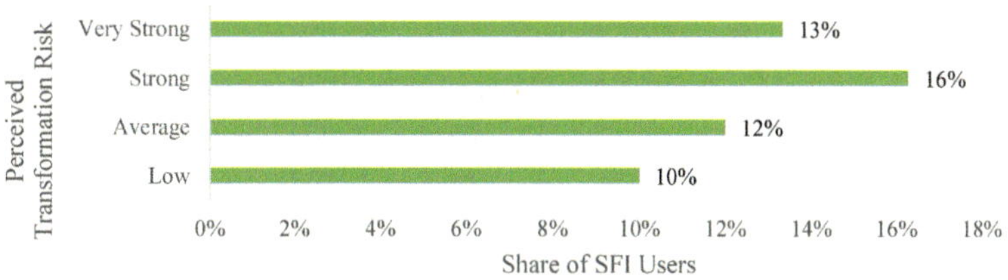

Source: This figure presents the share of SFI users for different levels of perceived transformation risk, based on the survey data reported in Appendix A, Table 8.

As seen in Figure 7, companies' perceived transformation risk substantially varies between company size groups, albeit not statistically significantly (see Appendix A, Table 9). The most pronounced difference can be found between medium-sized companies and multinational companies. Whilst 22 % of medium-sized companies perceive their business to be little affected by the economy's sustainability transition, none of multinationals perceive their business to be little affected. In contrast, none of medium-sized companies perceive their business to be very strongly affected, compared to 20 % of multinational companies. On average, larger companies appear to perceive a stronger transformation risk than smaller companies. A potential explanation could be that larger companies might experience more public pressure to transition, as they are more in the public eye, and thus perceive a stronger transformation risk.

Figure 7. Perceived Transformation Risk by Company Size

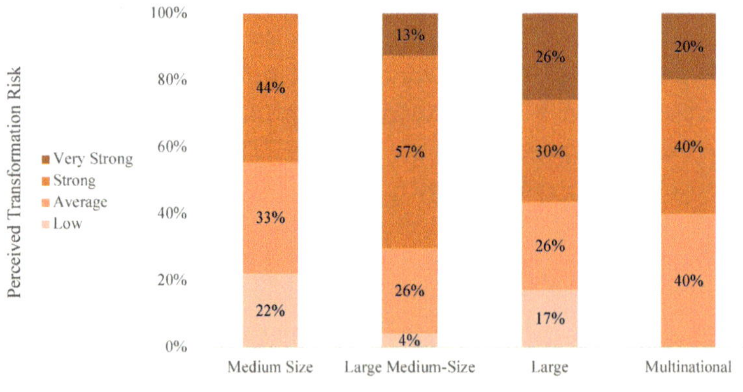

Source: This figure presents the respective share of different levels of perceived transformation risk by the four defined company size groups, based on the survey data reported in Appendix A, Table 10.

Furthermore, perceived transformation risk does not vary statistically significantly between the respective company capital market and sector groups, as seen in Appendix A, Table 9. Nevertheless, it should be noted that predominantly carbon-intensive sectors have a share of companies that perceive transformation risk as very strong. The largest share is observed for the utilities sector (44 %), followed by the consumer staples (33 %), materials (17 %), consumer discretionary (11 %) and industrials (10 %) sector (see Appendix A, Table 12). This is expected, as carbon-intensive industries are more affected by the economy's sustainability transition and thus perceive a stronger transition risk for their company.

2.5.1.3 Perceived Risk to Lose Financing Access

The third push factor is a company's perceived risk of losing its financing access should the company fail to achieve certain sustainability targets. An increasing number of financial institutions are already using negative screening as part of their sustainable investment methods, actively excluding certain companies or industries from their portfolios (United Nations Principles of Responsible Investment (UN PRI), 2020). Moreover, sustainability and ESG funds, which often include an ESG integration in the form of a cut-off value, are growing (PwC, 2022). As these developments suggest the potential of losing financing access in the case of failure to meet certain sustainability targets, SFIs can offer the opportunity to maintain financing access by making, for some instruments even binding[18], sustainability commitments. Consequently, a company's perceived risk of losing its financing access could affects its use of SFI. More precisely, if a company perceives a high risk of losing its financing access, it could incentivize a company to use SFIs.

However, according to the survey results seen in Figure 8, the share of SFI users is not higher among companies with a higher perceived risk to lose financing access. This is supported by the lack of associa-

18 An example for binding sustainability commitments are sustainability-linked instruments, which connect a financial characteristic of the instrument, most commonly the coupon, to the achievement of predetermined sustainability targets. Should the company fail to achieve the targets, the company is punished in form of a coupon step-up and thus higher financing costs (ICMA, 2023).

tion[19] between level of perceived risk to lose financing access and SFI use (see Appendix A, 7a). Interestingly, none of the companies that perceive the risk to lose financing access to be very high have used a SFI so far. A potential explanation could be that overall, the majority of companies (63 %) perceive the risk of losing financing access as low or average, only 25 % as high and only 4 % as very high (see Appendix A, Table 8), suggesting that the perceived risk of losing financing access itself is too low to show any significant effect on companies' SFI use.

Figure 8. SFI Use by Perceived Risk to Lose Financing Access

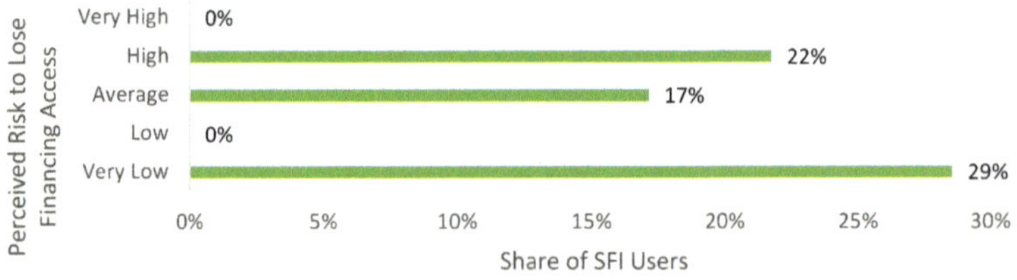

Source: This figure presents the share of SFI users for different levels of perceived risk to lose financing access, based on the survey data reported in Appendix A, Table 8.

Looking at the perceived risk to lose financing access by company size groups in Figure 9, the observed difference between company size groups is very small and statistically insignificant (see Appendix A, Table 9). Nevertheless, an increasing relation can be found for a very high perceived risk to lose financing access, as seen in Figure 9. Whilst none of medium-sized companies perceive the risk of losing their financing access due to failure to achieve certain sustainability targets as very high, the share increases with company size up to 10 % for multinational companies.

19 In fact, Fisher's exact test indicates a significant correlation (see Appendix A, Table 4). However, when looking at the logistic regression results in Appendix A, Table 7a, one can see that the correlation is driven by perfect predictions and that any association is in fact statistically insignificant.

Furthermore, half of multinational companies perceive the risk of losing financing access as high or very high, compared to none of medium-sized companies. Consequently, the observations of Figure 9 indicate that perceived risk to lose financing access differs particularly for medium-sized companies and is on average lower than for all other company size groups. This could potentially be caused by a lower awareness of smaller companies regarding how their financing access might be affected by their sustainability performance and is further analyzed in sections 5.1.5 to 5.1.7.

Figure 9. Perceived Risk to Lose Financing Access by Company Size

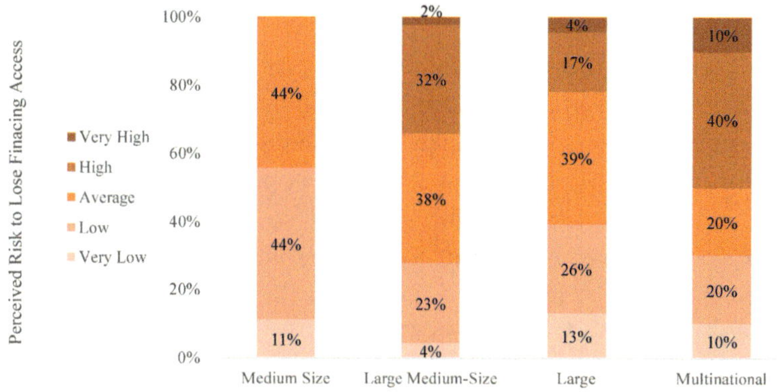

Source: This figure presents the respective share of different levels of perceived risk to lose financing access by the four defined company size groups, based on the survey data reported in Appendix A, Table 10.

In regard to company capital market groups, no significant relation with perceived risk to lose financing access can be found, whilst the correlation analysis indicates an association between company sector groups and perceived risk to lose financing access, statistically significant at the 1% level (see Appendix A, Table 9). In fact, only more carbon-intensive sectors perceive the risk to lose financing access as high or very high as seen in Appendix B, Figure 10. This suggests that the perceived risk to lose financing access is on average higher among more carbon-intensive companies.

2.5.1.4 Perceived Likelihood of Sustainability & Credit Condition Linkage

The fourth push factor is a company's perceived likelihood that sustainability criteria and credit conditions will be linked. With the advancing integration of sustainability criteria into investment and credit decisions, as well as risk management methods, companies are preparing for financing conditions to be linked to sustainability criteria (LBBW, 2022). As sustainability-linked financing instruments are demonstrating a potential pricing advantage in the current market (Berrada et al., 2022; CBI, 2022; Kölbel & Lambillon, 2022), a perceived higher likelihood of linkage could go hand in hand with a higher SFI use.

As seen in Figure 11, the share of SFI users is not higher among companies with a higher perceived likelihood that sustainability criteria and credit conditions will be linked. Even though overall, the majority of companies (66 %) think that a link between sustainability criteria and credit conditions is likely or very likely (see Appendix A, Table 8), the expectation does not appear to translate into a higher use of SFI. This is supported by the lack of any statistically significant association as seen in Appendix A, Table 4 and 7a.

Figure 11. Sustainable Finance Instrument Use by Perceived Likelihood of Linkage

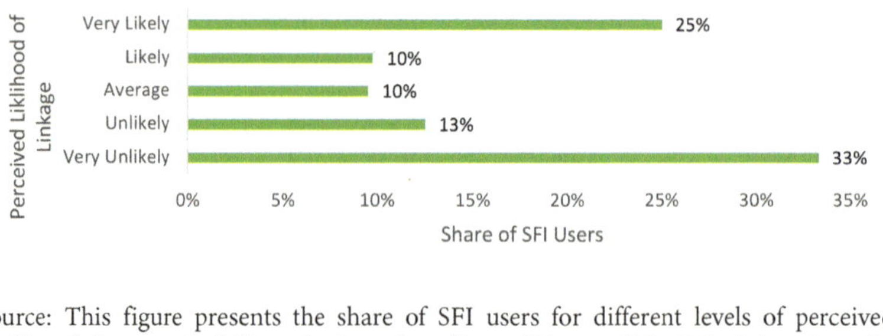

Source: This figure presents the share of SFI users for different levels of perceived likelihood that sustainability criteria and credit conditions will be linked, based on the survey data reported in Appendix A, Table 8.

Looking at the perceived likelihood of linkage among the different company size groups in Figure 12, the survey results indicate that the perceived likelihood on average increases with company size. This is supported by the correlation analysis results, which demonstrate a relation between levels of perceived likelihood of linkage and the four company size groups, statistically significant at the 5 % level (see Appendix A, Table 9). The variation among company size groups is most pronounced for companies which perceive the likelihood that sustainability criteria and credit conditions will be linked as likely or very likely, as seen in Figure 12. In fact, none of the medium-sized companies perceive the likelihood of linkage to be very likely, compared to 21 % of large medium-sized companies, 26 % of large companies and 30 % of multinational companies.

Figure 12. Perceived Likelihood of Linkage by Company Size

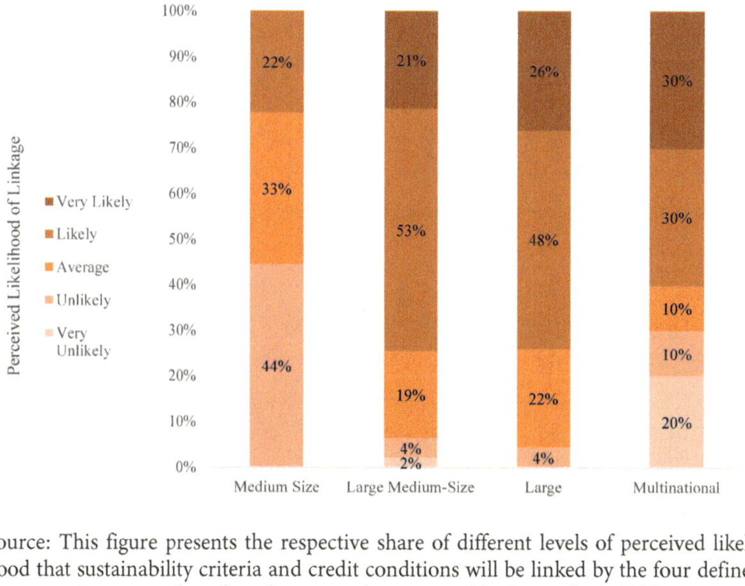

Source: This figure presents the respective share of different levels of perceived likelihood that sustainability criteria and credit conditions will be linked by the four defined company size groups, based on the survey data reported in Appendix A, Table 10.

Thus, on average, larger companies perceive the likelihood that sustainability criteria and credit conditions will be linked to be higher than smaller companies. The perceived higher likelihood of linkage for larger companies is likely caused by the more advanced sustainability disclosure regulations and measures for larger companies. For instance, banks need to report their green asset ratio (GAR) representing the sustainability of their lending activities, as explained in section 2.2. However, the GAR currently excludes lending to SMEs, as they cannot provide sustainability data in line with CSRD requirements yet. In contrast, larger companies already have to report their sustainability performance and therefore perceive a higher likelihood that this sustainability data might affect their financing conditions. Finally, in regard to perceived likelihood of linkage between company capital market and sector groups, no significant relation is found (see Appendix A, Table 9).

2.5.1.5 Company's Sustainability Awareness

The first pull factor is a company's sustainability awareness. In order to use a SFI, companies need to define company-level or project-level sustainability targets. Consequently, the hurdle to use a SFI is lower, if companies are already aware of their own sustainability performance. The survey measured companies' sustainability awareness through two measures. Firstly, respondents are asked whether the company is already determining its carbon footprint and secondly, whether the company has an ESG rating. Whilst the carbon footprint is a more fundamental measure and only captures a company's generated greenhouse gases, the ESG rating is a more complex indicator, measuring a company's environmental, social and governance performance, thus providing a more detailed understanding of a company's sustainability performance beyond its carbon footprint (UN PRI, 2023). A company does not need an ESG rating in order to use a SFI, but it reflects a company's more advanced awareness of its own sustainability performance. Therefore, one can expect to observe a higher share of SFI users amongst companies that have a carbon footprint and an even more pronounced difference for companies that have an ESG rating.

As seen in Figure 13, the survey results confirm a higher share of SFI users for companies with a higher sustainability awareness in terms of having a carbon footprint or ESG rating. In fact, 19 % of companies that have a carbon footprint have used a SFI, compared to only 6 % of companies that do not have a carbon footprint.

Figure 13. Sustainable Finance Instrument Use by Sustainability Awareness

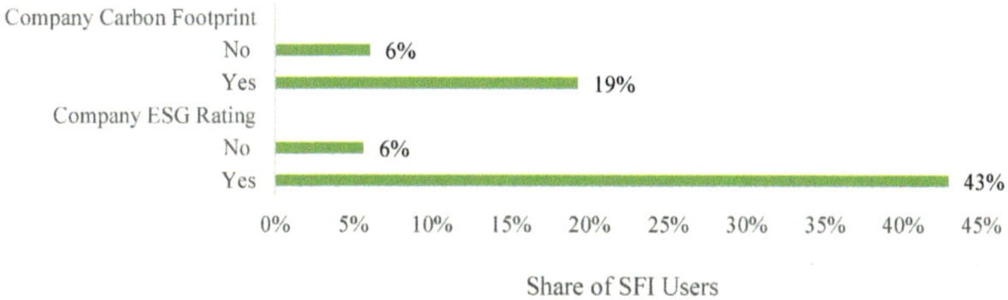

Source: This figure presents the share of SFI users for two indicators of sustainability awareness, namely having a carbon footprint and having an ESG rating, based on the survey data reported in Appendix A, Table 8.

This is supported by the logistic regression results as seen in Appendix A, Table 7b, which indicate higher odds, albeit not statistically significant, for companies with a carbon footprint to use a SFI compared to companies without a carbon footprint. As expected, the effect is more pronounced for having an ESG rating. In fact, 43 % of companies that have an ESG rating have used a SFI, compared to only 6 % of companies that do not have an ESG rating. The positive association between having an ESG rating and using a SFI is statistically significant at the 1 % level (see Appendix A, Table 7b).

Looking at sustainability awareness among the four defined company size groups in Figure 14, sustainability awareness appears to vary significantly amongst the four company size groups. In fact, only 22 % of medium-sized companies have a carbon footprint, which increases for larger medium-sized companies to 53 %, for large companies to 61 % and to 100 % for multinational companies.

Figure 14. Sustainability Awareness by Company Size

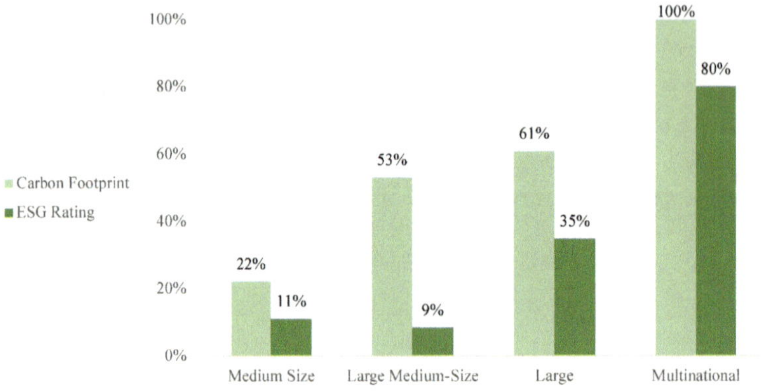

Source: This figure presents two indicators of sustainability awareness, namely having a carbon footprint and having an ESG rating, by the four defined company size groups, based on the survey data reported in Appendix A, Table 10.

The observed difference is similar for having an ESG rating, as a pronounced difference can be found for medium-sized and large medium-sized companies, of which 11 % and 9 % respectively have an ESG rating, compared to 35 % of larger companies and 80 % of multinational companies. Running Fisher's exact test confirms an association between company size and having a carbon footprint, as well as between company size and having an ESG rating. Both relations are statistically significant at the 1 % level (see Appendix A, Table 9). Thus, larger companies appear to have on average a higher sustainability awareness. This supports earlier assumptions that as larger companies have to adhere to more extensive sustainability disclosure regulations and since a longer time period, they have a higher sustainability awareness than smaller companies.

Regarding the defined company capital market groups, no significant variation for having a carbon footprint, but a significant variation for having an ESG rating is found. This is confirmed by the correlation results in Appendix A, Table 9, which indicate a statistically significant association between having an ESG rating and being active in capital markets. In fact, the share of companies that have an ESG rating (35 %)

is more than twice as high for capital market active companies, compared to companies that are not active in capital markets (16 %), as seen in Appendix A, Table 11. This is expected, as companies that are active in capital markets have a higher use case for an ESG rating, because for instance fund managers increasingly use ESG ratings in their investment strategies (Stackpole, 2021) and some ESG funds even only include companies with an existing ESG rating. Finally, regarding the company sector groups, no statistically significant variation in sustainability awareness between the different company sectors is found, as seen in Appendix A, Table 9.

2.5.1.6 Company's Sustainability Action

The second pull factor is a company's sustainability action, capturing whether a company has defined company-level sustainability targets and whether their achievement is ensured by a form of commitment scheme, such as board compensation being linked to sustainability target achievements. Similar to a company's sustainability awareness, implementing a SFI is easier if the company already has set company-level sustainability targets. Moreover, a company which has additionally already ensured its achievement by implementing a commitment scheme could be less inclined to refrain from using SFIs out of fear of not achieving the set sustainability targets. Therefore, a higher share of SFI users might be observed among companies with a more advanced sustainability action.

The survey results confirm a higher share of SFI users among companies that have company-level sustainability targets, as well as for companies that have a commitment scheme. As seen in Figure 15, 18 % of companies with company-level sustainability targets use SFIs, compared to only 4 % of companies without company-level sustainability targets.

Figure 15. Sustainable Finance Instrument Use by Sustainability Action

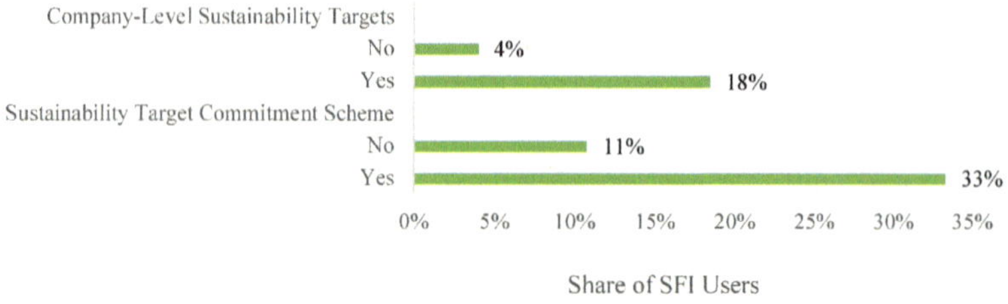

Source: This figure presents the share of SFI users for two indicators of sustainability action, namely having company-level sustainability targets and having a sustainability target commitment scheme, based on the survey data reported in Appendix A, Table 8.

The effect is even stronger for having an additional commitment scheme, as 33 % of companies with a commitment scheme in place have used a SFI, compared to only 11 % of companies without a commitment scheme, as seen in Figure 15. This observation is in line with the logistic regression results, which show statistically significant higher odds for companies that have a commitment scheme to be a SFI user, compared to companies that do not have a commitment scheme (see Appendix A, Table 7b).

Furthermore, sustainability action varies significantly between the four company size groups. As seen in Figure 16, medium-sized companies have the lowest share (56 %) of companies with company-level sustainability targets, which is continuously increasing for large medium-sized companies (60 %), large companies (87 %) up to 90 % for multinational companies. The difference is less pronounced for having an additional commitment scheme in place, for which medium-sized, large medium-sized and large companies have a similar share with 11 %, 9 % and 9 % respectively, compared to 40 % of multinational companies. This is reflected by the correlation results in Appendix A, Table 9, which demonstrate a statistically significant association between company size and having company-level sustainability targets, but no statistically significant association between company size and having an additional commitment scheme.

Figure 16. Sustainability Action by Company Size

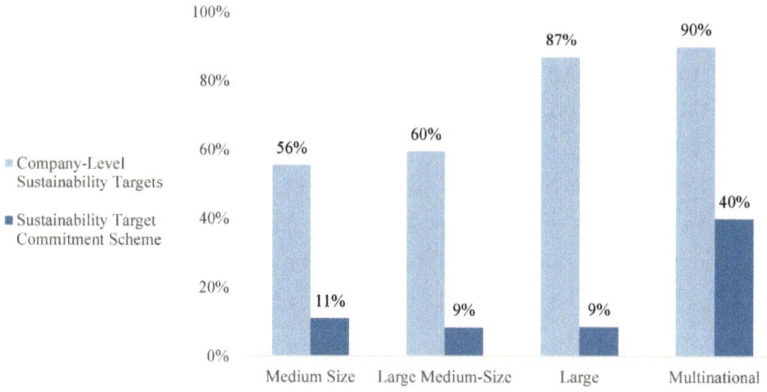

Source: This figure presents two indicators of sustainability action, namely having company-level sustainability targets and having a sustainability target commitment scheme, by the four defined company size groups, based on the survey data reported in Appendix A, Table 10.

Overall, it can be concluded that larger companies demonstrate on average a higher sustainability action. This is in line with advanced sustainability regulations for larger companies and the assumption that they are more likely to be in the public eye, which incentivizes them to set sustainability targets, as well as commitment schemes to achieve these targets. Finally, the survey results do not demonstrate a statistically significant variation in sustainability action among the different company capital market and company sector groups, as seen in Appendix A, Table 9.

2.5.1.7 Company's Sustainable Finance Knowledge

The third pull factor is a company's sustainable finance (instrument) knowledge. This pull factor is measured through two aspects. Firstly, whether the respondent is familiar with the term ESG. Secondly, whether the respondent is familiar with sustainable finance instruments. A company which has a basic understanding of sustainable finance and is familiar with SFIs is more likely to use SFIs, as the barrier of knowledge and implementation is lower.

The survey results support this hypothesis, as none of the companies that are unfamiliar with the term ESG have used a SFI, compared to 15 % of companies that are familiar with the term ESG, as seen in Figure 17. Moreover, 13 % of all respondents state that they did not know about SFIs prior to the survey, indicating that there is a significant number of companies that are lacking any SFI knowledge (see Appendix A, Table 6). Consequently, it can be said that companies with a higher sustainable finance (instrument) knowledge demonstrate a higher share of SFI users.

Figure 17. Sustainable Finance Instrument Use by Sustainable Finance Knowledge

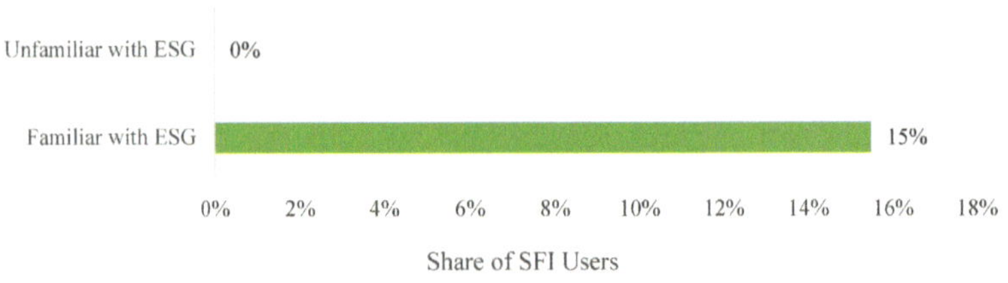

Source: This figure presents the share of SFI users for an indicator of sustainable finance knowledge, namely being familiar with the term ESG, based on the survey data reported in Appendix A, Table 8.

Furthermore, the results demonstrate a statistically significant variation in sustainable finance (instrument) knowledge amongst the four company size groups and the two company capital market groups, but no significant variation among the company sector groups (see Appendix A, Table 9). Whilst 44 % of medium-sized companies are unfamiliar with the term ESG, the share decreases for large medium-sized companies to 11 % and for large and multinational companies to 0 %, as seen in Figure 18.

Figure 18. Sustainable Finance Knowledge by Company Size

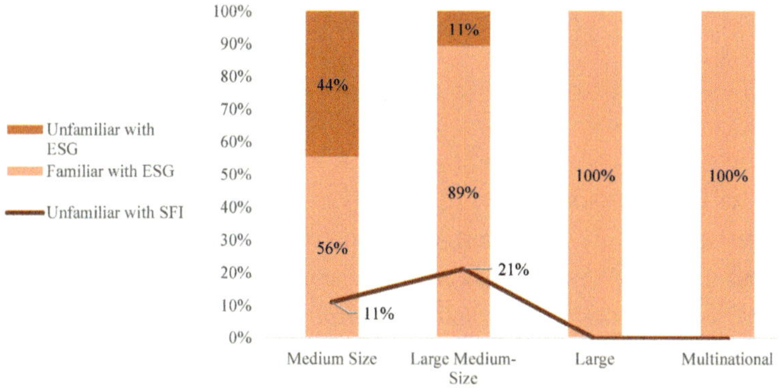

Source: This figure presents two indicators of sustainable finance knowledge, namely being familiar with the term ESG and being familiar with SFIs, by the four defined company size groups, based on the survey data reported in Appendix A, Table 6 and Table 10.

A similar pattern can be observed for companies being unfamiliar with SFIs, with a share of 11 % for medium-sized companies and 21 % for large medium-sized companies, compared to none for large and multinational companies. Again a potential explanation could be that larger companies are more exposed to the topic of sustainable finance due to higher sustainability regulatory requirements.

For the defined company capital market groups, the results show that companies which are active in capital markets have a higher sustainable finance instrument knowledge. In fact, only 3 % of companies that are active in capital markets were unfamiliar with SFIs before the survey, compared to 17 % of companies that are not active in capital markets (see Appendix A, Table 11). In contrast, there is no variation in regard to ESG term knowledge. A potential explanation for the higher SFI knowledge among capital market active companies could be that capital market SFIs, for example a green bond, are more well-known and more advanced in terms of standardization and processing than for example a green loan. Overall, larger companies and companies that are active in capital markets demonstrate a higher sustainable finance (instrument) knowledge.

2.5.2 Does This Translate Into Different Challenges & Barriers for Companies?

In order to fully understand the different sustainable finance needs and to subsequently provide tailored support to companies, one also has to understand the varying barriers that companies face in using SFIs, as well as the motivational factors. Therefore, the survey directly asks companies to state any barriers that might hinder them to use SFIs, as well as to rank provided reasons for and against the use of SFIs. As the pull and push factors differ most significantly for the four company size groups, the reported barriers will be analyzed in regard to their variation amongst the company size groups as well.

2.5.2.1 Companies' Reported Perceived Barriers to SFI Use

All companies were asked to state any potential perceived barriers regarding the use of SFIs, regardless of whether they have used a SFI before or not. Almost half of all companies (41 %) state that they perceive barriers to use a SFI, as seen in Appendix A, Table 13. Interestingly, the share of companies that perceive barriers is not significantly different for companies that have used SFIs before (31 %), companies that have not (45 %) and even companies that are unfamiliar with SFIs (33 %). Moreover, the share of companies that perceive barriers does not vary significantly between the four company group sizes, as seen in Appendix B, Figure 19. This is supported by the correlation analysis and logistic regression results which do not show any statistical significance (see Appendix A, Table 9 and Table 18).

In order to gain a deeper understanding of companies' perceived barriers, the survey used a mixed method approach and employed open questions, as explained in section 3.2. The answers were analyzed using a thematic content analysis framework (for further details, see section 3.2). The main thematic categories developed based on companies' stated barriers are applicability, company requirements, economic efficiency and implementation. Subsequently, subcategories for each main thematic category were developed inductively, following Kuckartz (2014), resulting in a categorical system reported in Appendix A, Table 14. The most often stated barriers are general additional efforts, reporting, KPI choice & tracking and risk of failure to achieve targets (see Appendix A, Table 14).

Using quantification (Kuckartz, 2014), the qualitative answers can be analyzed in regard to their variation among the four defined company size groups, as seen in Figure 20. The stated barriers differ between the respective company size groups and are discussed in the following section.

Figure 20. Stated Barriers by Company Size

Source: This figure presents the defined five groups of stated barriers by company size, based on the survey data reported in Appendix A, Table 13.

Applicability

As seen in Figure 20, smaller companies view applicability as a barrier to SFI use, whilst large and multinational companies do not state any applicability barriers. The applicability of SFIs to company characteristics, including company purpose, financing structure and industry, is a barrier for both, medium-sized and large medium-sized companies. In contrast, applicability to financing needs, including insufficient flexibility of SFIs and no use cases, is only stated as a barrier by large medium-sized companies.

Company Requirements

Company requirements is a barrier that is perceived by all companies, except medium-sized companies. All three company size groups perceive administrative work as a barrier, including general additional effort and work capacities, as well as reporting. Knowledge, which includes insufficient experience, consulting and regulatory uncertainty, is only reported as a barrier by large medium-sized and large companies. Interestingly, medium-sized companies did not state knowledge as a barrier, even though they demonstrated on average a lower sustainable finance (instrument) knowledge than larger companies, as described in section 5.1.7. A potential explanation could be that they have not advanced beyond the consideration of SFI use yet, to have been confronted with company requirement barriers.

Economic Efficiency

Regarding economic efficiency, the results show a more similar perception amongst the company size groups. All company groups view economic efficiency as a barrier, with costs being the most often stated barrier, followed by risk. Only large medium-sized and large companies state costs as a barrier, including higher implementation costs and insufficient promotional loans. In contrast, risk is stated as a barrier by all four company size groups. The reported risk barriers include regulatory risk, greenwashing risk and the risk of failure to achieve sustainability targets (see Appendix A, Table 14). The risk of failure to achieve sustainability targets is mentioned by medium-size, large and multinational companies, emphasizing that companies independent of their size are confronted with this barrier. This is an important observation, as it demonstrates an undesirable adverse effect of the SFI mechanism, which aims to incentivize companies to invest in their sustainability transition, rather than hindering companies to use SFI due to fear of failure to achieve their sustainability targets.

Implementation

Finally, all four company size groups report implementation as a barrier to SFI use. Both, small and large companies view the implementation of a SFI, in the form of size, KPI choice & tracking and data collection as a barrier to use SFIs. Moreover, large medium-sized, large and multinational companies state standards & regulations regarding data comparability, availability and investor requirements as a perceived barrier to SFI use. Overall, all four main reported barriers vary between company size groups and underline that companies face different barriers when considering the use of or implementing a SFI.

2.5.2.2 Ranking of Barriers and Motivations to Use SFIs

Subsequently, the survey asked respondents, which had stated that they have not used SFIs before, to rank potential reasons for not using SFIs, and companies that have used SFIs or are currently underway to use a SFI, to rank potential reasons for using SFIs, employing a display logic.

Barriers to SFI use

Firstly, looking at the ranking of reasons why companies have not used a SFI so far, but have considered using a SFI, we find that there is no difference among the various company size groups, as seen in Appendix A, Table 15. Ranked as the most influential reason is an insufficient SFI knowledge, followed by insufficient sustainability data, additional costs of implementing a SFI and the potential negative public reaction, for instance in the form of greenwashing accusations. However, medium-sized and large medium-sized companies state no financing needs as an additional reason for not using SFIs and large medium-sized companies additionally state low promotional loans, regulatory uncertainty, insufficient consultation and limited financing offers as further barriers.

Looking at companies which have not used SFIs and also have not considered using a SFI so far, the results also show no difference between the company size groups, as seen in Appendix A, Table 15. Moreover, the ranking order is the same as for companies which have considered using a SFI. Medium-sized, large medium-sized and large companies mention no financing needs as an additional reason for not using SFIs, large medium-sized companies additionally mention the lack of identified potential projects and multinational companies mention insufficient incentives. Overall, the results do not indicate a difference regarding potential barriers to SFI use among the four company size groups. For all company size groups, an insufficient knowledge about SFIs and insufficient sustainability data are ranked as the most prominent barriers to SFI use.

Motivations to use SFIs

In contrast, we do find differing patterns for motivation among those companies that have used SFIs. Whilst large medium-sized and large companies rank a potential pricing advantage compared to conventional financing as the most influential reason to use SFIs, multinational companies rank communication of their sustainability strategy to investors and customers as the most influential factor (see Appendix A, Table 15). Moreover, large medium-sized and multinational companies rank the recommendation of SFIs through their financing partner as a more influential factor than using SFIs because their competition is using SFIs as well. Both company size groups additionally mention the alignment of SFI use with the overall company strategy as an influential factor, as well as attracting a broader investor base, which is mentioned by large companies. The analysis does not include small medium-sized companies, as there were no respondents that have used a SFI so far. Overall, the results show a small difference in motivational factors to use SFIs amongst the four company size groups. For all company size groups, a potential pricing advantage and the opportunity to communicate their sustainability strategy are ranked as the most prominent motivational reasons to use SFIs.

2.6 Individual Sustainable Finance Support

Having gained a more profound understanding of companies' individual sustainable finance needs, as well as the individual barriers to SFI use, the study proceeds by using these insights to evaluate the role of banks in providing a fitting form of support. As explained in section 2, banks play a crucial role in the successful use and implementation of sustainable finance (instruments). However, as demonstrated in the previous sections, companies vary greatly in their sustainable finance needs and behavior. Consequently, this section analyzes whether banks are currently already fulfilling their role in providing effective and tailored support to their corporate customers in regard to sustainable finance, as well as potential improvements. Moreover, promotional loan programs are discussed as an additional approach to support companies in their sustainability transition.

2.6.1 The Desired Role of Banks in Providing Sustainable Finance Support

In order to evaluate whether banks are currently providing an effective and satisfactory level of support, the survey asked respondents to evaluate their banks' and financing partners' support regarding sustainability and whether they have ever suggested using a SFI. Furthermore, taking the point of view of the corporate customers themselves, the survey asked whether the respondents believe that their banks and financing partners can provide support regarding the company's sustainability transition and what form of support they would like to receive.

2.6.1.1 Bank Sustainability Support Rating

Firstly, banks' sustainable finance support quality is analyzed, as a good consultation regarding sustainable finance is crucial in regard to an effective use of SFIs. Only if companies understand the regulatory requirements that they have to adhere to, as well as the opportunities that sustainable finance can offer, will it enable them to effectively use SFIs for a successful sustainability transition. As seen in Figure 21, the majority of companies rate their banks' sustainability support as average (41 %) or good (34 %), but 12 % rate the support as bad and 5 % even as very bad. However, companies might be influenced in their rating by their SFI use and knowledge. Indeed, companies that have used SFIs rate their banks' sustainability support significantly better, with the majority giving a rating of good (54 %) and none giving a rating of very bad or bad. This relation is supported by the logistic regression results, which show that the odds of a company, which rates their bank's support as very good, being a SFI user are more than 8 times higher than the baseline of an average support rating (see Appendix A, Table 18). The positive association is significant at the 5 % level.

Figure 21. Rating of Banks' Sustainable Finance Support

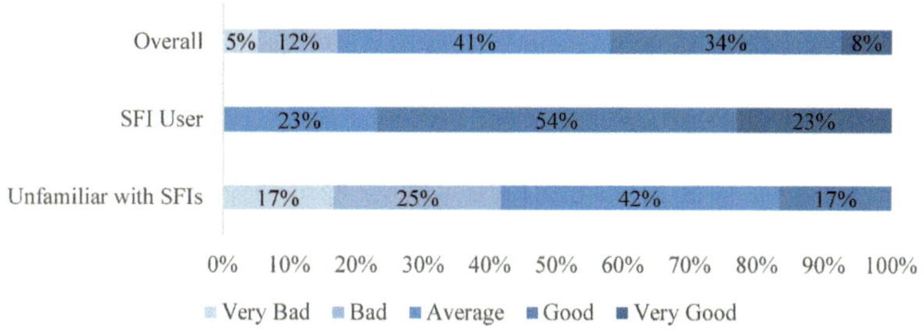

Source: This figure presents the companies' bank support ratings of the overall sample, of only companies that used SFIs and of only companies that were unfamiliar with SFIs before the survey, based on the survey data reported in Appendix A, Table 16.

Furthermore, looking only at companies' ratings that were unfamiliar with SFIs, the opposite effect can be observed. The share of companies that rate their banks' sustainability support as very bad or bad increases to 17 % and 25 % respectively. Based on the survey results it is not possible to evaluate whether companies' rated their banks' support on their past experience, for example as good because they successfully implemented a SFIs, or whether banks' support affected companies' SFI behavior, for instance in the form of a bad bank support leading to companies' being unfamiliar with SFIs. Nevertheless, these results indicate that a significant relation between banks' sustainability support and SFI use, as well as SFI knowledge, exists, and that banks generally still have room to improve their sustainability support.

2.6.1.2 Bank SFI Recommendation

Apart from a good level of support, banks also have the opportunity to actively suggest the use of sustainable finance structures to their corporate customers. This indicates a more precise sustainable finance consultation that goes beyond the general sustainability support in terms of sustainability awareness and regulations, and could subsequently be expected to lead to a higher use of SFIs. Indeed, the survey results indicate an increasing SFI use alongside a bank's sustainable finance suggestion. In fact, as seen in Figure 22, 32 % of companies that have been recommended SFI use also report that they have used a SFI, compared to only 4 % of companies that have not been recommended SFI use.

Figure 22. Sustainable Finance Instrument Use by Banks' SFI Recommendation

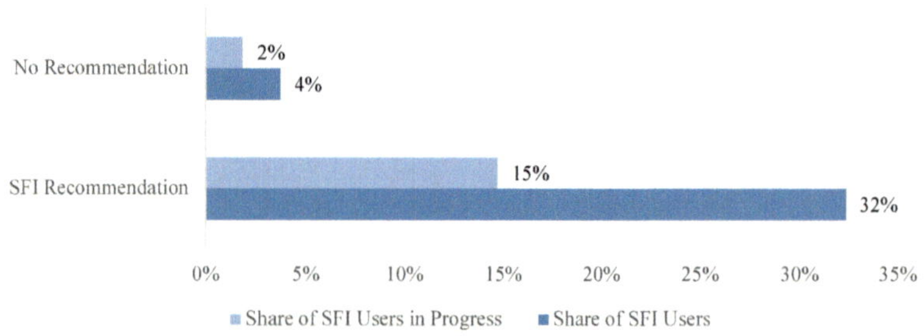

Source: This figure presents the share of SFI users and SFI users in progress based on whether companies have been recommended to use SFIs by their banks, based on the survey data reported in Appendix A, Table 16.

This is confirmed by the logistic regression results, which demonstrate higher odds for companies to be a SFI user, if their bank has recommended SFI use, statistically significant at the 1 % level (see Appendix A, Table 18). Furthermore, the share of companies that are currently implementing a SFIs is also significantly higher for companies that have been recommended SFI use (15 %), compared to companies that have not been recommended SFI use (2 %).

It should be noted that, as the timing of the SFI suggestion cannot be retrieved from the survey data, one cannot draw any conclusions on how close to the suggestion the SFI use was and whether this was indeed a significant driver to use SFIs. Instead, it should be interpreted as a more advanced sustainable finance consultation, as the suggestion of a sustainable finance structure entails a detailed explanation of the process, costs and opportunities. This is supported by the fact that having been recommended the use of SFIs reduces the share of companies that were unfamiliar with SFIs before the survey from 22 % to, as to be expected, zero (see Appendix A, Table 16). Therefore, it can be concluded that a more advanced SF consultation in the form of a SFI recommendation can increase SFI knowledge and likely also can increase companies' SFI use.

2.6.1.3 Bank's Role in Sustainability Transformation

Providing a good level of support regarding the use of SFIs is not sufficient, if the target group of corporate customers does not accept and use this support. Consequently, the survey asked respondents whether they believe that banks and financing partners can support them in their sustainability transition. Figure 23 shows that only a slight majority (51 %) thinks that their banks can support them in their sustainability transition and that a high share (32 %) is uncertain.

Figure 23. Banks' Support Potential

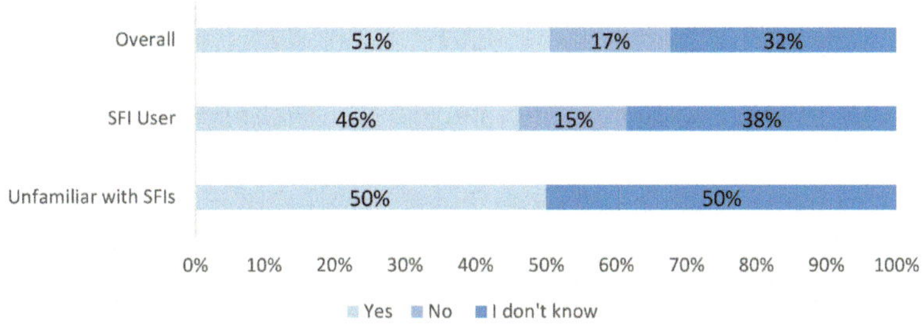

Source: This figure presents companies' evaluation of banks' potential to support them in their sustainability transition for the whole sample, for only SFI users and for only companies that were unfamiliar with SFIs before the survey, based on the survey data reported in Appendix A, Table 16.

Interestingly, the distribution does not change for companies that have used a SFI before, with a remaining high share (38 %) of uncertainty. For companies that were unfamiliar with SFIs before the survey, the share of companies that is uncertain about their banks' role even increases to 50 %, as seen in Figure 23. The uncertainty amongst all respondents suggests that companies do not have a clear understanding of their bank's role in regard to their sustainability transformation, but that the majority believes that there is a potential that could be used.

In order to gain a deeper understanding of companies' expectations regarding their banks' potential support, the survey included open questions asking respondents to state what form of support they would like to receive from their respective banks and financing partners. The qualitative answers were analyzed using thematic content analysis as described in section 3.2, specifying main thematic categories, inductively developing subcategories and coding all answers accordingly. The final categorical system of expectations, as seen in Appendix A, Table 17, is evaluated as follows.

Of the 47 companies which believe that their bank or financing partner can support them in their sustainability transition, 24 stated that they would like to receive consultation and 17 stated that they would like to receive information. Regarding consultation, the mentioned aspects are KPI choice, reporting, rating optimization, and promotional loans, as seen in Appendix A, Table 17. Furthermore, the information that companies would like to receive beyond general information can be divided into three areas, namely sustainable finance market, sustainable finance mechanism and sustainable finance use. Firstly, the information that companies would like to receive regarding the sustainable finance market includes a market overview and an insight into the expectations of banks and capital market participants, as seen in Appendix A, Table 17. Secondly, information on the sustainable finance mechanisms entails information on the impact of sustainability on a company's rating and financing, financing conditions and comparisons to conventional finance instruments. Finally, companies would like to receive information regarding sustainable finance use, particularly best practice examples and use cases built on experience with previous corporate customers.

Additionally, six companies stated their expectations regarding their bank's role and three companies shared their preferred modes of information. Regarding the bank's role, companies view their bank as a sparring partner and would like to see a clear commitment from their bank to sustainable finance, for instance through corresponding strategic asset allocations, as well as to receive concrete sustainable finance offers. Furthermore, the mentioned modes of information are personal talks, questionnaires, presentations, workshops and events around the topic of sustainable finance, as seen in Appendix A, Table 17.

2.6.2 Variation in Sustainable Finance Support Based On Company Size

Taking a closer look at banks' sustainable finance support for different company size groups in Figure 24, the survey results show that smaller companies on average rate their banks' financing support as lower than larger companies. This is supported by the correlation analysis results, which indicate an, at the 1 % level statistically significant, association between company size and bank financing support rating (see Appendix A, Table 20).

Figure 24. Rating of Banks' Sustainable Finance Support by Company Size Groups

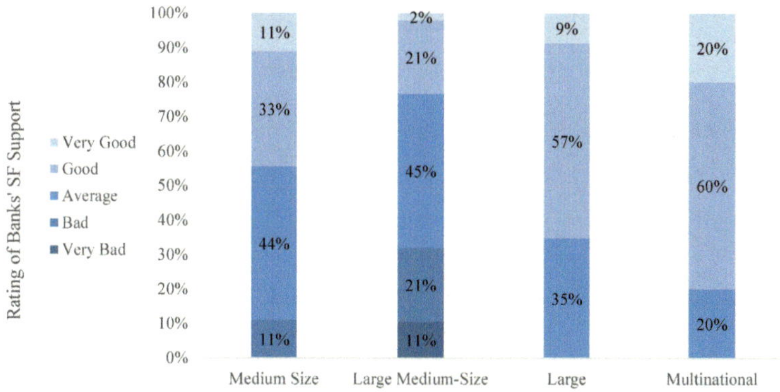

Source: This figure presents companies' bank support ratings by company size groups, based on the survey data reported in Appendix A, Table 16.

Nevertheless, the survey results also indicate that, even though smaller companies rate their banks' support lower than larger companies, they still believe that their banks and financing partners can provide the necessary support (see Appendix A, Table 16). However, medium-sized and large medium-sized companies also have a large share, 44 % and 34 % respectively, that is unsure about the role of their bank in supporting their sustainability transition (see Appendix A, Table 16). Moreover, as seen in Figure 25, the survey results show that a large share of medium-sized and large medium-sized companies state that their banks so far have never proposed the use of sustainable finance instruments. This could be due to smaller financing needs, but in combination with the lower sustainable finance knowledge and use among smaller companies, as pointed out in section 5.1.7, also demonstrates the need for an improved sustainable finance and sustainability disclosure regulation education.

Figure 25. Bank SFI Recommendation by Company Size Groups

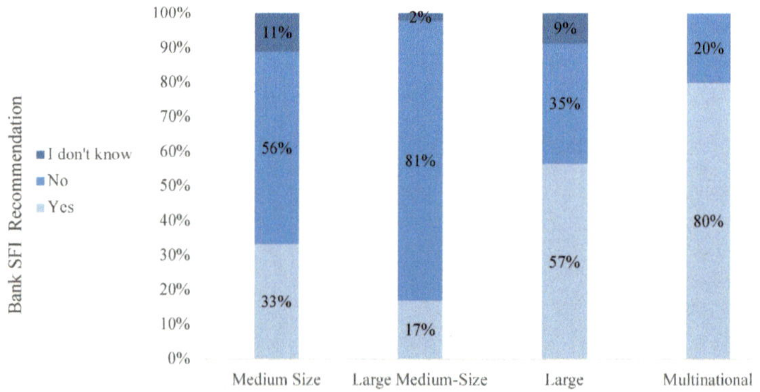

Source: This figure presents banks' SFI use recommendation by company size groups, based on the survey data reported in Appendix A, Table 16.

Overall, these observations indicate that the current level of sustainable finance support differs significantly with company size. Whilst section 6.1 discussed companies' desired role for banks in supporting them in their sustainability transition, this section demonstrates that medium-sized and large medium-sized companies experience a different sustainable finance support, both in terms of perceived quality and measurable SFI recommendations, compared to large and multinational companies. This suggests that banks should improve their sustainable finance support particularly for smaller companies, which is further discussed in section 7.

2.6.3 The Role of Promotional Loans

In order to further support companies' sustainability transition, alternative financing instruments such as promotional loans and grants are being offered through public financial institutions like the European Investment Bank (EIB, 2023) and Kreditanstalt für Wiederaufbau (KFW, 2023). The primary objective of these programs is to strengthen companies' investments into climate protection and resource efficiency by lowering financial barriers for companies to establish and implement their transition strategy. Potential financing instruments can be promotional loans, which have a lower interest rate than a conventional bank loan, partial risk coverage or include a repayment grant.

These alternative instruments can offer a great opportunity particularly to smaller and medium-sized companies. Acquiring a carbon footprint and developing a transition strategy are cost-intensive measures, which are relatively more expensive for smaller companies than larger companies. Consequently, some promotional loan and grant programs are especially targeted towards smaller and medium-sized companies. For instance, the Federal Ministry of Economic Affairs and Climate Action (BMWK, 2023) has established an energy efficiency grant program that among other things includes a transformation grant for smaller and medium-sized companies to finance the assessment and certification of their carbon footprint, as well as the commissioning of a professional energy efficiency consultant. Additionally, the program contains the option to apply for a promotional loan at the public financial institution KFW to strengthen investments into improved electricity and heat efficiency (BMWK, 2023).

As promotional loan programs provide an important financial support for companies to finance their sustainability transition, the survey asked respondents whether they are familiar with or have used any promotional loan programs, as well as whether they would be interested in these programs. As seen in Figure 26, the results show that whilst 48 % of respondents know promotional loan programs connected to sustainable finance, only 9 % have used such a promotional loan. Moreover, 43 % are not familiar with sustainable finance promotional loans yet.

Figure 26. Promotional Loan Interest and Use

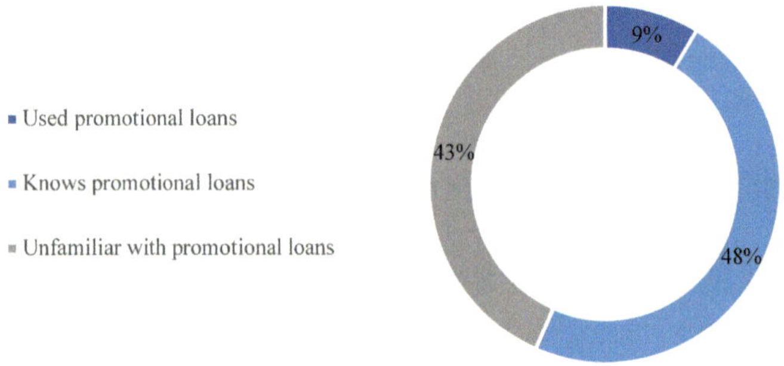

Source: This figure presents companies' promotional loan interest, knowledge and use, based on the survey data reported in Appendix A, Table 16.

Regarding promotional loan use among company size groups, a pronounced difference can be found for medium-sized companies, as no company with a revenue of €10 to €49 million has used a promotional loan compared to on average 10 % for all other company size groups (see Appendix A, Table 16). Moreover, medium-sized companies also have the highest share (55.6 %) of companies that are unfamiliar with sustainable finance promotional loans.

Even though a significant number of companies is not familiar with sustainable finance related promotional loan programs, the majority of respondents are interested in using these programs. This holds true among all company size groups, even though multinational companies demonstrate a comparatively high share (20 %) of companies that state they are not interested in sustainable finance promotional loans (see

Appendix A, Table 16). This is in line with a study by KFW (2022), which shows that SMEs use a higher share of promotional loans (20 %) to finance their sustainability transition compared to large companies (4 %). Consequently, promotional loan programs are an important lever to advance SMEs' sustainability transition, which is supported by the findings that insufficient financial resources are one of the biggest barriers for sustainable investments by SMEs (KFW, 2022).

Additionally, promotional loan programs can also provide the opportunity to connect traditional promotional loans with the elicitation of sustainability criteria. For instance, the L-Bank (2022), a public financial institution, offers an interest rate reduction for their innovation and growth promotional loan, if the company can prove the assessment of their carbon emissions and even a further reduction if the company has additionally defined carbon emission reduction goals and established a plan to achieve these. The program particularly targets smaller companies which have not assessed their carbon footprint yet and provides companies with a tool and personal support to assess their carbon emissions to receive the promotional loan interest rate reduction (L-Bank, 2022). Consequently, banks and public financial institutions can work together to increase the use and application of sustainability-related promotional loan programs, as well as to incentivize companies to collect the desired sustainability measures. This would not only lower companies' financial barrier to finance their sustainability transformation, but could also improve the sustainability data assessment and exchange, particularly between smaller companies and their banking partners.

2.7 Discussion

The aim of this paper is to identify companies' individual sustainable finance interests and needs, and to subsequently develop recommendations on how banks can provide better and tailored sustainable finance (instrument) support to their corporate customers, to thereby foster sustainability transition investments.

The survey results show that SFI use can be strengthened by improving sustainable finance support, with 41 % of companies rating their bank's support as average, 12 % as bad and 5 % even as very bad. Nevertheless, companies predominantly believe that banks can support them in their sustainable finance use and have clear expectations for their banks as a sparring partner, who provides consultation and information on sustainable finance and SFIs. So how can banks provide better and tailored support based on the research findings?

2.7.1 Improve Sustainable Finance Awareness and Knowledge

Firstly, banks can improve companies' awareness and knowledge regarding the sustainable finance market and sustainable finance instruments. The survey results show that 13 % of respondents were unfamiliar with SFIs prior to the survey and that 10 % were even unfamiliar with the term ESG. In order to efficiently use SFIs, companies need to understand how sustainability transparency regulations can impact their financing access and conditions, as well as how sustainable finance and SFIs work.

Whilst the survey results indicate a higher share of SFI users for companies that perceive a strong regulatory pressure, only a slightly higher share of SFI users is found for companies that perceive a strong transformation risk. Moreover, the majority of companies perceive an average or low risk to lose their financing access and even though the majority perceives a link between a company's sustainability performance and financing conditions to be likely or very likely, they do not demonstrate a higher SFI use. These results indicate that whilst companies do experience regulatory and transformative pressure,

1. they are not sufficiently aware how this can impact their financing access and conditions, and
2. they do not have sufficient knowledge on sustainable finance and how sustainable finance instruments work.

This is supported by the fact that companies ask their banks to provide information on the sustainable finance market, particularly on market expectations and a market overview, as well as on sustainable finance mechanisms. They want to understand what their financing partners require from them in terms of sustainability performance, as well as measures, and how this can affect their financing offers.

2.7.2 Simplify the Implementation and Communicate Expectations

Secondly, banks can provide more extensive support regarding the implementation of a SFI. Among the most often stated barriers to SFI use are the choice of sustainability targets, lack of sustainability data, implementation costs and bureaucracy. By providing corporate customers with clear-cut best practice examples as well as concise expectations and recommendations regarding their sustainability measures, the process of using a SFI could become simpler and more standardized.

Moreover, the survey results show that 56 % of companies already have a carbon footprint and that 23 % even have an ESG rating. Both are important sustainability measures and can be used as a foundation for a SFI. However, in the long run, all companies will be required to provide sustainability measures as part of mandatory sustainability disclosure regulations, their supply chain or their financing. Consequently, banks can prepare and support their corporate customers by explaining the need for sustainability performance measures, formulating clear expectations on what sustainability measures are required for future financing offers and by providing, for instance, industry examples. This is in line with the demand of companies for more information on SFI use and hands-on use cases. Furthermore, the survey results show that proactively suggesting a sustainable finance structure to companies can also likely increase SFI use.

2.7.3 Provide Tailored Sustainable Finance Support

Thirdly, banks need to tailor their sustainable finance information and support to their customer groups. The survey results show that smaller companies, in the case at hand medium-sized and large medium-sized companies, perceive lower regulatory pressure and transformation risk, as well as a lower likelihood to lose finance access and that the sustainability performance will be linked to their credit conditions. This indicates that smaller companies have a lower awareness and knowledge regarding the impact of sustainability disclosure regulations on a company's financing conditions and access, as well as the mechanisms of sustainable finance. This is supported by the fact that 44 % of medium-sized companies are not aware of the term ESG and that 11 % were unfamiliar with SFIs prior to the survey. For large medium-sized companies even 21 % were unfamiliar with SFIs prior to the survey. Furthermore, they particularly perceive the applicability of SFIs as a barrier, as well as insufficient consulting and low promotional loan funds.

Consequently, banks might need to provide a more fundamental consultation to smaller companies. As sustainability disclosure regulations predominantly do not apply to these companies yet, it is important to explain how sustainability measures, such as a carbon footprint, which only 22 % of medium-sized companies have, can still be required for financing offers or can be demanded by larger companies as part of their supply chain. It is particularly crucial, that clear expectations regarding the necessary sustainability measures are formulated and that the required measures are kept simple to minimize costs. For example, a complex ESG rating might not be necessary for a smaller company, but can be very cost-intensive to acquire. Finally, sustainable finance literature has been focused a lot on bonds as a SFI, but schuldscheindarlehen and loans also allow for a sustainable finance structure, which should be highlighted particularly to smaller companies.

2.8 Conclusion

In order to assess companies' individual sustainable finance interests and needs, and to subsequently develop recommendations for an improved and tailored sustainable finance support, this study conducted an online survey with 700 invited corporate customers of DZ BANK AG. Based on the recorded 93 answers, the study finds that SFI use significantly varies between the four defined company size groups. In fact, the survey results show a larger SFI use for large and multinational companies, as well as for companies that are active in capital markets.

In regard to identified and analyzed push and pull factors, as well as potential barriers in the sustainable finance market, the study finds a variation for both, SFI use and between company sizes. The share of companies that use SFIs increases with a higher perceived regulatory pressure and increases very slightly with a higher perceived transformation risk. Furthermore, smaller companies on average perceive regulatory pressure and transformation risk to be lower and demonstrate a lower level of sustainability awareness, sustainability action and sustainability knowledge than larger companies. Among the most often stated barriers to SFI use are the achievement of sustainability targets, lack of sustainability data, higher implementation costs, bureaucracy and choice of sustainability targets. The majority of respondents think that their bank can provide valuable support to overcome these barriers and view their bank as a sparring partner that provides information and consultation on sustainable finance. Furthermore, the results indicate that a bank's higher quality of sustainable finance support and actively suggesting the use of SFIs can potentially increase SFI use among all company size groups. Finally, promotional loan programs can function as an additional support to increase investments in companies' sustainability transition.

Based on these results, the study formulates three recommendations on how banks can improve their sustainable finance support to strengthen SFI use. Firstly, the study demonstrates that companies which are not using SFIs yet tend to be insufficiently aware of how regulatory requirements and an increase in sustainability transparency can potentially impact their financing access and conditions. Moreover, they tend to have insufficient knowledge regarding sustainable finance and on how sustainable finance instruments work. Consequently, banks can improve their corporate customers' sustainable finance awareness and knowledge. Secondly, companies view bureaucracy and high implementation costs as some of the biggest barriers to SFI use and are asking for best-practice examples, which suggests that banks can support their corporate customers' SFI use by simplifying the implementation and by communicating their expectations particularly regarding necessary sustainability measures clearly. Thirdly, the study results confirm that smaller companies have different sustainable finance interests and needs than larger companies. Therefore, banks should tailor their sustainable finance support, especially for smaller companies, but more generally by understanding and catering to companies' individual levels of sustainable finance awareness and knowledge.

This study analyzes companies' individual sustainable finance interests and needs using a mixed method approach to gain a deeper understanding of the detected relations. Regarding limitations, the results in respect to potential push and pull factors, as well as barriers in the sustainable finance market, cannot be interpreted as causal relations. Furthermore, a larger survey sample could allow for a better analysis of potential company sector differences, as in the case at hand the large variety of company sectors meant a lower number of respondents per sector. Moreover, further research could include respondents from various banks, including regional savings and cooperative banks, to better assess the difference in sustainable finance support between financial institutions, as well as it could elaborate how SMEs' general financing needs to achieve their sustainability transition differ compared to large companies.

Overall, the study's recommendations aim to increase SFI use and to thereby strengthen investments into companies' sustainability transitions. In regard to policy recommendations, the study results emphasize the importance of recognizing the difference in implications of sustainability regulations for SMEs compared to larger companies.

Therefore, regulatory requirements need to be adapted to SMEs and allow for simplified implementations to minimize costs and the administrative burden. Additionally, the study suggests how banks and public financial institutions could cooperate to increase the use and application of sustainability-related promotional loan programs, by simultaneously improving the sustainability data exchange between SMEs and their financing partners.

References

Berrada, T., Engelhardt, L., Gibson, R., & Krueger, P. (2022). The economics of sustainability linked bonds. *Swiss Finance Institute Research Paper No. 22–26.* https://dx.doi.org/10.2139/ssrn.4059299

Bogmans, C., Pescatori, A., & Prifti, E. (2023). The impact of climate policy on oil and gas investment: evidence from firm-level data. *International Monetary Fund Working Paper No. 2023/140.* https://dx.doi.org/10.5089/9798400247736.001

Buchner, B., Naran, B., Padmanabhi, R., Stout, S., Strinati, C., Wignarajah, D., Miao, G., Connolly, J., & Marini, N. (2023). *Global landscape of climate finance 2023.* Climate Policy Initiative. https://www.climatepolicyinitiative.org/wp-content/uploads/2023/11/Global-Landscape-of-Climate-Finance-2023.pdf

Bundesverband mittelständische Wirtschaft. (2023). *Der Mittelstand ist Garant für Stabilität und Fortschritt.* Retrieved November 21, 2023, from https://www.bvmw.de/de/der-verband/über-uns/zahlen-fakten

Climate Bonds Initiative. (2022). *Green bond pricing in the primary market: H1 2022.* https://www.climatebonds.net/files/reports/cbi_pricing_h1_2022_02g.pdf

Climate Bonds Initiative. (2023). *Green bond pricing in the primary market: H2 2022.* https://www.climatebonds.net/files/reports/cbi_pricing_h2_2022_01c.pdf

Coleton, A., Font Brucart, M., Gutierrez, P., Le Tennier, F., & Moor, C. (2020). Sustainable finance: market practices. *European Banking Authority Research Paper,* (6). https://dx.doi.org/10.2139/ssrn.3749454

Creswell, J. D., & Creswell, J. W. (2018). *Research design. qualitative, quantitative, and mixed methods approaches* (fifth edition). SAGE.

Deschryver, P., & De Mariz, F. (2020). What future for the green bond market? How can policymakers, companies, and investors unlock the potential of the green bond market?. *Journal of Risk and Financial Management, 13(3),* 61. https://doi.org/10.3390/jrfm13030061

Deutsche Bank. (2022). *Green Asset Ratio: die Nachhaltigkeits-Kennziffer für Banken.* Retrieved November 21, 2023, from https://www.deutsche-bank.de/ms/results-finanzwissen-fuer-unternehmen/zahlungsverkehr/09-2022-green-asset-ratio-die-nachhaltigkeits-kennziffer-fuer-banken.html

DZ BANK. (2023a). *First half of 2023: DZ BANK Group reports a profit before taxes of €1.95 billion.* Retrieved November 21, 2023 from https://www.dzbank.com/content/dzbank/en/home/we-are-dz-bank/press/news_archive/2023/first-half-of-2023dzbankgroupreportsaprofitbeforetaxesof195billi.html

DZ BANK. (2023b). *Research-Publikation der DZ BANK AG 3. Sonderumfrage Nachhaltigkeit.* Retrieved November 21, 2023, from https://firmenkunden.dzbank.de/content/firmenkunden/de/homepage/research/sonderumfrage-nachhaltigkeit3.html

European Investment Bank. (2023). *How to get help for your climate project.* Retrieved November 21, 2023, from https://www.eib.org/en/about/priorities/climate-action/get-support/index.htm

European Central Bank. (2022). *2022 climate stress test.* https://www.bankingsupervision.europa.eu/ecb/pub/pdf/ssm.climate_stress_test_report.20220708~2e3cc0999f.en.pdf

European Commission. (2019). *Financing sustainable growth.* https://finance.ec.europa.eu/system/files/2020-01/200108-financing-sustainable-growth-factsheet_en.pdf

European Commission. (2020a). *Financing the green transition: The European Green Deal Investment Plan and the Just Transition Mechanism.* https://ec.europa.eu/commission/presscorner/detail/en/ip_20_17

European Commission. (2020b). *Renewed sustainable finance strategy and implementation of the action plan on financing sustainable growth.* https://finance.ec.europa.eu/publications/renewed-sustainable-finance-strategy-and-implementation-action-plan-financing-sustainable-growth_en

European Commission. (2023a). *Overview of sustainable finance.* Retrieved November 21, 2023, from https://finance.ec.europa.eu/sustainable-finance/overview-sustainable-finance_en

European Commission. (2023b). *Sustainability-related disclosure in the financial services sector.* Retrieved November 21, 2023, from https://finance.ec.europa.eu/sustainable-finance/disclosures/sustainability-related-disclosure-financial-services-sector_en

European Commission. (2023c). *Corporate sustainability reporting.* Retrieved November 21, 2023, from https://finance.ec.europa.eu/capital-markets-union-and-financial-markets/company-reporting-and-auditing/company-reporting/corporate-sustainability-reporting_en

Fakis, A., Hilliam, R., Stoneley, H., & Townend, M. (2014). Quantitative analysis of qualitative information from interviews: A systematic literature review. *Journal of Mixed Methods Research, 8(2),* 139–161. https://doi.org/10.1177/1558689813495111

Federal Ministry for Economic Affairs and Climate Action. (2023). *Energy consulting and funding for companies.* Retrieved November 21, 2023, from https://www.bmwk.de/Redaktion/EN/Artikel/Energy/energy-consulting-and-funding-for-companies.html

Federal Ministry of Labour and Social Affairs. (2023). *Gesetz über die unternehmerischen Sorgfaltspflichten in der Lieferkette.* Retrieved November 21, 2023, from https://www.bmas.de/DE/Service/Gesetze-und-Gesetzesvorhaben/Gesetz-Unternehmerische-Sorgfaltspflichten-Lieferketten/gesetz-unternehmerische-sorgfaltspflichten-lieferketten.html

Flammer, C. (2020). Green bonds: effectiveness and implications for public policy. *Environmental and Energy Policy and the Economy, 1(1),* 95–128. https://doi.org/10.1086/706794

Georgieva, K. & Adrian, T. (2022). *Public sector must play major role in catalyzing private climate finance.* International Monetary Fund. https://www.imf.org/en/Blogs/Articles/2022/08/18/public-sector-must-play-major-role-in-catalyzing-private-climate-finance

Gianfrate, G., & Peri, M. (2019). The green advantage: exploring the convenience of issuing green bonds. *Journal of cleaner production, (219),* 127–135. https://doi.org/10.1016/j.jclepro.2019.02.022

Greene, J. C., Caracelli, V. J., & Graham, W. F. (1989). Toward a conceptual framework for mixed-method evaluation designs. *Educational evaluation and policy analysis, 11(3*), 255–274. https://doi.org/10.3102/01623737011003255

Hinsche, I. C. (2021). A greenium for the Next Generation EU Green Bonds analysis of a potential green bond premium and its drivers. *Center for Financial Studies Working Paper,* (663). https://dx.doi.org/10.2139/ssrn.3965664

Hinsche, I. C., & Klump, R. (2023). Mirror, mirror on the wall, who is transitioning amongst them all?. *Center for Financial Studies Working Paper,* (712). https://dx.doi.org/10.2139/ssrn.4464312

Intergovernmental Panel on Climate Change. (2021). Summary for policymakers. In: *Climate Change 2021: The Physical Science Basis. Contribution of Working Group I to the Sixth Assessment Report of the Intergovernmental Panel on Climate Change.* https://www.ipcc.ch/report/ar6/wg1/chapter/summary-for-policymakers/

International Capital Market Association. (2021). *Green Bond Principles.* https://www.icmagroup.org/assets/documents/Sustainable-finance/2022-updates/Green-Bond-Principles-June-2022-060623.pdf

International Capital Market Association. (2023). *Sustainability-Linked Bond Principles.* https://www.icmagroup.org/assets/documents/Sustainable-finance/2023-updates/Sustainability-Linked-Bond-Principles-June-2023-220623.pdf

Kapraun, J., Latino, C., Scheins, C., & Schlag, C. (2021). (In)-credibly green: which bonds trade at a green bond premium?. In *Proceedings of Paris December 2019 Finance Meeting EUROFIDAI-ESSEC.* https://dx.doi.org/10.2139/ssrn.3347337

Kölbel, J. F., & Lambillon, A. P. (2022). Who pays for sustainability? An analysis of sustainability-linked bonds. *Swiss Finance Institute Research Paper No. 23–07.* https://dx.doi.org/10.2139/ssrn.4007629

Kreditanstalt für Wiederaufbau. (2022). *KfW-Klimabarometer 2022.* KfW Research. https://www.kfw.de/PDF/Download-Center/Konzernthemen/Research/PDF-Dokumente-KfW-Klimabarometer/KfW-Klimabarometer-2022.pdf

Kreditanstalt für Wiederaufbau. (2023). *Förderprodukte für Energie und Umwelt.* Retrieved November 21, 2023, from https://www.kfw.de/inlandsfoerderung/Unternehmen/Energie-Umwelt/Förderprodukte/Förderprodukte-(S3).html

Kuckartz, U. (2014). *Mixed Methods: Methodologie, Forschungsdesigns und Analyseverfahren.* Springer-Verlag. https://doi.org/10.1007/978-3-531-93267-5

L-Bank. (2022). *Neues Förderprogramm ebnet Südwest-Unternehmen den Weg in eine nachhaltigere Wirtschaft: Nachhaltigkeitsbonus startet am 1. Juli.* Retrieved November 21, 2023 from https://www.l-bank.info/fuer-die-presse/presseinformationen/2022/pi2022_44_nachhaltigkeitsbonus.html

LBBW. (2022). *Ergebnisse Mittelstandsradar.* https://www.lbbw.de/konzern/research/2022/mittelstandsradar/lbbw-mittelstandsradar-2022_aezn797ua5_m.pdf

Maltais, A., & Nykvist, B. (2020). Understanding the role of green bonds in advancing sustainability. *Journal of Sustainable Finance & Investment,* 1–20. https://doi.org/10.1080/20430795.2020.1724864

Morgan, D. L. (2014). *Integrating qualitative and quantitative methods: A pragmatic approach.* SAGE. https://doi.org/10.4135/9781544304533

MSCI. (2023). *The global industry classification standard (GICS).* Retrieved November 21, 2023 from https://www.msci.com/our-solutions/indexes/gics

Partridge, C., & Medda, F. R. (2020). The evolution of pricing performance of green municipal bonds. *Journal of Sustainable Finance & Investment, 10(1),* 44–64. https://doi.org/10.1080/20430795.2019.1661187

PwC. (2022). *The growth opportunity of the century.* Retrieved November 21, 2023, from https://www.pwc.lu/en/sustainable-finance/esg-report-the-growth-opportunity-of-the-century.html

Stackpole, B. (2021). *Why sustainable business needs better ESG ratings.* Massachusetts Institute of Technology. Retrieved November 21, 2023, from https://mitsloan.mit.edu/ideas-made-to-matter/why-sustainable-business-needs-better-esg-ratings

Tang, D. Y., & Zhang, Y. (2020). Do shareholders benefit from green bonds?. *Journal of Corporate Finance, 61,* 101427. https://dx.doi.org/10.2139/ssrn.3259555

United Nations Principles of Responsible Investment. (2020). *Introductory guides to responsible investment – screening.* Retrieved November 21, 2023, from https://www.unpri.org/introductory-guides-to-responsible-investment/an-introduction-to-responsible-investment-screening/5834.article

United Nations Principles of Responsible Investment. (2023). *ESG in credit ratings and ESG ratings.* Retrieved November 21, 2023, from https://www.unpri.org/credit-risk-and-ratings/esg-in-credit-ratings-and-esg-ratings/11071.article#:~:text=ESG%20ratings%20are%20typically%20produced,address%20the%20needs%20of%20shareholders

Walther, U. (2023). *Climate stress tests: are banks fit for the green transition?.* Deutsche Bank Research. https://www.dbresearch.com/PROD/RPS_EN-PROD/PROD0000000000526206/Climate_stress_tests%3A_Are_banks_fit_for_the_green_.PDF?undefined&realload=OpesygUtqtzxvMXKvNDVo9yjgsFjYIVfbufAWIgtjioHB6L3/fB2U1mmG9haip1m

Zerbib, O. D. (2019). The effect of pro-environmental preferences on bond prices: evidence from green bonds. *Journal of Banking & Finance, (98),* 39–60. https://doi.org/10.1016/j.jbankfin.2018.10.012

Appendix A: Tables

Table 3. Summary Statistics – Respondents' Additional Information

	Observations	Percent of Data
Numer of Companies	93	100 %
<u>Company Department</u>		
Finance	86	94.5 %
Other Deparment	5	5.5 %
<u>Gender</u>		
Male	80	87.9 %
Female	9	9.9 %
Diverse	1	1.1 %
No Answer	1	1.1 %
<u>Age Group</u>		
20 to 29 years	2	2.2 %
30 to 39 years	21	23.1 %
40 to 49 years	28	30.8 %
50 to 59 years	28	30.8 %
60 years or older	12	13.2 %
<u>Study / Work Experience in Sustainability</u>		
Yes, study and work experience in sustainability	8	8.8 %
Yes, work experience in sustainability	27	29.7 %
No, neiter study nor work experience in sustainability	48	52.7 %
No Answer	8	8.8 %

Source: This table presents additional information regarding the 93 survey respondents, based on survey questions 26, 27, 28 and 29. Differences in the number of observations are due to the fact that the response was voluntary and not all survey participants answered these questions.

Table 4. Correlation Analysis Results SFI Use

	SFI Use		
	Fisher's Exact P-Value	Significance	Cramér's V
Company Size	.000	***	.5456
Capital Market Activity	.013	**	-.2712
Company Sector	.782		.2346
Regulatory Pressure	.697		.1425
Transformation Risk	.969		.0662
Financing Access	.067	*	.2789
Financing Link	.307		.2054
Carbon Footprint	.204		.1774
ESG Rating	.001	***	.4545
CLST	.168		.1979
STCS	.138		.2156
Barriers	.549		.0828

Source: Fisher's exact test and Cramér's V calculation run in Stata using the data from Table 6 and Table 8. The number of observations for company size groups is 89, for capital market activity groups 92 and for company sector groups 75, as recorded "no answer" options were excluded. Note: "CLST" denotes company level sustainability targets. "STCS" denotes sustainability target commitment scheme. Significance levels are denoted as follows: *** p<.01, ** p<.05, * p<.1.

Table 5. Logistic Regression Analysis Results – Company Groups

Logistic Regression: SFIUse – Company Size

SFIUser	Odds Ratio	Robust Std. Err.	z	P >|z|	95 % Confidence Interval		Significance/ Comment
Medium-Sized	1	.	.	.	.	.	PFP
Large Medium-Sized	1	.	.	.	.	.	Baseline
Large	12.778	14.532	2.24	.025	1.375	118.721	**
Multinationals	69	83.276	3.51	0	6.479	734.792	***
Constant	.022	.022	-3.76	0	.003	.16	***

Number of obs	=	*80*	*Log pseudol.*	=	*-23.612035*
Wald chi2(2)	=	*12.69*	*Pseudo R2*	=	*.3018*
Prob > chi2	=	*.0018*			

Logistic Regression: SFIUse – Capital Market Activity

SFIUser	Odds Ratio	Robust Std. Err.	z	P >|z|	95 % Confidence Interval		Significance/ Comment
Capital Market Active	4.86	3.166	2.43	.015	1.356	17.42	**
Not Capital Market A.	1	.	.	.	.	.	Baseline
Constant	.074	.039	-5.00	0	.027	.206	***

Number of obs	=	*92*	*Log pseudol.*	=	*-34.20472*
Wald chi2(1)	=	*5.89*	*Pseudo R2*	=	*.0872*
Prob > chi2	=	*.0152*			

<u>Logistic Regression: SFIUse – Company Sector</u>

SFIUser	Odds Ratio	Robust Std. Err.	z	P >|z|	95 % Confidence Interval		Significance/ Comment
Communication S.	1	.	.	.	.	.	PFP
Consumer Disc.	2.476	2.514	0.89	.372	.339	18.112	
Consumer Staples	1.083	1.336	0.06	.948	.097	12.145	
Financials	2.889	3.802	0.81	.42	.219	38.108	
Health Care	2.889	3.802	0.81	.42	.219	38.108	
Industrials	1	.	.	.	.	.	Baseline
Information Tech.	1	.	.	.	.	.	PFP
Materials	1	.	.	.	.	.	PFP
Real Estate	1	.	.	.	.	.	PFP
Utilities	2.476	2.514	0.89	.372	.339	18.112	
Constant	.115	.071	-3.51	0	.035	.385	***

Number of obs	=	*64*	*Log pseudol.*	=	*-26.818114*
Wald chi2(5)	=	*1.77*	*Pseudo R2*	=	*.0331*
Prob > chi2	=	*.8801*			

Source: Logistic regression analysis with robust standard errors run in Stata using data from Table 6. The dependent variable is a binary variable for which 1 denotes SFI use and 0 no SFI use. The independent variables are the respective company groups. The notation "PFP" means "predicts failure perfectly" and indicates that the respective group level 100 % predicts no SFI use. Significance levels are denoted as follows: *** p<.01, ** p<.05, * p<.1.

Table 6. Sustainable Finance Instrument Use

	Implementation					Consideration		
	Yes	No	In Process	Unfamiliar with SFIs	I don't know	Yes	No	I don't know
All Companies	13	60	6	12	2	25	33	4
<u>Company Size</u>								
€10 million to €49 million	0	7	0	1	1	3	4	1
€50 million to €499 million	1	34	2	10	0	12	21	1
€500 million to €5 billion	5	14	4	0	0	6	7	1
Bigger than €5 billion	6	4	0	0	0	3	1	0
<u>Company Capital Market Activity</u>								
Active	9	22	1	1	1	11	11	1
Not Active	4	38	5	10	1	14	22	3
<u>Company Sector</u>								
Communication Services	0	0	1	0	0	0	0	0
Consumer Discretionary	2	5	0	2	0	1	4	0
Consumer Staples	1	7	0	0	1	2	5	1
Financials	1	2	0	0	1	2	0	1
Health Care	1	1	2	0	0	1	0	0
Industrials	3	17	2	7	0	5	12	0
Information Technology	0	0	1	1	0	0	0	0
Materials	0	5	0	2	0	1	4	0
Real Estate	0	1	0	0	0	1	0	0
Utilities	2	7	0	0	0	5	2	0

Source: This table presents the recorded data based on survey questions 1 and 3 by company groups. The difference in number of observations between SFI implementation and consideration is due to the fact that question 3 is a follow-up question for all respondents that answered question 1 with "No" or "I don't know", thus only recording 62 answers.

Table 7a. Logistic Regression Analysis Results – Push Factors

Logistic Regression: SFIUse – Regulatory Pressure

SFIUser	Odds Ratio	Robust Std. Err.	z	P >|z|	95 % Confidence Interval		Signifi-cance / Comment
Low	1	.	.	.	.	.	PFP
Average	1	.	.	.	.	.	Baseline
Strong	2.183	1.617	1.05	.292	.511	9.327	
Very Strong	1.812	1.593	0.68	.499	.324	10.147	
Constant	.103	.063	-3.72	0	.031	.342	***
Number of obs	=	*89*			*Log pseudol.*	=	*-36.396517*
Wald chi2(2)	=	*1.12*			*Pseudo R2*	=	*.0165*
Prob > chi2	=	*.5718*					

Logistic Regression: SFIUse – Transformation Risk

SFIUser	Odds Ratio	Robust Std. Err.	z	P >|z|	95 % Confidence Interval		Signifi-cance / Comment
Low	1	.	.	.	.	.	Baseline
Average	1.227	1.506	0.17	.867	.111	13.601	
Strong	1.75	1.992	0.49	.623	.188	16.291	
Very Strong	1.385	1.809	0.25	.803	.107	17.916	
Constant	.111	.118	-2.07	.038	.014	.887	**
Number of obs	=	*93*			*Log pseudol.*	=	*-37.417624*
Wald chi2(3)	=	*.40*			*Pseudo R2*	=	*.0055*
Prob > chi2	=	*.9405*					

Logistic Regression: SFIUse – Financing Access

SFIUser	Odds Ratio	Robust Std. Err.	z	P >|z|	95 % Confidence Interval		Signifi-cance / Comment
Very Low	1	.	.	.	.	.	Baseline
Low	1	.	.	.	.	.	PFP
Average	.517	.495	-0.69	.491	.079	3.373	
High	.694	.684	-0.37	.711	.101	4.788	
Very High	1	.	.	.	.	.	PFP
Constant	.4	.337	-1.09	.277	.077	2.088	
Number of obs	=	*65*			*Log pseudol.*	=	*-32.265419*
Wald chi2(2)	=	*.53*			*Pseudo R2*	=	*.0080*
Prob > chi2	=	*.7684*					

Logistic Regression: SFIUse – Financing Link

SFIUser	Odds Ratio	Robust Std. Err.	z	P >|z|	95 % Confidence Interval		Signifi-cance / Comment
Very Unlikely	1	.	.	.	.	.	Baseline
Unlikely	.286	.467	-0.77	.443	.012	7.034	
Average	.211	.303	-1.08	.279	.013	3.544	
Likely	.216	.29	-1.14	.253	.016	2.99	
Very Likely	.667	.891	-0.30	.762	.049	9.15	
Constant	.5	.616	-0.56	.574	.045	5.586	
Number of obs	=	*93*			*Log pseudol.*	=	*-35.882057*
Wald chi2(4)	=	*3.59*			*Pseudo R2*	=	*.0463*
Prob > chi2	=	*.4649*					

Source: Logistic regression analysis with robust standard errors run in Stata using data from Table 8. Further details see Table 5. Note: "PFP" = predicts failure perfectly. Significance levels: *** p<.01, ** p<.05, * p<.1.

Table 7b. Logistic Regression Analysis Results – Pull Factors

Logistic Regression: SFIUse – Carbon Footprint

SFIUser	Odds Ratio	Robust Std. Err.	z	P >|z|	95 % Confidence Interval		Significance/ Comment
Yes	3.69	3.005	1.60	.109	.748	18.209	
No	1	.	.	.	.	.	Baseline
I don't know	2.214	2.881	0.61	.541	.173	28.372	
Constant	.065	.047	-3.74	0	.015	.272	***
Number of obs	=	*93*			*Log pseudol.*	=	*-36.015712*
Wald chi2(2)	=	*2.63*			*Pseudo R2*	=	*.0428*
Prob > chi2	=	*.2689*					

Logistic Regression: SFIUse – ESG Rating

SFIUser	Odds Ratio	Robust Std. Err.	z	P >|z|	95 % Confidence Interval		Significance/ Comment
Yes	12.5	9.307	3.39	.001	2.905	53.788	***
No	1	.	.	.	.	.	Baseline
I don't know	1.852	2.254	0.51	.613	.17	20.131	
I don't know, unfamiliar	1	.	.	.	.	.	PFP
Constant	.06	.036	-4.70	0	.019	.194	***
Number of obs	=	*84*			*Log pseudol.*	=	*-29.120384*
Wald chi2(2)	=	*12.33*			*Pseudo R2*	=	*.1954*
Prob > chi2	=	*.0021*					

Logistic Regression: SFIUse – CLST

SFIUser	Odds Ratio	Robust Std. Err.	z	P >|z|	95 % Confidence Interval		Signifi-cance/ Comment
Yes	5.434	5.844	1.57	.116	.66	44.729	
No	1	.	.	.	.	.	Baseline
I don't know	1	.	.	.	.	.	PFP
Constant	.042	.043	-3.10	.002	.006	.311	***
Number of obs	=	*90*			*Log pseudol.*	=	*-35.289425*
Wald chi2(1)	=	*2.48*			*Pseudo R2*	=	*.0505*
Prob > chi2	=	*.1155*					

Logistic Regression: SFIUse – STCS

SFIUser	Odds Ratio	Robust Std. Err.	z	P >|z|	95 % Confidence Interval		Signifi-cance/ Comment
Yes	4.143	3.047	1.93	.053	.98	17.512	*
No	1	.	.	.	.	.	Baseline
I don't know	1.184	1.018	0.20	.845	.219	6.386	
Constant	.121	.049	-5.26	0	.055	.266	***
Number of obs	=	*93*			*Log pseudol.*	=	*-35.874599*
Wald chi2(2)	=	*3.83*			*Pseudo R2*	=	*.0465*
Prob > chi2	=	*.1473*					

Source: Logistic regression analysis with robust standard errors run in Stata using data from Table 8. Further details see Table 5. Note: "PFP" = predicts failure perfectly. Significance levels: *** p<.01, ** p<.05, * p<.1.

Table 8. SFI Use for the Seven Defined Push and Pull Factors

	SFI Implementation				
	Yes	No	In Process	Unfamiliar with SFIs	I don't know
Perceived Regulatory Pressure					
None	0	0	0	0	0
Low	0	4	0	0	0
Average	3	21	2	6	0
Strong	7	24	3	4	0
Very Strong	3	11	1	2	2
Perceived Transformation Risk					
None	0	0	0	0	0
Low	1	7	0	2	0
Average	3	14	3	4	1
Strong	7	29	2	5	0
Very Strong	2	10	1	1	1
Perceived Risk to Lose Financing Access					
Very Low	2	2	1	1	1
Low	0	17	2	5	0
Average	6	24	2	3	0
High	5	14	1	3	0
Very High	0	3	0	0	1
Perceived Likelihood that Sustainability Criteria & Credit Conditions will be linked					
Very Unlikely	1	2	0	0	0
Unlikely	1	5	0	1	1
Average	2	14	1	4	0
Likely	4	27	5	5	0
Very Likely	5	12	0	2	1
Company Carbon Footprint					
Yes	10	31	5	5	1
No	2	23	1	7	0
I don't know	1	6	0	0	1

	SFI Implementation				
	Yes	No	In Process	Unfamiliar with SFIs	I don't know
Company ESG Rating					
Yes	9	9	3	0	0
No	3	37	3	9	1
I don't know	1	7	0	2	0
I don't know, unfamiliar with ESG term	0	7	0	1	1
Company-Level Sustainability Targets					
Yes	12	40	5	8	0
No	1	19	1	4	0
I don't know	0	1	0	0	2
Sustainability Target Commitment Scheme					
Yes	4	6	1	1	0
No	7	43	5	10	0
I don't know	2	11	0	1	2

Source: This table presents the recorded answers regarding the push and pull factors from the survey questions 14, 15, 16, 17, 21, 22, 23 and 24, as well as the recorded SFI use for each push and pull factor.

Table 9. Correlation Analysis Results – Push and Pull Factors & Barriers

	Company Size		CMA		Company Sector	
	Fisher's Exact P-Value	Cramér's V	Fisher's Exact P-Vale	Cramér's V	Fisher's Exact P-Value	Cramér's V
Regulatory Pressure	.764	.1481	.555	.1662	.728	.3056
Transformation Risk	.175	.2144	.710	.1234	.157	.3929
Financing Access	.377	.1978	.832	.1199	.077*	.4323
Financing Link	.022**	.3345	.941	.0907	.768	.2986
Carbon Footprint	.007***	.2990	.237	.1710	.257	.4121
ESG Rating	.000***	.3960	.079*	.2685	.509	.3300
CLST	.062*	.2516	.511	.1237	.111	.4024
STCS	.165	.2408	.275	.1716	.435	.3383
Unfamiliar with ESG	.005***	.4159	.721	-.0511	.329	.3758
Unfamiliar with SFI	.040**	.3020	.049**	.2127	.357	.3571
Barriers	.555	.1507	.273	.1352	.775	.2714

*** p<.01, ** p<.05, * p<.1

Source: Fisher's exact test and Cramér's V calculations run in Stata using the data from Table 10, 11 and 12. The number of observations for company size groups is 89, for capital market activity groups 92 and for company sector groups 75, as recorded "no answer" options were excluded. Note: "CMA" denotes capital market activity, "CLST" denotes corporate level sustainability targets and "STCS" denotes sustainability target commitment scheme. Significance levels are denoted as follows: *** p<.01, ** p<.05, * p<.1.

Table 10. Push and Pull Factors by Company Size Group

	Company Size				
	Medium-Size	Large Medium-Size	Large	Multi-nationals	No Answer
Perceived Regulatory Pressure					
None	0	0	0	0	0
Low	1	2	1	0	0
Average	4	17	6	2	3
Strong	3	19	12	4	0
Very Strong	1	9	4	4	0
Perceived Transformation Risk					
None	0	0	0	0	0
Low	2	2	4	0	2
Average	3	12	6	4	0
Strong	4	27	7	4	1
Very Strong	0	6	6	2	0
Perceived Risk to Lose Financing Access					
Very Low	1	2	3	1	0
Low	4	11	6	2	1
Average	4	18	9	2	2
High	0	15	4	4	0
Very High	0	1	1	1	0
Perceived Likelihood that Sustainability Criteria & Credit Conditions will be Linked					
Very Unlikely	0	1	0	2	0
Unlikely	4	2	1	1	0
Average	3	9	5	1	3
Likely	2	25	11	3	0
Very Likely	0	10	6	3	0
Company Carbon Footprint					
Yes	2	25	14	10	0
No	5	20	6	0	2
I don't know	2	2	3	0	1

	Company Size				
	Medium-Size	Large Medium-Size	Large	Multi-nationals	No Answer
Company ESG Rating					
Yes	1	4	8	8	0
No	2	33	13	2	2
I don't know	2	5	2	0	1
I don't know, unfamiliar with ESG term	4	5	0	0	0
Company-Level Sustainability Targets					
Yes	5	28	20	9	3
No	3	18	3	1	0
I don't know	1	1	0	0	0
Sustainability Target Commitment Scheme					
Yes	1	4	2	4	1
No	7	37	15	5	1
I don't know	1	6	6	1	1

Source: This table presents the recorded answers regarding the push and pull factors from the survey questions 14, 15, 16, 17, 21, 22, 23 and 24 by company size groups.

Table 11. Push and Pull Factors By Company Capital Market Activity Group

	Company Capital Market Activity		
	Active	Not Active	I don't know
Perceived Regulatory Pressure			
None	0	0	0
Low	0	4	0
Average	13	19	0
Strong	14	23	1
Very Strong	7	12	0
Perceived Transformation Risk			
None	0	0	0
Low	3	7	0
Average	10	14	1
Strong	14	29	0
Very Strong	7	8	0
Perceived Risk to Lose Financing Access			
Very Low	3	4	0
Low	10	13	1
Average	11	24	0
High	8	15	0
Very High	2	2	0
Perceived Likelihood that Sustainability Criteria & Credit Conditions will be Linked			
Very Unlikely	1	2	0
Unlikely	4	4	0
Average	7	14	0
Likely	15	25	1
Very Likely	7	13	0
Company Carbon Footprint			
Yes	19	33	0
No	10	22	1
I don't know	19	33	0
Company ESG Rating			
Yes	12	9	0
No	14	39	0
I don't know	4	5	1
I don't know, unfamiliar with ESG term	4	5	0

	Company Capital Market Activity		
	Active	Not Active	I don't know
Company-Level Sustainability Targets			
Yes	24	40	1
No	8	17	0
I don't know	2	1	0
Sustainability Target Commitment Scheme			
Yes	9	3	0
No	21	44	0
I don't know	4	11	1

Source: This table presents the recorded answers regarding the push and pull factors from the survey questions 14, 15, 16, 17, 21, 22, 23 and 24 by capital market activity groups.

Table 12. Push and Pull Factors by Company Sector Group

Company Sector	Perceived Regulatory Pressure					Perceived Transformation Risk				
	None	Low	Average	Strong	Very Strong	None	Low	Average	Strong	Very Strong
Communication S.	0	0	1	0	0	0	0	0	1	0
Consumer Discr.	0	0	5	3	1	0	1	2	5	1
Consumer Staples	0	1	2	3	3	0	1	0	5	3
Financials	0	0	2	1	1	0	2	1	1	0
Health Care	0	0	0	4	0	0	0	3	1	0
Industrials	0	2	9	11	7	0	3	7	16	3
Information Techn.	0	0	0	1	1	0	0	2	0	0
Materials	0	0	3	3	1	0	0	3	3	1
No Answer	0	1	4	8	5	0	2	7	6	3
Real Estate	0	0	1	0	0	0	0	0	1	0
Utilities	0	0	5	4	0	0	1	0	4	4

Company Sector	Perceived Risk to Lose Financing Access					Perceived Likelihood of Linkage				
	Very Low	Low	Average	High	Very High	Very Unlikely	Unlikely	Average	Likely	Very Likely
Communication S.	0	1	0	0	0	0	0	0	1	0
Consumer Discr.	1	2	3	3	0	0	0	4	3	2
Consumer Staples	0	2	2	3	2	0	1	1	4	3
Financials	2	0	2	0	0	0	2	1	0	1
Health Care	2	0	2	0	0	0	0	2	2	0
Industrials	1	8	14	6	0	1	2	7	15	4
Information Techn.	0	2	0	0	0	0	1	0	1	0
Materials	0	3	1	3	0	0	1	2	2	2
No Answer	1	4	7	4	2	2	1	2	7	6
Real Estate	0	0	0	1	0	0	0	0	1	0
Utilities	0	2	4	3	0	0	0	2	5	2

Company Sector	Company Carbon Footprint			Company ESG Rating			
	Yes	No	I don't know	Yes	No	I don't know	Unfamiliar with ESG
Communication S.	0	1	0	0	1	0	0
Consumer Discr.	4	4	1	1	7	1	0
Consumer Staples	6	3	0	3	4	1	1
Financials	1	1	2	1	1	1	1
Health Care	4	0	0	2	2	0	0
Industrials	14	13	2	6	16	3	4
Information Techn.	2	0	0	1	1	0	0
Materials	5	2	0	2	2	0	3
No Answer	12	3	3	3	11	4	0
Real Estate	1	0	0	1	0	0	0
Utilities	3	6	0	1	8	0	0

Company Sector	Sustainability Targets			Commitment Scheme		
	Yes	No	I don't know	Yes	No	I don't know
Communication S.	0	1	0	0	1	0
Consumer Discr.	7	2	0	2	4	3
Consumer Staples	6	2	1	0	8	1
Financials	3	0	1	1	2	1
Health Care	4	0	0	1	3	0
Industrials	21	8	0	3	22	4
Information Techn.	1	1	0	1	1	0
Materials	4	3	0	0	6	1
No Answer	15	2	1	3	11	4
Real Estate	1	0	0	0	0	1
Utilities	3	6	0	1	7	1

Source: This table presents the recorded answers regarding the push and pull factors from the survey questions 14, 15, 16, 17, 21, 22, 23 and 24 by company sector groups.

Table 13. Barriers to SFI Use by SFI Implementation and Company Size Groups

	Implementation				
	Yes	No	Currenly in Process	Unfamiliar with SFIs	I don't know
<u>Barriers</u>					
Yes	4	27	3	4	0
No	9	33	3	8	2

	Company Size				
	Medium-Size	Large Medium-Size	Large	Multinational	No Answer
<u>Barriers</u>					
Yes	5	16	9	5	3
No	4	31	14	5	0
<u>Stated Barriers</u>					
Applicability	1	4	0	0	1
Company Requirements	0	6	4	2	2
Economic Efficiency	3	6	3	1	1
Implementation	1	2	3	3	0

Source: This table presents the recorded answers from survey question 2.

Table 14. Stated Perceived Barriers to SFI Use

Main Categories	Subcategories Level 1	Subcategories Level 2	Number of Observations
Applicability	Company Characteristics	*Company purpose*	1
		Financing structure	2
		Industry	1
	Financing Need	*Insufficient flexibility*	1
		Use Case	1
Company Requirements	Administrative Work	*Add. work capacities needed*	1
		General add. effort	7
		Reporting	4
	Knowledge	*Insufficient consulting*	1
		No experience	1
		Regulatory uncertainty	2
Economic Efficiency	Cost	*Costs higher than benefits*	3
		Higher costs	3
		Insufficient promotional loans	2
	Risk	*Greenwashing risk*	1
		Regulatory risk	1
		Risk of failure to achieve targets	4
Implementation	Instrument	*Data collection*	2
		KPI choice & tracking	4
		Size	1
	Standards & Regulations	*Data availability*	3
		Data comparability	1
		Investor requirements	1

Source: This table shows the categorical system developed based on companies' stated perceived barriers using thematic content analysis following Kuckartz's (2014) seven steps and the survey data recorded for survey question 2.

Table 15. Ranking of Potential SFI Use Barriers by Company Size Group

		Medium- Size	Large Medium-Size	Large	Multinational
Considered SFI					
	1	Knowledge	Knowledge	Knowledge	Knowledge
	2	Data	Data	Data	Data
	3	Costs	Costs	Costs	Costs
	4	Publicity	Publicity	Publicity	Publicity
	5	No financing needs	Promotional loans exhausted / too low, no financing needs, regulatory uncertainty, complicated application, insufficient consultation / advice, limited financing offers	No financing needs	-
Not Considered SFI					
	1	Knowledge	Knowledge	Knowledge	Knowledge
	2	Data	Data	Data	Data
	3	Costs	Costs	Costs	Costs
	4	Publicity	Publicity	Publicity	Publicity
	5	No financing needs	No needs, no project identified	No financing needs	Insufficient incentive
Implemented SFI					
	1	-	Pricing	Pricing	Communication
	2	-	Communication	Communication	Pricing
	3	-	Competition	Competition	Recommendation
	4	-	Recommendation	Recommendation	Competition
	5	-	-	Company strategy, broader investor base	Company strategy
SFI Implementation Underway					
	1	-	Pricing	Communication	-
	2	-	Communication	Pricing	-
	3	-	Competition	Competition	-
	4	-	Recommendation	Recommendation	-
	5	-	-	-	-

Source: This table shows the ranking of potential barriers to SFI use, as recorded by the survey data from questions 4, 5, 6 and 7. It should be noted that none of the medium-sized companies have implemented or are currently underway to implement a SFI. Furthermore, none of the multinational companies are currently underway to implement a SFI.

Table 16. The Role of Banks and Promotional Loans in Regard to SFI Use

	Implementation				
	Yes	No	Currenly in Process	Unfamiliar with SFIs	I don't know
Bank Support					
Very Bad	0	3	0	2	0
Bad	0	8	0	3	0
Average	3	28	2	5	0
Good	7	18	4	2	1
Very Good	3	3	0	0	1
Bank Recommendation to Use SFIs					
Yes	11	17	5	0	1
No	2	39	1	12	0
I don't know	0	4	0	0	1
Bank Role					
Yes	6	31	4	6	0
No	2	11	2	0	1
I don't know	5	18	0	6	1

	Company Size				
	Medium-Size	Large Medium-Size	Large	Multinational	No Answer
Promotional L. Interest					
Yes	6	38	18	7	1
No	0	4	1	2	0
I don't know	3	5	4	1	2
Promotional L. Use					
Yes, we use PL	0	5	2	1	0
No, we do not use PL	9	42	21	9	3
Promotional L. Knowledge					
Yes, PL are known	4	19	13	6	2
No, unfamiliar with PL	5	23	8	3	1
Bank Support					
Very Bad	0	5	0	0	0
Bad	1	10	0	0	0
Average	4	21	8	2	3
Good	3	10	13	6	0
Very Good	1	1	2	2	0
Bank Recommendation					
Yes	3	8	13	8	2
No	5	38	8	2	1
I don't know	1	1	2	0	0
Bank Role					
Yes	4	23	12	8	0
No	1	8	5	1	0
I don't know	4	16	6	1	3

Source: This table shows companies' evaluation of banks' role and support in regard to SFI use, as well as their interest in and use of promotional loans. The data is based on the recorded answers for survey questions 9, 10, 11, 12 and 13.

Table 17. Desired Form of Bank Support in Regard to SFI Use

Main Categories	Subcategories Level 1	Subcategories Level 2	Number Of Observations
Consultation	General Consultation		14
	KPI Choice		4
	Optimizing Rating		1
	Promotional Loans		3
	Reporting		2
Information	General Information		3
	Sustainable Finance Market	*Expectation of bank / capital market participants*	2
		Market overview	2
	Sustainable Finance Mechanisms	*Comparison to conv financing*	1
		Impact of sustainability on rating / financing	1
		Information on conditions	1
	Sustainable Finance Use	*Best Practice*	2
		Experience (with other customers)	4
		Use Cases	1
Mode of Information	Event		1
	Personal Talks		1
	Presentation		1
	Questionnaire		1
	Workshop		1
Role of Bank	Clear Commitment with Strategic Allocation		1
	Financing (Offers)		4
	Sparring Partner		1

Source: This table presents companies' desired support that they would like to receive from their banks and financial partners in regard to sustainable finance, based on the survey data recorded for question 12. The qualitative answers were categorized using a thematic content analysis method based on the seven steps by Kuckartz (2014).

Table 18. Logistic Regression Analysis Results – Barriers & Company Bank Relation

Logistic Regression: SFIUse – Barriers

SFIUser	Odds Ratio	Robust Std. Err.	z	P >|z|	95 % Confidence Interval		Significance/ Comment
Yes	.601	.388	-0.79	.431	.17	2.131	
No	1	.	.	.	.	.	Baseline
Constant	.196	.072	-4.45	0	.095	.401	***
Number of obs	=	*93*			*Log pseudol.*	=	*-37.297639*
Wald chi2(1)	=	*.62*			*Pseudo R2*	=	*.0087*
Prob > chi2	=	*.4307*					

Logistic Regression: SFIUse – Bank Support

SFIUser	Odds Ratio	Robust Std. Err.	z	P >|z|	95 % Confidence Interval		Significance/ Comment
Very Bad	1	.	.	.	.	.	PFP
Bad	1	.	.	.	.	.	PFP
Average	1	.	.	.	.	.	Baseline
Good	3.267	2.427	1.59	.111	.762	14.011	
Very Good	8.75	8.563	2.22	.027	1.285	59.566	**
Constant	.086	.052	-4.06	0	.026	.281	***
Number of obs	=	*77*			*Log pseudol.*	=	*-32.085894*
Wald chi2(2)	=	*5.22*			*Pseudo R2*	=	*.0822*
Prob > chi2	=	*.0737*					

Logistic Regression: SFIUse – Bank Recommendation

SFIUser	Odds Ratio	Robust Std. Err.	z	P >|z|	95 % Confidence Interval		Significance/ Comment
Yes	12.435	10.111	3.10	.002	2.527	61.2	***
No	1	.	.	.	.	.	Baseline
I don't know	1	.	.	.	.	.	PFP
Constant	.038	.028	-4.50	0	.009	.159	***
Number of obs	=	*88*			*Log pseudol.*	=	*-29.957214*
Wald chi2(1)	=	*9.61*			*Pseudo R2*	=	*.1870*
Prob > chi2	=	*.0019*					

Logistic Regression: SFIUse – Bank Role

SFIUser	Odds Ratio	Robust Std. Err.	z	P >|z|	95 % Confidence Interval		Significance/ Comment
Yes	1.024	.899	0.03	.978	.183	5.725	
No	1	.	.	.	.	.	Baseline
I don't know	1.4	1.268	0.37	.71	.237	8.261	
Constant	.143	.109	-2.56	.01	.032	.634	**
Number of obs	=	*93*			*Log pseudol.*	=	*-37.495085*
Wald chi2(2)	=	*.26*			*Pseudo R2*	=	*.0035*
Prob > chi2	=	*.8770*					

Source: Logistic regression analysis with robust standard errors run in Stata using data from Table 13 and Table 16. Further details see Table 5. Note: "PFP" = predicts failure perfectly. Significance levels: *** p<.01, ** p<.05, * p<.1.

Table 19. Logistic Regression Results Analysis Promotional Loans

Logistic Regression: SFIUse – Promotional Loan Interest

SFIUser	Odds Ratio	Robust Std. Err.	z	P >|z|	95 % Confidence Interval		Significance / Comment
Yes	.443	.397	-0.91	.363	.076	2.563	
No	1	.	.	.	.	.	Baseline
I don't know	.462	.517	-0.69	.49	.051	4.155	
Constant	.333	.274	-1.34	.181	.067	1.666	
Number of obs	*=*	*93*			*Log pseudol.*	*=*	*-37.245138*
Wald chi2(2)	*=*	*.84*			*Pseudo R2*	*=*	*.0101*
Prob > chi2	*=*	*.6574*					

Logistic Regression: SFIUse – Promotional Loan Knowledge

SFIUser	Odds Ratio	Robust Std. Err.	z	P >|z|	95 % Confidence Interval		Significance / Comment
No	1	.	.	.	.	.	Baseline
Yes	1.936	1.249	1.02	.306	.547	6.852	
Constant	.108	.057	-4.20	0	.038	.305	***
Number of obs	*=*	*93*			*Log pseudol.*	*=*	*-37.065362*
Wald chi2(1)	*=*	*1.05*			*Pseudo R2*	*=*	*.0149*
Prob > chi2	*=*	*.3056*					

Logistic Regression: SFIUse – Promotional Loan Use

SFIUser	Odds Ratio	Robust Std. Err.	z	P >|z|	95 % Confidence Interval		Signifi-cance / Comment
No	1	.	.	.	.	.	Baseline
Yes	2.242	1.98	0.91	.36	.397	12.654	
Constant	.149	.048	-5.87	0	.079	.281	***
Number of obs	=	*93*			*Log pseudol.*	=	*-37.246373*
Wald chi2(1)	=	*.84*			*Pseudo R2*	=	*.0101*
Prob > chi2	=	*.3604*					

Source: Logistic regression analysis with robust standard errors run in Stata using data from Table 16. Further details see Table 5. Note: "PFP" = predicts failure perfectly. Significance levels: *** p<.01, ** p<.05, * p<.1.

Table 20. Correlation Analysis Results Company Bank Relation & Promotional Loans

	Company Size	
	Fisher's Exact	Cramér's V
Bank SF Support Rating	.008***	.3040
Bank SFI Recommendation	.000***	.3689
Banks Potential Role	.637	.1632
Promotional Loan Knowledge	.498	.1690
Promotional Loan Use	.942	.1091
Promotional Loan Interest	.421	.183

Source: Fisher's exact test and Cramér's V calculations run in Stata using the data from Table 16. Note: Significance levels are denoted as: *** p<.01, ** p<.05, * p<.1.

Appendix B: Figures

Figure 3. Sustainable Finance Instrument Use by Company Sector

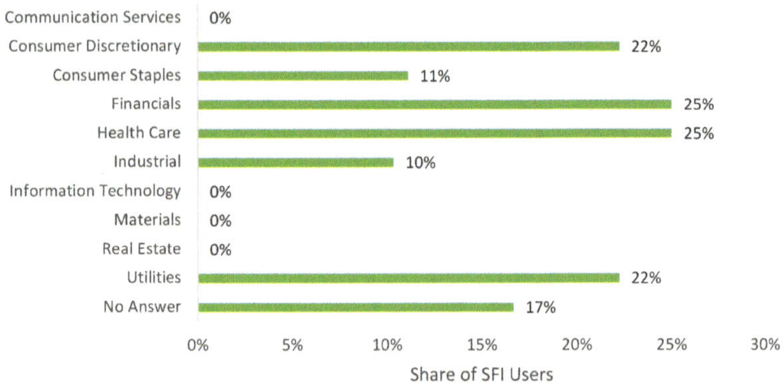

Source: This figure presents the share of SFI users for the ten defined company sector groups, based on the survey data reported in Appendix A, Table 6.

Figure 10. Perceived Risk to Lose Financing Access by Company Sector

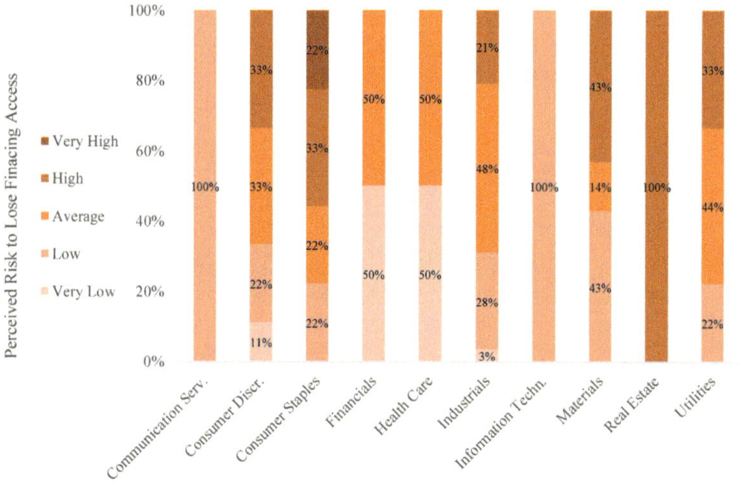

Source: This figure presents the respective share of different levels of perceived risk to lose financing access by the ten defined company sector groups, based on the survey data reported in Appendix A, Table 12.

Figure 19. Barriers to SFI Use by Company Size Group

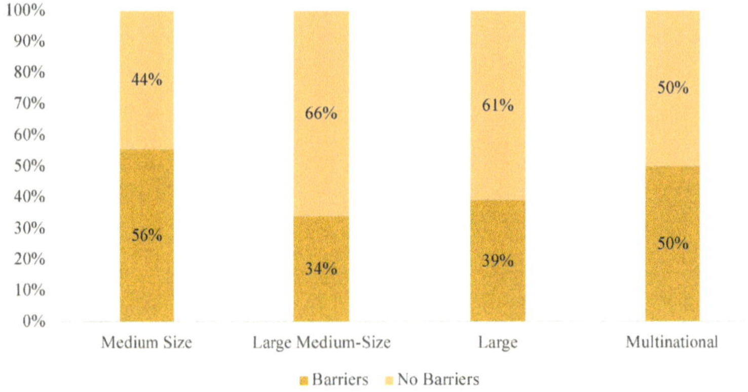

Source: This figure presents the share of companies that state they view barriers to SFI use by the four defined company size groups, based on the survey data reported in Appendix A, Table 13.

Appendix C: Survey

Appendix C: Survey

Start of Block: Introduction

Welcome Message
Goethe University Study: More Favorable Financing through Sustainability ?!

The European Green Deal is changing financing: it is to be expected that financing conditions will become more favorable due to sustainability criteria . But how can the potential of sustainable finance instruments be used in the best possible way?

This study, in cooperation with DZ BANK AG and Goethe University Frankfurt, examines the advantages and opportunities of sustainable finance for companies. **It takes 5 minutes to answer the questions**. At the end you have the opportunity to write down any additional information or comments.

If you have any questions or require assistance in completing the survey, please contact Mrs. Isabelle Hinsche (hinsche@econ.uni-frankfurt.de). All answers are anonymous and the results of the study will be made available to all participants.

Data Protection
All answers are anonymous and cannot be traced back to you personally. The answers will be stored on an EU server and will only be used for the research project Sustainable Finance by Goethe University Frankfurt.

What are Sustainable Finance Instruments?

In the following section, two best-known instruments will be explained. The respective sustainable financing structure can be applied to any traditional credit financing instrument, such as a loan, schuldscheindarlehen or bond.

A green financing instrument:
is a financing instrument whose funds may only be used for a predefined green project that contributes to environmental protection. The sustainability of the issuer is irrelevant. There are also social or combined instruments whose projects are classified as social or social and green.

A sustainability-linked instrument:
is a financing instrument that is linked to company-level sustainability criteria. The issuer defines company-specific sustainability targets and commits to reaching these targets within a set time frame. In the event that the sustainability targets are not met, a financial penalty, for example in the form of a coupon step-up, is defined in advance.

End of Block: Introduction

Start of Block: SF Instruments

Q1 Has your company ever used a sustainable finance instrument (e.g.: green loan / schuldscheindarlehen / bond)?

○ Yes. *Please briefly name the sustainable finance instrument(s) used:* (1) ________________________________

○ No. (2)

○ Is currently being implemented. *Please briefly name the planned sustainable financing instrument:* (3) ________________________________

○ I was not familiar with sustainable finance instruments so far. (4)

○ I don't know. (5)

Q2 Do you see any barriers in regard to sustainable finance instrument use for your company? *(If yes, please name them: keywords are possible)*

○ Yes: (1) ________________________________

○ No. (2)

Display This Question:

If "Has your company ever used a sustainable finance instrument" = No.
Or "Has your company ever used a sustainable finance instrument" = I don't know.

Q3 Has your company ever considered using a sustainable finance instrument?

○ Yes. (1)

○ No. (2)

○ I don't know. (3)

Display This Question:
If "Has your company ever considered using a sustainable finance instrument?" = Yes.

Q4 Why has your company nevertheless not used a sustainable finance instrument so far? *(Please rank the potential reasons according to their influence: category 1 indicates the greatest influence)*

_____ Insufficient knowledge of sustainable finance instruments. (1)
_____ Insufficient data on company's sustainability. (2)
_____ Additional costs of a sustainable finance structure (consultation, reporting). (3)
_____ Potential negative public reaction (e.g. greenwashing accusations). (4)
_____ Further: (5)

Display This Question:
If "Has your company ever considered using a sustainable finance instrument?" = No.

Q5 Why has your company not used a sustainable finance instrument so far? *(Please rank the potential reasons according to their influence: category 1 indicates the greatest influence)*

_____ Insufficient knowledge of sustainable finance instruments. (1)
_____ Insufficient data on the company's sustainability. (2)
_____ Additional costs of a sustainable finance structure (consultation, reporting). (3)
_____ Potential negative public reaction (e.g. greenwashing accusations. (4)
_____ Further: (5)

Display This Question:
If "Has your company ever considered using a sustainable finance instrument?" = Is currently being implemented.

Q6 Why does your company plan to use a sustainable finance instrument? *(Please rank the potential reasons according to their influence: category 1 indicates the greatest influence)*

_____ Potential pricing advantage compared to conventional financing structure. (1)
_____ Communication of own sustainability strategy to investors and customers. (2)
_____ The competition has already used a sustainable financing structure. (3)
_____ Recommendation of sustainable finance structure by financing partner/Hausbank. (4)
_____ Further: (5)

Display This Question:
If "Has your company ever used a sustainable finance instrument" = Yes.

Q7 Why has your company used a sustainable finance instrument?
(Please rank the potential reasons according to their influence: category 1 indicates the greatest influence)

_____ Potential pricing advantage compared to conventional financing structure. (1)
_____ Communication of own sustainability strategy to investors and customers. (2)
_____ The competition has already used a sustainable financing structure. (3)
_____ Recommendation of sustainable finance structure by financing partner/Hausbank. (4)
_____ Further: (5)

Q8 Does your company plan to use (further) sustainable finance instruments in the future?

- ○ Yes, because (1) ____
- ○ No, because (2) ____
- ○ I don't know. (3)

Q9 Are you familiar with promotional loans in connection with sustainable finance?

- ○ Yes, we are already using the following promotional loans: (1)
____
- ○ Yes, I am familiar with sustainable finance related promotional loans. (2)
- ○ No, I am not familiar with sustainable finance related promotional loans. (3)

Q10 Would you be interested in promotional loans in connection with sustainable finance?

- ○ Yes. (1)
- ○ No. (2)
- ○ I don't know. (3)

End of Block: SF Instruments

Start of Block: Sustainability, Banks & Regulation

Q11 How well do you feel supported by your bank(s) on the subject of sustainability?

- ◯ Very bad (1)
- ◯ Bad (2)
- ◯ Average (3)
- ◯ Good (4)
- ◯ Very good (5)

Q12 Do you believe that your financing partner / bank can support you in your sustainability transformation?

- ◯ Yes, in the form of: (1) ____
- ◯ No. (2)
- ◯ I don't know. (3)

Q13 Have your financing partners (e.g. Hausbank) ever suggested a sustainable financing structure to you?

- ◯ Yes. (1)
- ◯ No. (2)
- ◯ I don't know. (3)

Q14 How likely do you think is the linkage of sustainability criteria and credit conditions for your future financing?

- Very unlikely (1)
- Unlikely (2)
- Average (3)
- Likely (4)
- Very likely (5)

Q15 How high do you estimate the risk of losing access to the capital / credit market to be, if you do not meet certain sustainability targets?

- Very low (1)
- Low (2)
- Average (3)
- High (4)
- Very high (5)

Q16 How strongly do you think is your company affected by the sustainability transformation of the economy?

- Not at all (1)
- Little (2)
- Average (3)
- Strongly (4)
- Very strongly (5)

Q17 How much pressure to you experience as a company from regulatory sustainabilty requirements (NFRD, CSRD, Supply Chain Act)?

- None (1)
- Little (2)
- Average (3)
- Strong (4)
- Very strong (5)

End of Block: Sustainability, Banks & Regulation

Start of Block: Company Information

Q18 Which industry does your company belong to?
Please select the appropriate industry group.

- Automobiles and Parts (1)
- Banks (2)
- Construction and Materials (3)
- Chemicals (4)
- Retail (5)
- Utilities (6)
- Oil and Gas (7)
- Financial Services (8)
- Health Care (9)
- Real Estate (10)
- Industrial Goods & Services (11)
- Media (12)
- Food, Beverages and Tobacco (13)
- Personal and Household Products (14)
- Basic Resources (15)
- Travel and Leisure (16)
- Technology (17)
- Telecommunications (18)
- Insurance (19)
- No Answer (20)

Q19 How big is your company?
Please select the appropriate annual revenue range (rounded to millions)

- Up to €9 million (1)
- From €10 million to €49 million (2)
- From €50 million to €499 million (3)
- From €500 million to €5 billion (4)
- Greater than €5 billion (5)
- No Answer (6)

Q20 Does your company acquire financing on the capital market?

- Yes. (1)
- No. (2)
- I don't know. (3)

Q21 Does your company already determine its carbon footprint?

- Yes. (1)
- No. (2)
- I don't know. (3)

Q22 Does your company have an ESG rating?

- Yes. (1)
- No. (2)
- I don't know. (3)
- I don't know, I am not familiar with the term ESG. (4)

Q23 Has your company defined sustainability targets at the company level?

- Yes. (1)
- No. (2)
- I don't know. (3)

Q24 Is the achievement of these targets ensured by a form of commitment? *(e.g. management compensation is linked to the achievement of sustainability targets)*

- Yes, through (1) ____
- No. (2)
- I don't know. (3)

Q25 For which company are you answering this questionnaire?

(Voluntary information. All answers are anonymous, this information is only used to link company-specific data for research purposes and will also be anonymized and aggregated in the analysis). We would be happy to send you, as a participant, the results of the study. However, as all answers are anonymous, we do not have any contact details for the distribution of the survey results. Consequently, we would kindly ask you to state your company name if you would like to receive the survey results.

____

End of Block: Company Information

Start of Block: Personal Information

Q26 Please select your gender:

- Male (1)
- Female (2)
- Diverse (3)
- No Answer (4)

Q27 Please select your age group:

- Younger than 20 years (1)
- 20 to 29 years (2)
- 30 to 39 years (3)
- 40 to 49 years (4)
- 50 to 59 years (5)
- 60 years or older (6)
- No Answer (7)

Q28 Please select your work department within your company:

- Finance (1)
- Sustainability (2)
- Other Area (3)
- No Answer (4)

Q29 Do you have any study and / or work experience in the field of sustainability?

- Yes, I have study and work experience in the field of sustainability. (1)
- Yes, I have study experience in the field of sustainability. (2)
- Yes, I have work experience in the field of sustainability. (3)
- No, I do not have study or work experience in the field of sustainability. (4)
- No Answer (5)

Q30 Additional information / comments from your side:

____

End of Block: Personal Information

Chapter 3 Sustainable Finance in House Bank Relations

Enabling the Effective Use of Sustainable Finance in a Bank-Based Financial System – With Special Consideration of SMEs –

Isabelle Cathérine Hinsche[*]

Abstract

This paper analyzes whether and how the currently implemented sustainable finance incentive mechanism needs to be adapted to and utilize the characteristics of house bank relations, particularly in regard to SMEs, to achieve the desired and necessary sustainability transition investments. The analysis is conducted based on a survey with 700 corporate customers of DZ BANK AG and uses a mixed method research approach to investigate how companies that rely solely on bank-based financing differ in their motivational, implementation and enabling factors to use sustainable finance instruments (SFIs). The results show that they can primarily be incentivized by a potential pricing advantage. Furthermore, they demonstrate a low sustainable finance knowledge and perceive data collection, reporting and insufficient consulting amongst the biggest barriers to SFI use. In regard to their bank relation, less than a third of companies have been recommended SFI use by their bank. To overcome these barriers, they would like to receive information on SFI use, concrete financing offers and are interested in promotional loan use. Based on the findings, the study formulates recommendations on how to ensure an effective use of sustainable finance in a bank-based financial system, as well as how to use the potential of promotional loan programs.

JEL Classification: C83, G21, G23, G28, G32, G38, H23, Q01, Q58

Keywords: Sustainable Finance, Sustainable Finance Instruments, Sustainable Finance Support, Bank Advisory, Corporate Customers, House Bank

---

[*] I would like to thank Rainer Klump and Tim Buchholz for intriguing discussions, valuable input and support. Furthermore, I thank DZ BANK Stiftung for providing the funds to implement the research project. The usual disclaimer applies.

3.1 Introduction

In December 2019, the European Commission presented the European Green Deal, an ambitious undertaking to make Europe the first climate-neutral continent by 2050 and thereby contribute to the global effort to limit global temperature rise to 2°C (European Commission, 2024a). In September 2020, the European Green Deal was extended to include a 2030 climate target plan with the plan to reduce the European Union's greenhouse gas emissions by 55 % until 2030 (European Commission, 2024b). Both targets are part of the European Climate Law, which entered into force on the 29th of July 2021 (European Commission, 2024c). In order to achieve these sustainability targets, the European Commission (2020) has introduced the sustainable finance action plan to foster investments into sustainable activities. The action plan includes several sustainability regulations meant to incentivize sustainability investments. The two main objectives are to establish a transparent and comparable sustainability reporting, as well as to integrate sustainability criteria into risk assessments (European Commission, 2020).

The currently implemented sustainable finance incentive mechanism, in terms of sustainability transparency and sustainability risk, differs in its effect on companies' motivation to invest into their sustainability transition. Regarding the integration of sustainability risk and potential financial consequences, the existence of a risk differential between green and non-green assets still needs to be proven (Network for Greening the Financial System (NGFS), 2020; NGFS, 2022; Neagu et al., 2024). Consequently, regulatory authorities are hesitant to introduce risk-weighted adjustment factors into pillar I of the Basel framework, such as a green supporting factor (Deutsche Bundesbank, 2023; European Banking Authority (EBA), 2023). In contrast, the increased transparency regarding companies' sustainability performance appears to already have the intended effect. Companies are motivated to invest into their sustainability transition and use sustainable finance instruments (SFIs) by their sustainability reputation and its effect on their financial performance (Bachelet et al., 2019; Tang & Zhang, 2020;

Friede et al., 2015), as well as a potential pricing advantage of SFIs compared to a conventional financing instrument (Berrada et al., 2022; Gianfrate & Peri, 2019; Hinsche, 2021; Kapraun et al., 2021).

Generally, academic and market research suggest that companies are currently primarily incentivized to use SFIs due to a potential pricing advantage, the anticipation of a potential risk differential and the reputational effect of their sustainability transparency (Bachelet et al., 2019; Gerstenberger, 2024; Gianfrate & Peri, 2019; Kapraun et al., 2021). However, companies which are not active in capital markets and thus rely solely on bank-based financing are not exposed to the same sustainability regulations and market environment, which could alter how they are affected by the current sustainable finance incentive mechanism. The same holds for small and medium-sized companies (SMEs). This is crucial, as in the European Union (EU), and particularly Germany, banks-based financing is still prevalent and banks are often the main external provider of financing to companies (Franke & Krahnen, 2017; Schmidt & Tyrell, 2004). Furthermore, SMEs make up 99 % of Germany's companies (Bundesverband mittelständische Wirtschaft (BVMW), 2023). Consequently, in order to achieve the EU's sustainability targets, companies not active in capital markets, including SMEs, need to invest in their sustainability transition.

In fact, the corporate sector has to invest €120 billion annually to achieve the goal of climate neutrality, of which around half, approximately €60 billion annually, have to be borne by SMEs (Gerstenberger et al., 2023). However, current investment efforts indicate a gap of €32 billion in sustainability investments for SMEs alone (Gerstenberger et al., 2023). Moreover, a study by Hinsche (2024) demonstrates that SFI use among companies which are not active in capital markets is statistically significantly lower (7 %) than for companies active in capital markets (26 %). These observations suggest that the currently implemented sustainable finance incentive structure might not work effectively for companies relying on bank-based financing instead of capital markets.

Consequently, the question arises *whether and how the currently implemented sustainable finance incentive mechanism might need to be adapted to companies not active in capital markets, and particularly SMEs.* This paper analyzes whether companies active and not active in capital markets differ significantly in their sustainable finance interests and characteristics, and how the sustainable finance incentive mechanism might need to be adapted accordingly to companies not active in capital markets, to ensure sufficient sustainability transition investments. Furthermore, close and long-term relations between companies and their banks, so-called house bank relations, are a common characteristic in Germany's bank-based financial system (Hackethal, 2004) and could influence the SFI behavior of companies not active in capital markets. Thus, this paper additionally evaluates how the characteristics of house bank relations might be utilized for an efficient SFI use as well. Finally, SMEs not active in capital markets might deviate in their interests and in regard to their established house bank relations, and are thus evaluated additionally.

In order to answer these research questions, this study uses a mixed method research approach and conducted a survey with 700 corporate customers of DZ BANK AG in June 2023. The online survey included questions regarding companies' sustainable finance interest, knowledge and use, as well as perceived barriers and expectations regarding their banks' sustainable finance support. Furthermore, using a mixed method approach, the survey contains both, quantitative and qualitative questions. The response rate was 17.6 % and yielded 93 fully completed surveys. Analyzing the survey data, the quantitative analysis is conducted using correlation and logistic regression analysis, whilst the qualitative analysis is done based on the seven steps thematic content analysis by Kuckartz (2014).

Firstly, the survey results show that companies active and not active in capital markets differ in regard to their motivation to use SFIs. Companies not active in capital markets perceive lower regulatory pressure and slightly lower transition risk. Furthermore, both, companies active and not active in capital markets, believe it to be likely that credit conditions will be linked to sustainability criteria, whilst they are more hesitant to believe that they could lose financing access should they fail to achieve certain sustainability targets. Moreover, companies not active in capital markets are less likely to benefit from any reputational advantages from SFI use, compared to capital market active companies. Instead, the results indicate that companies not active in capital markets can be predominantly incentivized to use SFIs by a potential pricing advantage. In regard to SMEs not active in capital markets, there is no significant difference in observations, apart from a lower perceived regulatory and transition risk.

In regard to SFI implementation, the analysis demonstrates that companies not active in capital markets have a lower sustainability awareness and sustainable finance knowledge. In fact, only 16 % of companies not active in capital markets have an ESG rating and 17 % were unfamiliar with SFIs before the survey. This is further reflected in their reported perceived barriers to SFI use, which state that particularly data collection and reporting pose a challenge for companies not active in capital markets, as well as insufficient consulting and a lack of experience. Regarding the SME share of companies not active in capital markets, the low sustainability awareness is even more pronounced. None of the companies have an ESG rating and only 50 % have a carbon footprint. Nevertheless, the share of companies that perceive barriers is similar to all companies not active in capital markets.

Taking a closer look at the (house) bank relation of companies not active in capital markets, this paper shows that 47 % believe that their banks can support them in their sustainability transition, whilst 36 % are uncertain about their banks' role. Furthermore, the share of companies that have been recommended SFI use is statistically significantly lower for companies not active in capital markets (28 %) compared to capital market active companies (53 %). When asked to rate their banks' sustainable finance support, the highest share of companies not active in capital markets rates it only as average (48 %). These observations are also reflected in companies' expectations regarding their banks' support. Companies not active in capital markets would like a clear commitment from their banks and for them to be their sparring partner to acquire financing for their sustainability transition. More precisely, they would like to receive guidance regarding KPI choice and reporting, as well as information on SFI use and concrete financing offers. In regard to SMEs not active in capital markets, the bank support evaluation indicates that none have been recommended SFI use and a lower share of only 33 % that believe in their banks' support.

Finally, the survey also assessed companies' interest, knowledge and use of promotional loans as an alternative sustainable finance instruments to green and sustainability-linked loans. The results show that whilst 57 % of companies not active in capital markets know promotional loans connected to sustainable finance, only 14 % have used one. Nevertheless, the share of promotional loan users is statistically significantly higher for companies not active in capital markets, suggesting that promotional loans could be an effective instrument to support particularly companies not active in capital markets in financing their sustainability transition. Regarding SMEs not active in capital markets, the analysis demonstrates a lower promotional loan knowledge and that none have used a promotional loan connected to sustainable transition investments so far.

Based on the research findings, this paper concludes that the currently implemented sustainable finance incentive structure needs to be adapted to the characteristics of companies not active in capital markets. Furthermore, SFIs need to offer a clear pricing advantage to foster sustainability investments among companies not active in capital markets. A potentially effective, at least temporary, option are promotional loans connected to sustainable finance, as they have a lower sustainability data barrier, compared to green or sustainability-linked loans, whilst offering a clear pricing or risk advantage compared to conventional financing instruments. However, from a social market economy perspective, the preferred option would be to improve the applicability and implementation of SFIs, as well as to establish a link between companies' sustainability and risk performance, thereby returning to market-based structures, rather than relying on public funds. This would be in line with the overarching aim of sustainable finance to mobilize private sector sustainability investments in addition to public sector sustainability investments.

The paper contributes to the existing literature by using a mixed methods research approach to analyze the differences between companies active and not active in capital markets with respect to their sustainable finance interests and characteristics. It demonstrates that the current sustainable finance incentive mechanism needs to be adapted to companies not active in capital markets and particularly SMEs not active in capital markets, in order to ensure sufficient investments into their sustainability transition to successfully reach the set sustainability targets.

This paper is structured as follows: section 2 explains the desired and current sustainable finance incentive mechanism, incorporating sustainability regulations and research on the existence of a risk differential. Section 3 gives an overview of the German financial system, namely the characteristics of a bank-based financial system and house bank relations. Section 4 begins by developing the research question based on the theoretical background of Section 2 and 3, and subsequently outlines the existing literature on sustainable finance in house bank relations and details this study's methodology and data sample. Section 5 presents the results regarding any differences in motivational, implementation and enabling factors between companies active and not active in capital markets. Moreover, promotional loan use, interest and knowledge among companies active and not active in capital markets is analyzed, and all results are additionally evaluated with respect to SMEs not active in capital markets. Section 6 discusses the findings in terms of existing differences between companies active and not active in capital markets, an effective sustainable finance mechanism, and the role of banks, and particularly regional banks, in relation to SMEs' sustainability transition. Finally, section 7 summarizes the papers' results and formulates a recommendation regarding how companies not active in capital markets, and particularly SMEs, can be effectively incentivized to invest into their sustainability transition.

3.2 The Sustainable Finance Mechanism

In order to analyze the sustainable finance mechanism in house bank relations, it is helpful to first understand and assess how the sustainable finance mechanism works in capital markets. The following section explains the existing sustainability regulations, their intended effect, as well as how the mechanism is currently incentivizing companies active in capital markets to invest into their sustainability transition.

3.2.1 Desired Sustainable Finance Mechanism

In order to finance the sustainability transition, the European Commission has introduced the sustainable finance action plan, which aims to foster sustainable finance growth (European Commission, 2020). The action plan encompasses several sustainability regulations to redirect capital flows towards sustainable economic activities. The two overarching goals of sustainable finance regulations can be summarized as establishing transparency and comparability in regard to companies' sustainability performance and integrating sustainability criteria into risk assessments of financial institutions. Thereby, they are the main drivers meant to incentivize sustainable investments and are further discussed in the following sections.

By making companies' sustainability performance transparent and comparable, whilst simultaneously requesting financial institutions to incorporate sustainability criteria into their risk assessments, sustainability becomes an influential factor in investment and credit decisions of investors. Consequently, companies are incentivized to invest in their sustainability transition and thereby improve their sustainability performance. This is supported by the use of sustainable finance instruments, such as green or sustainability-linked bonds, which offer companies the possibility to invest in their sustainability transformation whilst obligating them to credibly and transparently communicate their progress to their investors.

3.2.1.1 Transparency & Comparability

In order to establish transparency and comparability in regard to companies' sustainability performance, the European Union has introduced several sustainability disclosure regulations, as well as a unified classification system for sustainable activities. First, in order to establish a common definition of sustainable economic activities for companies and financial institutions, the EU has developed the EU Taxonomy, which entered into force on July 12th 2020 (European Commission, 2024d). Moreover, since January 5th 2023, the EU requires all large and listed companies to report on their sustainability performance according to the Corporate Social Responsibility Directive (CSRD) (European Commission, 2024e). The first CSRD reports will be due 2025 for the financial year 2024 and over time will be rolled out to apply to smaller companies as well[20]. Finally, the EU also introduced the Sustainable Finance Disclosure Regulation (SFDR), which applies to financial market participants and advisers (European Commission, 2024f). The SFDR requires financial institutions to report on their sustainability performance on both, the entity and financial product level (European Commission, 2024f). This establishes a unified sustainable classification system of investment products and thereby advances the integration of sustainability criteria into investment decisions.

20 For the financial year 2024, the CSRD applies to all large public-interest companies that already had to adhere to the non-financial reporting directive, and for the financial year 2025 to all large companies that fulfil two of the following three criteria: they have a net turnover of more than €50 million, total assets of more than €25 million or more than 250 employees. Finally, for the financial year 2026, the CSRD applies to all listed SMEs (European Parliament, 2022).

3.2.1.2 Sustainability Criteria in Risk Assessments

As a second driver to incentivize sustainable investments, the European Banking Authority (EBA), the European Central Bank (ECB) and the Federal Financial Supervisory Authority (BaFin) have introduced several recommendations and regulatory adjustments requesting financial institutions to incorporate sustainability criteria into their risk assessments.

In 2019, the ECB published guidelines and recommendations on the definition and integration of climate-related and environmental risk. The guide states that the ECB expects banks to incorporate climate-related and environmental risk into their risk management, including credit, operational, market and liquidity risk, as well as scenario analysis and stress testing (ECB, 2020). Subsequently, the ECB conducted a climate-risk stress test in 2022, in order to assess banks' progress regarding the integration of climate-related risks according to the guide (ECB, 2022a). The stress test did not have any effect on banks' Basel framework pillar II guidance, which serves as an indicator for banks' level of capital that needs to be maintained as a stress buffer, additionally to their binding capital requirements (ECB, 2022a). However, following the stress test results, the ECB (2022b) announced that it requires banks to reach full alignment with all expectations set in the ECB's guide on climate-related and environmental risk by the end of 2024.

For banks that are supervised on a national level, so-called less significant institutions (LSIs), the BaFin published a guide on how to deal with sustainability risks for German banks (BaFin, 2020). The guide only entailed non-binding recommendations on, for example, the integration of sustainability risks into risk management practices. However, these recommendations became legally binding in the newest publication of the minimum requirements for risk management (MaRisk). The publication states that banks are to incorporate ESG risks with "due and explicit account" into their risk management practices, including for instance the loan granting process and annual credit risk classification (BaFin, 2023, p. 10).

The regulatory adjustments by the ECB and BaFin primarily target pillar II of the Basel framework, which focuses on qualitative banking supervision and banks' risk management (Deutsche Bundesbank, 2023). Pillar III, which encompasses supervisory disclosure requirements is targeted by EBA's binding technical standards on ESG risk disclosure. The standards include comparable key performance indicators such as the green asset ratio (GAR)[21] and the banking book taxonomy alignment ratio (BTAR), which aim to establish transparency regarding bank portfolios' sustainability (EBA, 2022).

However, the integration of sustainability risks into pillar I, which calculates banks' capital requirements based on banks' respective credit, operational and market risks, is still being discussed (Deutsche Bundesbank, 2023). A potential adjustment could be the introduction of a green or brown supporting factor, which would decrease capital requirements for green assets or increase capital requirements for environmentally harmful assets respectively[22]. In its newest publication, EBA (2023) states that they recommend to enhance the existing risk categories of pillar I by incorporating environmental and social risks. But, at this point in time, the EBA (2023) does not support the introduction of a green supporting or brown penalizing factor.

3.2.2 Current Sustainable Finance Mechanism

Transparency and reporting regulations are coming into action, as large and listed companies will need to report on their sustainability

21 The GAR measures lenders' asset share invested in sustainable activities. However, only CSRD-level sustainability reporting measures are used to calculate the GAR. Therefore, SMEs that do not report their sustainability performance according to CSRD guidelines yet, cannot be included in the ratio. Instead, the BTAR can be used, which includes SMEs sustainability data based on bilateral data exchange (Deutsche Bank, 2022).

22 In the case of a green supporting factor, prudential capital requirements could be decreased through lower risk weights or the application of an adjustment factor smaller than one to risk-weighted assets (EBA, 2023). For a brown supporting factor, higher risk weights would be used or an adjustment factor larger than one would be applied to risk-weighted assets.

performance in line with the CSRD for the first time in 2025 for the financial year 2024 (European Commission, 2024e) and since January 2023 large financial market participants already have to comply with the SFDR (European Commission, 2024f). Beyond increasing sustainability performance transparency, the integration of sustainability criteria into risk assessment methods is progressing as well. Nevertheless, the existence and mechanism of a link between sustainability and financial risks are still being investigated and discussed. The existence of a risk differential between green and non-green assets and activities, however, is a necessity to warrant further regulatory adjustments, such as a closer risk monitoring and subsequently higher regulatory capital requirements (NGFS, 2020). The following section presents the current research on a potential risk differential, as well as the respective regulatory perspective.

3.2.2.1 Existence of a Risk Differential

A risk differential between green and non-green assets could exist due to non-green assets' higher exposure to transition risk. However, in a survey conducted with 49 banks worldwide, the Network for Greening the Financial System (NGFS, 2020) finds that the majority of financial institutions do not have sufficient evidence to prove the existence of a risk differential between green, non-green and brown assets. Also, the research findings of credit rating agencies fail to establish a clear link between a company's final credit rating and the ESG credit factors that could affect a company's creditworthiness (NGFS, 2022). Moreover, banks' motivation to green their balance sheet appears to be currently guided by the desire to mitigate reputational, business model or legal risks, rather than based on a distinct relation between their portfolios' greenness and credit risk (NGFS, 2020).

Nevertheless, several academic studies analyzing a potential link between sustainability and financial risks find some supporting evidence. Analyzing the relation between firms' climate metrics, such as carbon emissions, and credit risk measures, Carbone et al. (2021) find that higher emissions are associated with higher credit risk. Furthermore, disclosing emissions and setting emission targets can be observed in line with a lower credit risk. This is supported by Saffiulah et al. (2021), who also detect a negative impact of firms' carbon emissions on their respective credit ratings. Further studies also suggest a relation between a company's emissions and distance-to-default (Kabir et al., 2021; Capasso et al., 2020). However, a most recent study by Neagu et al. (2024) fails to detect the existence of a clear risk differential, as no significant credit risk reduction for green loans compared to conventional loans is found. Generally, research on the existence of a risk differential is still inconclusive and regulatory authorities so far take the lack of evidence regarding a risk differential between green and non-green assets and activities as a baseline for their decision-making (Rismanchi et al., 2022).

3.2.2.2 Sustainability Risk Regulations

In line with the uncertainty regarding the existence of a relation between sustainability and financial risks, authorities are so far cautious to introduce financial consequences, such as a green supporting factor, linked to financial institutions' sustainability risk performance indicators, such as the GAR for banks. Based on academic literature and a public consultation conducted in 2022, the European Banking Authority (EBA, 2023), decided that the current empirical evidence on the existence of risk differentials is not sufficient to warrant the introduction of specific risk-weighted adjustment factors into pillar I of the Basel framework, as explained in section 2.1.2. Instead, environmental and social risks should be integrated into the existing internal market and credit risk models of pillar I, in line with the sustainability risk integration into risk management and supervision method of pillar II and market transparency measures under pillar III (EBA, 2023).

Some of the biggest challenges in regard to analyzing and detecting a potential risk differential are the lack of harmonized data, both in terms of quantity and quality, a lack of internal resources, as well as classification difficulties, such as the classification at activity or asset level rather than company level and the heterogenous methods of financial institutions (NGFS, 2020; NGFS, 2022; EBA, 2023; Walther, 2023; Deutsche Bundesbank, 2023). Consequently, the current priority for financial institutions is the identification of a potential link between sustainability and financial risks, understanding whether markets already price environmental risks, and further promoting the integration of sustainability measures into their own risk assessments (EBA, 2023). Nevertheless, the European Banking Authority leaves the door open for potential pillar I adjustments, should a clear link between sustainability and financial risk be established (EBA, 2023).

3.2.2.3 Reputation and Pricing as Additional Motivational Factors

As explained above, the existence of a risk differential between green and non-green assets is still to be proven and regulatory authorities are thus cautious to introduce measures that would introduce direct financial consequences linked to sustainability performance. However, even though the market is still uncertain regarding the link between sustainability and financial risk, companies and financial institutions are already using sustainable finance instruments. This might be due to the anticipation and thus preparation for a proven risk differential and subsequently regulatory adjustments.

Nevertheless, research is pointing towards additional motivational factors, namely public pressure for companies and financial institutions to become more sustainable, as well as the potential existence of a pricing advantage of sustainable instruments compared to conventional financing instruments. In recent years, climate change awareness has increased and companies, as well as financial institutions, have been moved into the limelight regarding their sustainability performance. A company's sustainability performance is becoming transparent due to increased sustainability disclosure regulations and can have an effect on its financial performance (Friede et al., 2015), for instance stock price and stock liquidity (Tang and Zhang, 2020), as well as on employer attractiveness (Bachelet et al., 2019).

Furthermore, the effect of a company's sustainability reputation can be both, positive or negative. Greenwashing controversies are the most prominent example how a company's negative sustainability image can also impact its general public image. However, in regard to sustainable finance, companies have also discovered the potential effects of a positive sustainability reputation, using sustainable finance instruments to communicate their transition willingness and strategy (Bachelet et al., 2019). Moreover, research shows that sustainable finance instruments can, in some instances, have a greenium, a green premium, which means that the yield is slightly lower compared to a conventional finance instrument with the same characteristics (Gianfrate & Peri, 2019; Hinsche, 2021; Kapraun et al., 2021).

Overall, academic and market research suggest that companies active in capital markets are currently primarily incentivized to use sustainable finance instruments due to the anticipation of a potential risk differential, a potential pricing advantage and the reputational effect of their sustainability transparency. These drivers in turn are fueled by the implementation of sustainability disclosure and risk assessment regulations. But how does the incentivization scheme work for companies that are not active in capital markets, relying solely on (house) bank financing, and are thus for instance not (yet) exposed to sustainability disclosure regulations already mandatory for capital market participants?

3.3 German Financial System

Before analyzing the above explained sustainable finance mechanism in house bank relations, the following section gives an overview of the main characteristics regarding a bank-based financial system and a traditional house bank relation. Furthermore, this section describes how small and medium-sized companies' financing needs and relations might differ compared to large companies.

3.3.1 Germany's Bank-Based Financial System

Generally, financial systems can be classified as market or bank-based. Germany, as well as other European countries, are known for their bank-based financial systems, whilst the United States is known for its market-based financial system (Allen & Gale, 2000; Franke & Krahnen, 2017). In a bank-based financial system, banks tend to have a more important role in regard to financing and saving than the organized capital markets and other financial intermediaries (Allen & Gale, 2000; Behr & Schmidt, 2016). In fact, banks are often the main external providers of financing to companies (Schmidt & Tyrell, 2004).

The German financial system, which will be the focus of the analysis of this paper, is classified by a three pillar system including private commercial banks, savings banks and cooperative banks (Behr & Schmidt, 2016)[23]. The first pillar consists of three big banks, Deutsche Bank, Commerzbank and UniCredit, as well as 237 smaller or foreign private credit institutions (Deutsche Bundesbank, 2024). The second pillar consists of 354 legally independent, municipality sponsored small and medium-sized savings banks and 6 Landesbanken (Behr & Schmidt, 2016; Deutsche Bundesbank, 2024). Finally, the third pillar comprises 694 local small and medium-sized cooperative banks and the central financial institution DZ BANK AG (Behr & Schmidt, 2016; Deutsche Bundesbank, 2024).

Both, savings and cooperative banks are not strictly profit-maximizing entities (Allen & Gale, 2000; Schmidt & Tyrell, 2004). Savings banks are institutions under public law, which means that they have a strong tie to public bodies such as municipalities and districts, whilst still being legally and economically independent (Deutscher Sparkassen- und Giroverband (DSGV), 2017). Furthermore, they follow a public mandate with the main purpose to serve the common good by providing financial access to all private customers and supporting the development of local businesses (DSGV, 2017). Cooperative

23 Other banks, such as promotional banks are considered in a fourth pillar (Behr & Schmidt, 2016).

banks are member-owned and their main purpose is to support the business of their members (Schmidt & Tyrell, 2004).

Furthermore, savings and cooperative banks adhere to the regional principle[24], which means that banks can only operate in their designated region (Schmidt & Tyrell, 2004; Behr & Schmidt, 2016). This in turn leads to low competition within their respective pillars, but to a high competition between the cooperative and savings bank pillars (Schmidt & Tyrell, 2004; Fischer & Pfeil, 2004). Overall, savings (23 %) and cooperative (17 %) banks make up 40 % in terms of total assets of German banks[25], whilst 46 % are private and exclusively profit-oriented (Deutsche Bundesbank 2024; DZ BANK, 2023).

3.3.2 The House Bank Model

A close and long-term relation between companies and their banks is called relationship banking or house bank model (Hackethal, 2004; Behr & Schmidt, 2016). A house bank model can be characterized by a long-term relationship between the respective company and bank. In Germany, such a relation exists on average for 29 years for companies' most important bank and 23 years for the second most important bank (Hainz & Wiegand, 2013). The relation takes time to grow (Hackethal & Schmidt, 2000) and thereby leads to a strong trust between companies and their house banks (Fuest et al., 2020). Furthermore, the house bank relation is known for its high exclusivity (Elsas, 2005), as companies, depending on size, often only have one or two house banks. This bank is not necessarily the only bank, but the main bank, with the closest relation and which provides all core services in terms of payment services, lines of credit and financing (Hainz & Wiegand, 2013; Elsas & Krahnen, 2004). Additional characteristics of a house

---

24 In the following analysis, the term regional bank refers to banks that adhere to the regional principle, which are predominantly savings and cooperative banks, but can also be private banks (Deutsche Bundesbank, 2024).

25 The remaining 14 % consist of mortgage banks, building and loan associations and banks with special, development or other central support tasks (Deutsche Bundesbank, 2024).

bank relation include the repetitive use of financial services, such as credit financing, personal support and an often small distance between the house bank and the companies' headquarters (Hainz & Wiegand, 2013; Handke, 2011).

As a further advantage, a house bank relation can overcome information asymmetry between companies and their banks. In a bank-based financial system, information is predominantly private, but banks require a high level of information, including proprietary data, to assess companies' creditworthiness and provide financing (Schwartz & Gerstenberger, 2019; Schmidt & Tyrell, 2004). This is particularly crucial in bank-based financial systems, as an individual bank's view on a company's creditworthiness determines the lending decision (Hardie & Howarth, 2013). In fact, banks often have difficulty assessing companies' creditworthiness, due to missing credit history, or are faced with high costs to acquire the necessary information (Schwartz & Gerstenberger, 2019). This is termed information asymmetry and in turn can lead to interest rate risk premiums, higher security and documentation requirements, as well as generally more expensive or scarer credit offers (Schwartz & Gerstenberger, 2019).

The information asymmetry between companies and their lenders can be overcome through house bank relations, as the long-term duration and exclusivity of the relation incentivize the bank to obtain the required and costly information to assess the company's creditworthiness (Handke, 2011). This in turn can improve a firm's access to credit, as well as their financing conditions (Schwartz & Gerstenberger, 2019; Hainz & Wiegand, 2013). Nevertheless, the presence of information asymmetry and subsequently high cost intensity to acquire the necessary credit information can also lead to a house bank developing an information monopoly (Sharpe, 1990). Having several bank relations can strengthen companies' bargaining power against each individual bank, which increases competition (Hainz & Wiegand, 2013). Therefore, having only one house bank can negatively affect companies' credit conditions. This can be particularly relevant for smaller and medium-sized firms, which tend to have a smaller financing demand

and thus often have only one house bank, as discussed in the next section.

3.3.3 SMEs and the House Bank Model

Traditionally, big banks, as part of pillar one's private banks, used to be house banks of large firms, being their main provider of financial services, such as credit lending and investment banking, as well as playing an important role in the governance of the respective firm (Behr & Schmidt, 2016). However, this traditional house banking role was discontinued by big banks around 2000 and they focused on the international markets of investment banking instead (Behr & Schmidt, 2016; Schmidt, 2019).

In contrast, savings and cooperative banks have always been and still are focused on lending to SMEs (Behr & Schmidt, 2016). In fact, SMEs often have one or two house banks that implement all their financing (Behr & Schmidt, 2016). A study by Schwartz and Gerstenberger (2019) analyzing house bank relations in 2018 shows that 93 % of SMEs in Germany have a primary credit institution in the form of a house bank. These are primarily savings or cooperative banks, as they are market leaders in lending to SMEs (Behr & Schmidt, 2016). As universal banks, they offer a wide range of banking services (Schmidt & Tyrell, 2004), which allows companies to obtain all their banking services from one institution (Behr & Schmidt, 2016). The duration of the house bank relation is on average 20 years and 80 % of an SME's credit financing is done through their house bank (Schwartz & Gerstenberger, 2019). In fact, more than 50 % of all SMEs only obtain credits through their house bank (Schwartz & Gerstenberger, 2019). In terms of financial instruments, SMEs predominantly finance their investments through own funds (32 %), bank loans (51 %) and promotional loans (14 %) (Kreditanstalt für Wiederaufbau (KFW), 2023).

3.4 Sustainable Finance Mechanism in House Bank Relations

3.4.1 Research Questions

As explained in section 3, bank-based financing is still the prevalent form of financing in a bank-based financial system and therefore an important channel to foster sustainable investments through sustainable finance. A study by Hinsche (2024), analyzing companies' individual sustainable finance needs, finds that the majority (63 %) of companies are not active in capital markets, in line with Germany's bank-based financial system. Moreover, the high share of companies not active in capital markets holds true for all company size groups (medium-sized, large medium-sized and large companies), apart from multinational companies[26]. This emphasized the importance of considering the characteristics of bank-based financing and house bank relations for an effective SFI use.

However, the study by Hinsche (2024) demonstrates that SFI use among companies who are not active in capital markets, and thus only obtain bank-based financing, is very low. In fact, SFI use is more than twice as high for companies that are active in capital markets (26 %), compared to companies that are not active in capital markets (7 %). Furthermore, not being active in capital markets decreases the odds of being a SFI user and the negative association is statistically significant at the 5 % level (Hinsche, 2024). The relation holds true, even when grouping the results based on company size as seen in Figure 1, supporting the observation that SFI use significantly differs for companies' capital market activity. The share of SFI users who are not active in capital markets is especially low for smaller companies, with medium-size companies having no SFI users and with large medium-sized companies having only 3 % that are SFI users and not active in capital markets.

26 Medium-sized companies have a revenue of €10 to €49 million, large medium-sized from €50 to €499 million, large companies from €500 million to €5 billion and multinational companies larger than €5 billion (Hinsche, 2024).

Figure 1. Companies' SFI Use by Capital Market Activity and Company Size

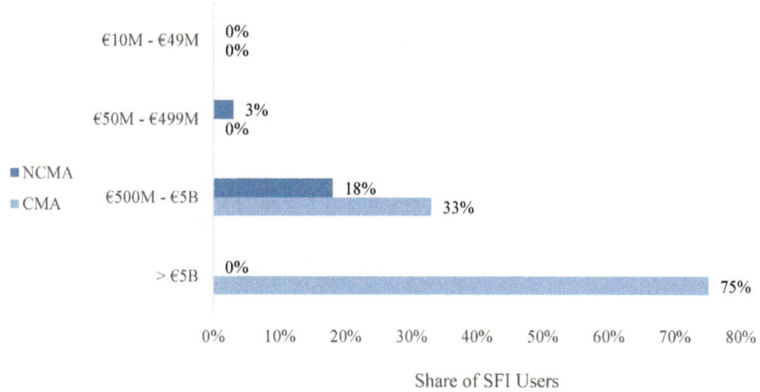

Source: This figure presents companies' SFI use by capital market activity and grouped by the four defined company size groups medium-size, large medium-size, large and multinationals as depicted in Hinsche (2024). Note: "NCMA" denotes not capital market active and "CMA" denotes capital market active. "M" denotes million and "B" denotes billion.

The lack of SFI use amongst companies not active in capital markets could indicate that the currently implemented sustainable finance incentive structure, as explained in section 2, does not work effectively for companies financing themselves through their (house) banks instead of capital markets. This leads to the research question, whether the currently implemented sustainable finance incentive structure is tailored to capital market structures and thus cannot simply be applied to house bank relations. Instead, the incentive structure might need to be adapted to and utilize the characteristics of house bank relations. Moreover, this might be particularly true for small and medium-sized companies, as they rely more heavily on bank financing, have smaller financing demands and simultaneously face relatively higher administrative costs to implement a SFI.

3.4.2 Existing Literature

The literature on sustainable finance use in house bank relations is still developing as the topic gains more attention with discussions on sustainable finance regulations being extended to SMEs and the implementation of sustainability regulations through regional banks.

In a conceptual research paper discussing the integration of climate financing into SME lending in Germany, Flögel et al. (2023) emphasize the importance of house bank financing for a successful sustainability transformation, as regional banks are responsible for 54.2 % of total lending volume to non-financial firms and self-employed. Moreover, they also point out the challenges that regional banks face in adopting sustainable finance measures, such as the integration of climate impact assessments into lending processes. Firstly, regional banks have a lower capacity and resources than larger banks. Secondly, the borrowers, which are mainly SMEs, often have no knowledge or disclosure of their sustainability performance. Thirdly, most regional banks are savings or cooperative banks, which are obliged to fulfil additional social requirements apart from profit maximization, as explained in section 3.3. Therefore, a restriction to or exclusion of certain industries would violate their mandate to provide local credit and meet the financial needs of their members (Fölgel et al., 2023). Finally, long-term house bank relations have the potential to undermine the impact of a sustainability assessment in the lending process, as house banks might be too lenient with their clients.

In contrast, Greitens (2023) focuses on the applicability of the sustainable finance framework and stresses that regulations need to take bank-based financing characteristics into account, allowing for individual transition financing options. Furthermore, regional banks often have an information advantage, due to their close relation with their clients, which gives them access to private information. This can be used as an advantage in regard to sustainability information availability and assessment. Greitens's (2023) conceptual paper advocates for a more flexible sustainability and green loan concept for SMEs compared to the capital market-oriented framework. Moreover, banks should clearly specify the information needed from their clients to be able to assess their sustainability risk.

In order to understand whether and how sustainability criteria are currently being integrated into banks' credit assessments and management, Strube et al. (2023a; 2023b) conduct a survey with 28 savings banks and 84 cooperative banks. They find that 35.5 % of banks are not performing any sustainability risk or ESG screening of their portfolios at the time of the survey. Reasons include insufficient data availability, no consistent methods, a lack of personal and technical capacities, as well as the extent of regulatory requirements (Strube et al., 2023a). Furthermore, only 18.8 % of banks require sustainability data from their lenders. The most common sustainability data provided are energy certificates, real estate related information and qualitative ESG criteria (Strube et al., 2023a). In regard to sustainability risk, the majority of surveyed savings and cooperative banks (74.3 %) stated that reputational risk is relevant or very relevant for them (Strube et al., 2023b). Moreover, 55 % think that the effect of sustainability risk on credit risk is also relevant or very relevant, but think that it has only a very limited effect on banks' financials and revenue. Additionally, the study by Strube et al. (2023b) finds that the majority of regional banks (81.7 %) currently do not offer any sustainability-linked loans.

Taking a closer look at the impact of sustainability regulations on SMEs' sustainability data collection and sustainable investments in Germany, Löher et al. (2022) conducted a quantitative survey with 199 companies that are members of the chamber of commerce and industry Siegen (IHK Siegen). Their research confirms that, even though SMEs might not be directly affected by sustainability disclosure regulations, they are affected indirectly through the supply chain. Customers and suppliers demand sustainability data most often and companies expect their requests to increase even more in the future.[27] However, only

27 The European Financial Reporting Advisory Group (EFRAG, 2024) is currently developing voluntary European Sustainability Reporting Standards for non-listed SMEs (VSME ESRS), which aim to establish a market standard that avoids individual sustainability data inquiries and satisfies demands from lenders and companies

2.8 % of companies state that they have received a sustainability data inquiry from their bank so far (Löher et al., 2022). In regard to sustainability investments, Löher et al. (2022) find that SMEs plan to finance their sustainability investments mainly through own funds, followed by bank and promotional loans.

Finally, Scharf (2022) analyzed SMEs' willingness to integrate sustainable finance measures into their established financing structures. Interviewing 100 German SMEs based on a survey with closed questions and running a linear regression analysis, Scharf (2022) finds a significant positive correlation between the willingness to integrate sustainable finance into their established financing structure and personnel resources, but no significant correlation for knowledge, profitability, administrative work or company size. The willingness to integrate sustainable finance into established financing structure was calculated using five different survey questions with a Likert scale, measuring companies' attitudes towards and interest in sustainable finance.

Overall, current studies have opened up the discussion regarding sustainable finance in house bank relations. However, apart from Strube et al. (2023a; 2023b); Löher et al. (2022) and Scharf (2022), the papers have not conducted any research to acquire or analyze existing data to gain a deeper insight into SFI use in bank-based financing. Furthermore, Strube et al. (2023a; 2023b) focus on the bank perspective, particularly on the integration of sustainability criteria into credit risk assessment methods. In contrast, Scharf (2022) concentrates on SMEs' perspectives regarding sustainable finance integration and use. However, the calculated measure of willingness to integrate sustainable finance in established financing structures does not reflect companies' actual sustainable finance behavior and the research did not examine the difference between capital-market and bank-based financing for SMEs and larger companies. Finally, Löher et al. (2022) focus on the impact of sustainability disclosure regulations primarily on SMEs' sustainability data collection and the planned form of sustainable invest-

---

along the supply chain, thereby simplifying and standardizing the sustainability data exchange for SMEs.

ments, but do not discuss the actual use and implementation of SFIs, as well as potential barriers.

Consequently, this research contributes to the existing literature by acquiring data on the current state of SFI use among companies that rely on bank-based financing, and by subsequently analyzing and interpreting the data using a mixed method approach. This will allow for a more precise understanding of how companies not active in capital markets can be motivated and supported to use SFIs, as well as how the sustainable finance incentive structure might need to be adapted accordingly. Furthermore, based on the results, the study will formulate recommendations on how to ensure an effective use of sustainable finance in a bank-based financial system and identify points for further research.

3.4.3 Methodology

This research aims to fill the aforementioned research gap using a mixed method approach, thus applying both, quantitative and qualitative methods. The study follows a convergent parallel design (Creswell & Creswell, 2018; Kuckartz, 2014), including quantitative and qualitative methods in the survey and subsequent analysis simultaneously. The research data is collected using a survey which is predominantly quantitative, but also includes some qualitative parts in the form of open questions. This qualifies as a concurrent embedded strategy (Creswell & Creswell, 2018) and allows for a more in-depth understanding of the quantitative analysis results through additional qualitative coverage and evaluation (Greene et al., 1989; Morgan, 2014).

The quantitative analysis entails a correlation analysis to test for an existing association between variables using Fisher's exact measure and for the strength of the association using Cramér's V. However, the correlation analysis does not indicate the direction of association. Consequently, a logistic regression with robust standard errors is run as well, to gain an insight based on the resulting odds ratios, whether an existing association is positive or negative. In regard to the qualitative analysis, a thematic content analysis is performed using the seven steps of Kuckartz (2014). This entails first coding all the existing material, which in the case at hand is also translated from German into English and subsequently developing main thematic categories. Once all the existing material is coded according to the main thematic categories, subcategories are defined inductively and the data material is coded again with the more advanced categorical system (Kuckartz, 2014). Finally, the qualitative results are integrated into the quantitative results using quantification (Fakis et al., 2014; Kuckartz, 2014) and thus interpreted together.

3.4.4 Data and Data Summary

In order to investigate the two research questions, this study uses the company and survey data provided through a survey study conducted by Hinsche (2024) in cooperation with DZ BANK AG. The online survey[28] was conducted in June 2023 with 700 invited corporate customers to record their individual sustainable finance interests and needs. An overview of the survey can be found in Chapter 2, Appendix C. The response rate was 17.6 %, with 123 recorded responses, and yielded 93 fully completed surveys.

Looking at the data summary in Table 1, the highest share of companies is from the industrials sector (31.2 %), followed by the utilities (9.7 %), consumer staples (9.7 %) and materials sector (9.7 %). Furthermore, more than half of the sample has a company size of €50 million to €499 million (50.5 %), followed by €500 million to €5 billion (24.7 %)[29].

---

28 For a more detailed description of the survey structure see Hinsche (2024).

29 In the following analysis, companies with a revenue lower than or equal to €49 million are denoted as small and medium-sized companies, based on DZ BANK AG's internal allocation.

Table 1. Summary Statistics – Company Characteristics

	Survey Sample Characteristics	
	Observations	**Percent of Data**
Number of Companies	93	100 %
Company Sector		
Industrials	29	31.2 %
Consumer Discretionary	9	9.7 %
Utilities	9	9.7 %
Consumer Staples	9	9.7 %
Materials	7	7.5 %
Financials	4	4.3 %
Health Care	4	4.3 %
Information Technology	2	2.2 %
Communication Services	1	1.1 %
Real Estate	1	1.1 %
No Answer	18	19.4 %
Company Size		
Up to €9 million	1	1.1 %
€10 mm to €49 million	9	9.7 %
€50 mm to €499 million	47	50.5 %
€500 mm to €5 billion	23	24.7 %
Bigger than €5 billion	10	10.8 %
No Answer	3	3.2 %
Company Capital Market Activity		
Yes	34	36.6 %
No	58	62.4 %
I don't know	1	1.1 %

Source: This table presents the company summary statistics of the 93 survey respondents. Companies' sectors are classified based on the Global Industry Classification Standard by MSCI and companies' sizes in terms of revenue are rounded to millions and divided into five respective revenue groups.

Finally, the majority of companies are not active in capital markets (62.4 %), whilst 35.5 % are active and 1.1 % answer that they do not know. Being active in capital markets is defined by the survey as acquiring any form of financing through the capital market. For the subsequent analysis, only respondents who answered company capital market activity with yes or no are included, thus reducing the data sample by one respondent to 92 companies. An overview of companies' sustainability characteristics and respondent information can be found in Appendix A, Table 2 and Table 3[30].

3.5 Results

In order to assess whether the currently implemented sustainable finance incentive structure works effectively for companies not active in capital markets, one first has to understand the potential differences in regard to SFI use between companies active and not active in capital markets. The following sections analyze any potential differences in the motivation to use SFIs, as well as whether companies can and will use SFIs. Moreover, the survey results are additionally evaluated with special regard to small and medium-sized companies not active in capital markets.

3.5.1 Motivation: Want to Use SFI

One potential difference in regard to SFI use between companies active and not active in capital markets could be their motivation to use SFIs. As discussed in section 2.2.1, regulatory authorities are still hesitant to introduce risk-weighted adjustment factors, such as a green supporting factor, as long as the existence of a risk differential between green and non-green assets is still debated. Nevertheless, companies might anticipate the existence of a risk differential and subsequent introduction of further regulatory adjustments, such as higher capital requirements, in the future. This in turn could incentivize them to already invest in

30 A more detailed data sample analysis, including company sustainability characteristics, as well as a representativeness analysis can be found in Hinsche (2024).

their sustainability transition through SFIs now. Moreover, companies could also be incentivized by regulatory pressure, pricing, and reputational advantages, as discussed in section 2.2.3. The following section analyzes the potential motivational influence of these factors, as well as the observed respective differences for companies active and not active in capital markets, based on the survey results.

3.5.1.1 Motivational Factors

Regulatory requirements such as the CSRD are mandatory for companies active in capital markets, whilst companies not active in capital markets have more time to adhere to sustainability disclosure regulations, depending on their company size (see section 2.1.1). Therefore, companies active in capital markets might experience a higher regulatory pressure. Moreover, companies might experience a higher transition risk not only influenced by their industry, for instance carbon-intensive industries such as oil and gas, but also due to their capital market activity. Companies active in capital markets are often faced with higher public awareness, due to the transparency and publicity that come with acquiring financing through the capital market. Consequently, they are more likely to experience a strong societal pressure to transition and invest in their sustainability and do not have the possibility to fly under the radar. The survey asked respondents to report on their perceived regulatory pressure and transition risk to evaluate both potential effects.

Looking at Figure 2, the survey results indeed indicate a slightly lower perceived regulatory pressure and transition risk for companies not active in capital markets compared to companies active in capital markets. The most prominent difference is that whilst 7 % of companies not active in capital markets perceive little regulatory pressure, none of the companies active in capital markets perceive such a low regulatory pressure. However, no statistically significant association between capital market activity (CMA) and levels of perceived regulatory pressure or levels of perceived transition risk can be found (see Appendix A, Table 4 and Table 8).

Figure 2. Regulatory Pressure and Transition Risk by Capital Market Activity

a. Regulatory Pressure

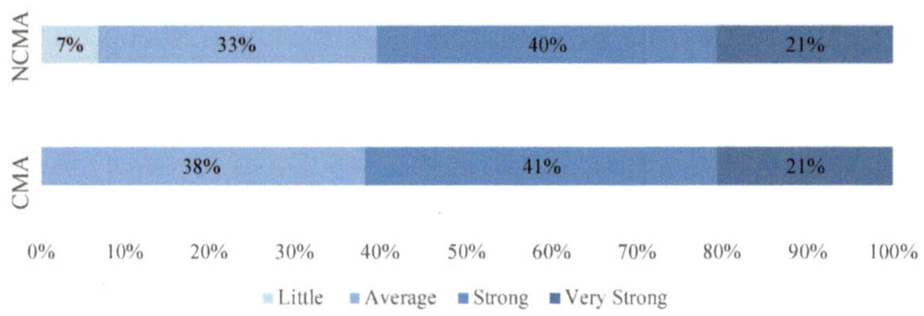

b. Transition Risk

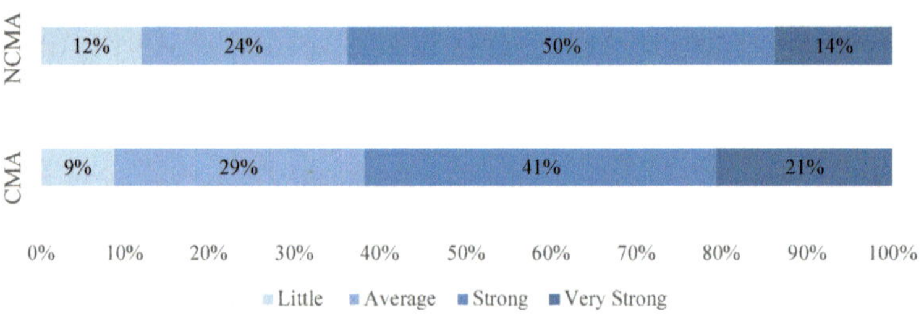

Source: This figure presents companies' perceived regulatory pressure and transition risk by capital market activity, based on the survey results reported in Appendix A, Table 7. Note: "NCMA" denotes not capital market active and "CMA" denotes capital market active.

Another potential difference in motivation between companies active and not active in capital markets could be due to varying levels of anticipation regarding the introduction of risk adjustment factors such as a brown penalizing factor and subsequent impacts on credit conditions and financing access. This was measured by inquiring companies to report on their credit link and financing access beliefs. The survey asked companies to assess the likelihood that sustainability criteria and credit conditions will be linked, as well as the risk to lose financing access in case they should fail to achieve certain sustainability targets. Looking at

Figure 3, no significant differences between companies active and not active in capital markets can be observed.

Figure 3. Credit Link and Financing Access Belief by Capital Market Activity

a. Credit Link

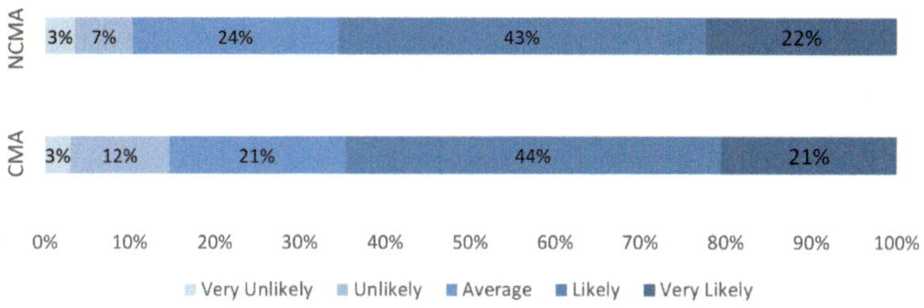

b. Financing Access

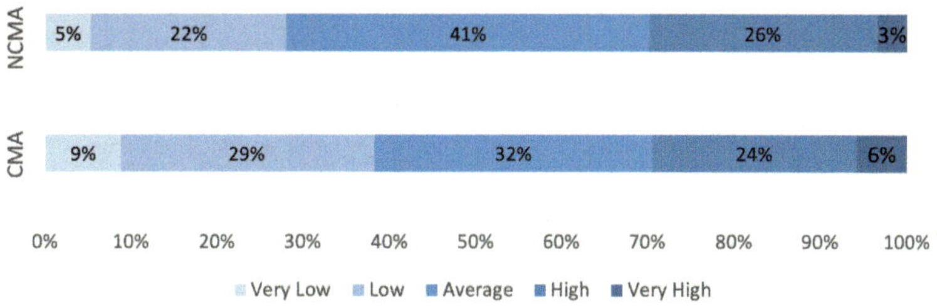

Source: This figure presents companies' credit link and financing access beliefs by capital market activity, based on the survey results reported in Appendix A, Table 7. Note: "NCMA" denotes not capital market active and "CMA" denotes capital market active.

This is supported by the correlation and linear regression analysis results which do not show any statistically significant association as seen in Appendix A, Table 4 and Table 8. Interestingly, both company groups demonstrate a strong belief that sustainability criteria and credit conditions will be linked, with more than 60 % stating likely or very likely. In contrast, when asked about their belief that they could lose their financing access in case of failure to achieve certain sustainability targets, more than 60 % stated average or unlikely.

Generally, companies perceive on average a strong regulatory pressure and transition risk. Moreover, they strongly believe that credit conditions will be linked to sustainability criteria, but are still hesitant to believe that they could lose their financing access in case of failure to achieve certain sustainability targets. However, an analysis of the respective four criteria regulatory pressure, transition risk, linkage and financing access, and their relation with SFI use, indicates no statistically significant association (Hinsche, 2024). These observations suggest that instead of regulatory pressure, transition risk or the anticipation of a risk differential, companies are currently primarily incentivized to use SFIs by a potential pricing or reputational advantage. This is confirmed by the findings that companies rate a potential pricing advantage and the communication of their sustainability strategy as the most influential factors to use SFIs (Hinsche, 2024).

However, companies not active in capital markets are less likely to benefit from any reputational advantages in regard to SFI use, compared to companies active in capital markets. Most of the reputational advantages are due to the publicity and transparency of the capital market. This is supported by the fact that smaller companies rank a potential pricing advantage as the most influential reason, compared to larger companies that rate the communication of their sustainability strategy as the most influential factor to use SFIs (Hinsche, 2024).

Consequently, the survey results suggest that companies not active in capital markets are or can be predominantly incentivized to use SFI by a potential pricing advantage compared to using a conventional financing instrument. This is an important observation and needs to be taken into consideration when evaluating how the current sustainable finance incentivization scheme can be applied to companies not active in capital markets.

3.5.1.2 Motivational Factors of SMEs Not Active in Capital Markets

Only looking at the SME share of companies not active in capital markets, it can be observed that the majority perceive transition risk (66 %)

and regulatory pressure (67 %) as little or average (see Appendix A, Table 7). Moreover, whilst 50 % of SME companies not active in capital markets state that the risk of credit linkage is average or unlikely, 50 % state that it is likely or very likely. In contrast, the majority (83 %) believe that the risk of losing their financing access due to not achieving certain sustainability targets is low or average. Nevertheless, 17 % believe that the risk is very high (see Appendix A, Table 7). These results show that regulatory pressure and transition risk are perceived as lower by smaller companies not active in capital markets.

Moreover, high uncertainty regarding the risk of credit linkage and financing access can be observed among smaller companies not active in capital markets. It should be noted that the share of companies which believe the risk of losing their financing access to be average or low is higher for SMEs not active in capital markets (83 %) compared to all companies not active in capital markets (63 %) (see Appendix A, Table 7). This could indicate companies' trust in their house bank relations, as particularly SMEs are relying on house bank financing through their local savings or cooperative banks (see section 3.3).

3.5.2 Implementation: Can Use SFI

Apart from motivation, companies need to have sufficient knowledge regarding sustainable finance instruments, as well as to fulfil necessary requirements such as sustainability performance data collection and monitoring, in order to use SFIs. As explained in section 2.1.1, sustainability disclosure regulations, such as the CSRD, aim to establish a transparent and comparable sustainability reporting, which in turn makes it easier for companies to use SFIs. However, capital market active companies might be more advanced in their implementation of sustainability regulations, as they already have to adhere to these regulations for a longer time than companies not active in capital markets (see section 2.1.1). Consequently, companies active and not active in capital markets might differ in regard to their SFI knowledge, data assessment and perceived barriers. The following section analyzes these potential differences and also examines any potential differences particular to SMEs.

3.5.2.1 Implementation Factors

Firstly, looking at Figure 4, the study results demonstrate that the share of companies which have a carbon footprint does not differ significantly with a company's capital market activity. This is supported by the correlation and logistic regression results which do not show any statistically significant association (see Appendix A, Table 4 and Table 10). However, the logistic regression results show a positive, at the 5 % level statistically significant, association between having an ESG rating and being active in capital markets (see Appendix A, Table 4 and Table 10). This can also be seen in Figure 4, as the share of companies that have an ESG rating is more than twice as high for companies active in capital markets (35 %) compared to companies not active in capital markets (16 %). Furthermore, the share of companies that are not familiar with the term ESG, which is denoted by "IDK ESG Term" is similar for both company groups.

Figure 4. Carbon Footprint and ESG Rating by Capital Market Activity

a. Carbon Footprint

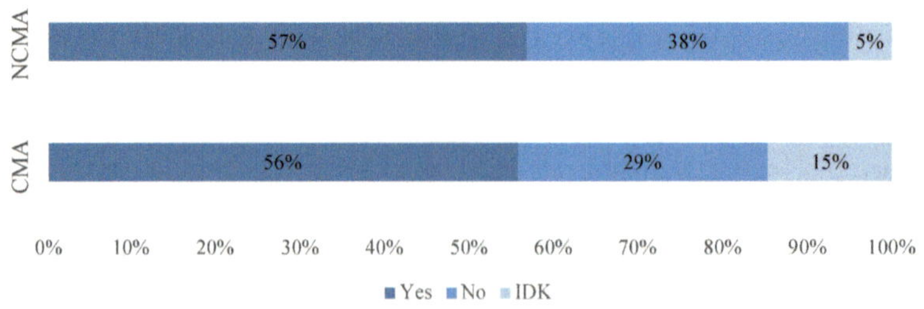

b. ESG Rating

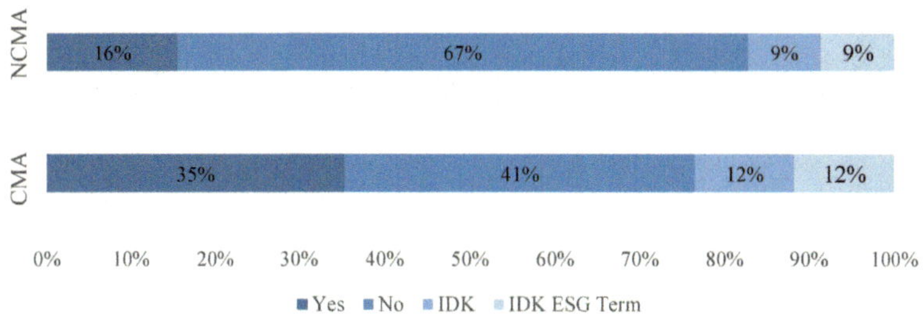

Source: This figure presents whether companies have a carbon footprint or ESG rating by capital market activity, based on the survey results reported in Appendix A, Table 9. Note: "IDK" = I don't know. Note: "NCMA" denotes not capital market active and "CMA" denotes capital market active.

In regard to having company-level sustainability targets, Figure 5 shows no significant difference between companies active and not active in capital markets. This is supported by the correlation and logistic regression results (see Appendix A, Table 4 and Table 10). Nevertheless, Figure 5 demonstrates that the share of companies with a sustainability target commitment scheme is more than twice as high for companies active in capital markets (21 %) compared to companies not active in capital markets (9 %). A potential explanation could be that companies active in capital markets are subject to higher transparency requirements. Consequently, they might use sustainability target commitment schemes, for instance in the form of management compensation linked to sustainability targets, as a public sustainability commitment and thereby improve the company's sustainability reputation. In fact, in case that companies report their type of sustainability target commitment scheme, they state that it is in the form of management compensation in 100 % of the answers (see Appendix A, Table 9).

Figure 5. CLST and STCS by Capital Market Activity

a. Company Level Sustainability Target (CLST)

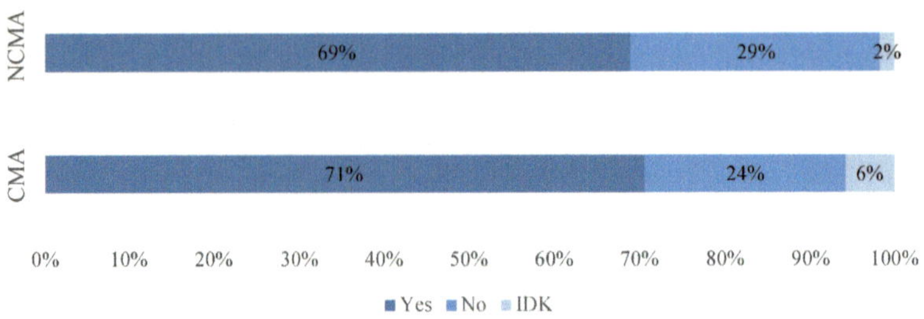

b. Sustainability Target Commitment Scheme (STCS)

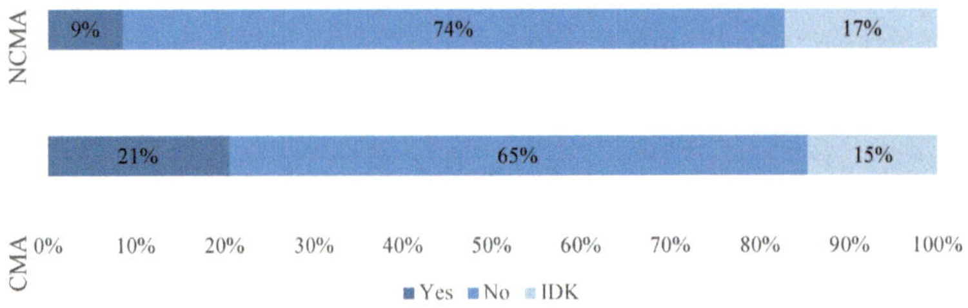

Source: This figure presents whether companies have company-level sustainability targets (CLST) and a sustainability target commitment scheme (STCS) by capital market activity, based on the survey results reported in Appendix A, Table 9. Note: "IDK" denotes I don't know. "NCMA" denotes not capital market active and "CMA" denotes capital market active.

Regarding companies' sustainable finance instrument knowledge, the survey results show that whilst only 3 % of companies active in capital markets are unfamiliar with SFIs, 17 % of companies not active in capital markets are unfamiliar with SFIs (see Appendix A, Table 9). This relation is confirmed by a statistically significant negative association between being unfamiliar with SFIs and being active in capital markets (see Appendix A, Table 4 and Table 10). Finally, the analysis results show that the share of companies which perceive SFI barriers is slightly higher for companies active in capital markets (50 %) than for companies not active (36 %) (see Appendix A, Table 9).

3.5.2.2 Qualitative Assessment of Companies' Implementation Barriers

In order to gain a deeper understanding of companies' perceived barriers, this study uses a mixed method research approach and integrated open questions into the survey. The answers are coded using thematic content analysis, as explained in section 4.3. Firstly, all answers were coded and simultaneously translated from German to English, as the survey language was German. Subsequently, main thematic categories were developed. As seen in Figure 6, the main thematic categories are applicability, company requirements, economic efficiency and implementation. Finally, further subcategories were developed inductively and attributed to the thematic main categories in line with the overarching categorical system. The resulting overview of perceived barriers can be seen in Appendix A, Table 12.

Figure 6. Reported Perceived Main Barriers

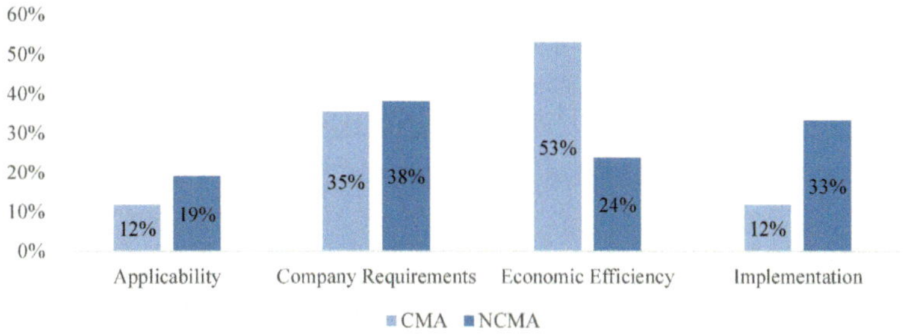

Source: This figure presents companies' reported perceived main barriers by capital market activity, coded and assigned using thematic content analysis. The full overview of coded reported barriers can be seen in Appendix A, Table 12. Note: "NCMA" denotes not capital market active and "CMA" denotes capital market active.

Capital market active companies are generally more concerned with the economic efficiency of SFIs, whilst companies not active in capital markets reported more often that they perceive the applicability and implementation of SFIs as a barrier, as seen in Figure 6. Furthermore, the number of times that company requirements were stated as a barrier is similar for both, companies active and not active in capital markets.

However, taking a closer look at company requirements subcategories in Figure 7 shows significant differences in the barriers perceived. In fact, capital market active companies state administrative work as a barrier relatively more often than companies not active in capital markets. The reported barriers that are part of the administrative work barrier subgroup are general additional effort, additional work capacities needed and reporting. Interestingly, reporting is predominantly stated as a barrier by companies not active in capital markets (see Appendix A, Table 12). Furthermore, the subgroup knowledge, containing regulatory uncertainty, no experience and insufficient consulting as barriers, is more often perceived as a barrier by companies not active in capital markets.

In regard to economic efficiency barriers, the survey results show that both, cost and risk barriers are stated more often by companies active in capital markets, as seen in Figure 7. The perceived barriers attributed to the cost subgroup are higher costs, insufficient promotional loans and costs higher than benefits. Furthermore, the risk subgroup contains the reported barriers regulatory and greenwashing risk, as well as the risk of failure to achieve sustainability targets. Interestingly, regulatory risk is only stated by a company not active in capital markets, whilst greenwashing risk is only stated by a company active in capital markets. This supports the claim in section 4.5.1 that capital market active companies can be incentivized to use SFIs by potential sustainability reputation effects, whilst companies not active in capital markets are rather incentivized by regulations or pricing.

Figure 7. Barrier Subcategories by Capital Market Activity

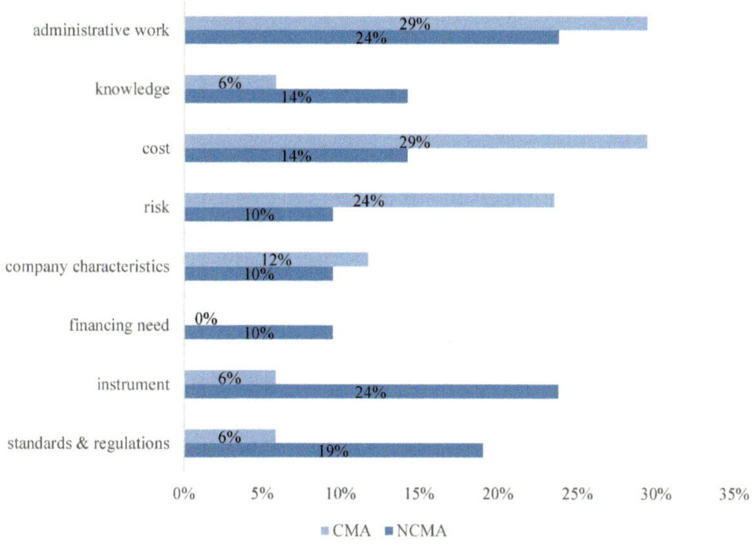

Source: This figure presents the subcategories of companies' reported perceived barriers by capital market activity, coded and assigned using thematic content analysis. The full overview of coded reported barriers can be seen in Appendix A, Table 12. The percentage indicates the share of companies that stated the respective barrier in relation to all companies that stated they perceive a barrier, which are 17 capital market active companies and 21 companies that are not active in capital markets. Note: "NCMA" denotes not capital market active and "CMA" denotes capital market active.

Moreover, it is striking that 18 % of capital market active companies, that perceive barriers, stated risk of failure to achieve sustainability targets as a barrier, as seen in Figure 7. Sustainable finance instruments such as the sustainability-linked bond only work efficiently, if companies are penalized for not achieving their targets. However, the stated barrier suggests that companies might be choosing not to use SFIs for fear of precisely this penalty, in the form of financial payments or reputational damage. This would be an unintentional and conflicting effect of SFIs characteristics and should be considered during further developments of SFIs.

Looking at applicability barriers, the survey results show that the applicability of SFIs to company characteristics, namely financing structure, industry and company purpose, is perceived equally as a barrier by companies active and not active in capital markets (see Figure 7 and Appendix A, Table 12). However, the applicability of SFIs to a company's financing needs is only stated as a barrier by companies not active in capital markets, more precisely they name the lack of use cases and insufficient flexibility as barriers to SFI use.

Finally, implementation barriers are predominantly stated by companies not active in capital markets. In regard to the subgroup instrument implementation, the most stated barrier is KPI choice and tracking, followed by data collection and size. Furthermore, taking a closer look at the reported barriers of the subgroup standard and regulations, it is striking that only companies not active in capital markets state data comparability and availability. In contrast, capital market active companies state investor requirements as a barrier to SFI use (see Appendix A, Table 12).

Overall, the qualitative survey results and analysis allow for a deeper understanding of the differences in barriers between companies active and not active in capital markets. The barriers stated by companies not active in capital markets demonstrate that they experience a high uncertainty regarding sustainability regulations and that particularly data collection and reporting pose a challenge. This supports the quantitative results which show that companies not active in capital markets have a significantly lower share that has an ESG rating. This could be due to data availability, as well as costs associated with data collection and obtaining an ESG rating. Furthermore, the recorded barriers of insufficient consulting and no experience underline the quantitative results that companies not active in capital markets have a lower share that already was familiar with SFIs prior to the survey. This emphasizes the lack of sustainable finance knowledge of companies not active in capital markets. Both aspects are discussed in more detail in section 6.

3.5.2.3 Implementation Factors of SMEs Not Active in Capital Markets

Regarding the SME share of companies not active in capital markets and their sustainable finance instrument knowledge and implementation, it is striking that none of the companies have an ESG rating (see Appendix A, Table 9). Moreover, only 50 % have a carbon footprint, compared to 57 % when looking at the whole sample of companies not active in capital markets. The same holds true for having company-level sustainability targets, with also a lower share of 50 % compared to 69 % of all companies not active in capital markets. This underlines the issue of data availability and monitoring for SMEs when considering the use of SFIs. Furthermore, the share of companies unfamiliar with SFIs is the same for SMEs and all companies not active in capital markets (17 %). Finally, also the share of companies that perceive barriers to SFI use is similar (33 % vs. 36 %), as seen in Appendix A, Table 9.

3.5.3 Enabler: Will Use SFI

As explained in Section 3, companies that are not active in capital markets rely on their (house) banks for financing. Therefore, banks play an important role in enabling them to use SFIs. This section reports the survey results in regard to banks' sustainable finance support, as well as companies' expectations regarding their financing partners. On the one hand, companies that are not active in capital markets might benefit from their very close (house) bank relation when considering SFI use. On the other hand, they also rely heavily on their banks to support them in their sustainable finance use and particularly SMEs, who often only have one or two close house bank relations, might be at a disadvantage as long as their bank is not suggesting and supporting SFI use.

3.5.3.1 Enabling Factors

Looking at the survey results, the difference between companies active and not active in capital markets is very apparent. As seen in Figure 8, more than half of capital market active companies (53 %) have been recommended by their bank to use SFIs, whilst only 28 % of companies not active in capital markets have had SFIs recommended to them by their bank. This relation is supported by the correlation and logistic regression results, which demonstrate a positive, at the 5 % level statistically significant, association between having been recommended a SFI and being active in capital markets (see Appendix A, Table 15).

Figure 8. Bank Recommendation by Capital Market Activity

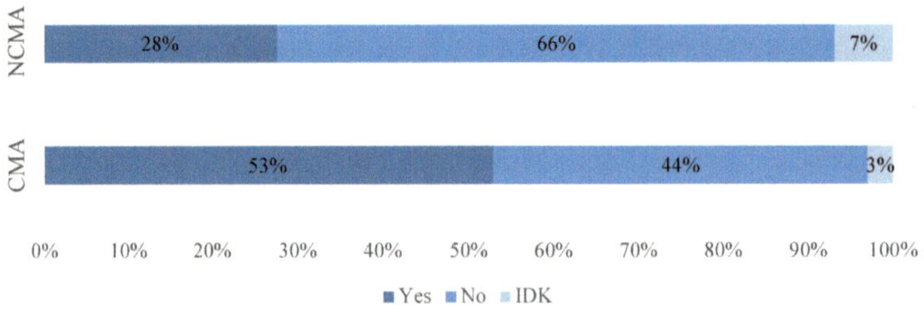

Source: This figure presents the share of companies that have been recommended SFIs by their banks by capital market activity, based on the survey results reported in Appendix A, Table 13. Note: "NCMA" denotes not capital market active and "CMA" denotes capital market active.

Nevertheless, companies believe in their banks' capability to support them in their sustainability transition is quite similar, as seen in Figure 9. Capital market active companies have a slightly higher share that believes in their banks' support (56 %) compared to companies not active in capital markets (47 %). In contrast, the latter have a higher share that is uncertain about their banks' role (36 %) in comparison to capital market active companies (26 %).

This is an interesting observation, as one could expect companies that rely solely on bank financing to have a stronger belief in their banks' support. Instead, the results suggest that companies not active in capital markets still experience a high uncertainty regarding how their banks can support them in their sustainability transition. This uncertainty could hinder positive characteristics of house bank relations, such as long-time trust and experience, to reach their full potential to support SFI use.

Figure 9. Bank Believe by Capital Market Activity

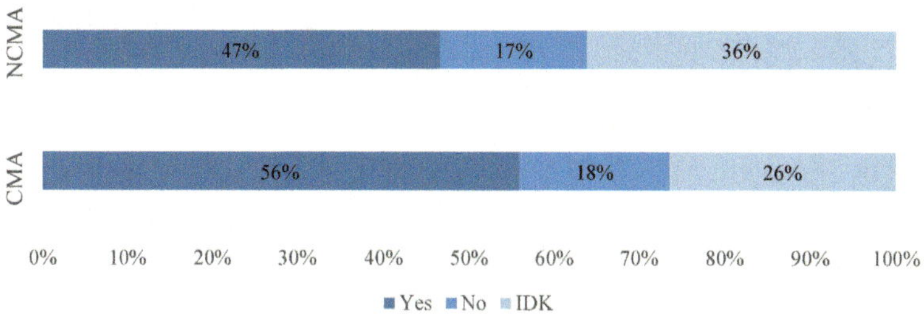

Source: This figure presents the share of companies that believe their bank(s) can support them with their sustainability transition by capital market activity, based on the survey results reported in Appendix A, Table 13. Note: "NCMA" denotes not capital market active and "CMA" denotes capital market active.

The survey also asked companies to rate their banks' sustainable finance support. As seen in Figure 10, the highest share of capital market active companies rates their banks' support as good (41 %), whilst the highest share of companies not active in capital markets rates their banks' support only as average (48 %).

However, banks' ratings might be influenced by companies' sustainable finance experience, as 17 % of companies not active in capital markets were unfamiliar with SFIs before the survey. Excluding these observations changes the distribution only very slightly for capital market active companies (see Appendix A, Table 14), but the distribution becomes on average more positive for companies not active in capital markets, as seen in Figure 10. The highest share still rated their banks' support as average (50 %), however, the ratings very bad and bad decreased to 0 % and 6 % respectively.

Figure 10. Bank Support Rating by Capital Market Activity

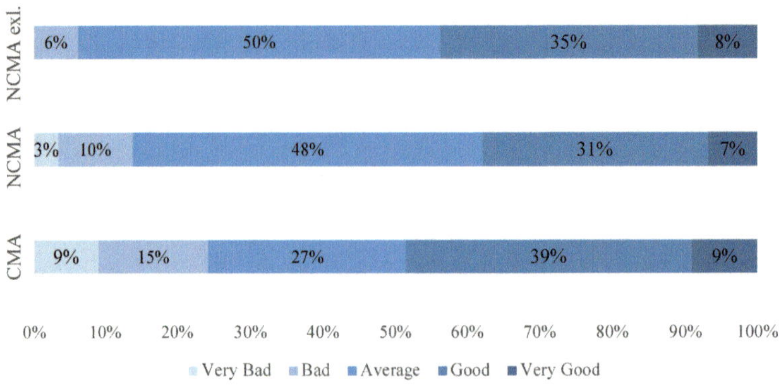

Source: This figure presents the share of companies that believe their bank(s) can support them with their sustainability transition, based on the survey results reported in Appendix A, Table 13 and Table 14. Note: "NCMA" denotes not capital market active and "CMA" denotes capital market active.

3.5.3.2 Qualitative Assessment of Companies' Bank Support Expectations

In order to gain a deeper understanding of companies' expectations regarding their banks' support and potential differences between companies active and not active in capital markets, the survey included a second open question section. The qualitative data are coded, grouped and analyzed in the same manner as described in Section 4.3 and 5.2.2, using thematic content analysis. As seen in Figure 11, the main thematic categories are consultation, information, mode of information and role of bank. More than half (53 %) of companies active in capital markets that would like to receive their banks' support stated that they would like to receive consultation and almost a third (26 %) that they would like to receive information. For companies not active in capital markets, the share of companies that would like to receive consultation is similar (48 %), but the share that would like to receive information is significantly higher (44 %). Moreover, 19 % had very clear expectations regarding the role of their banks.

Figure 11. Bank Expectations by Capital Market Activity

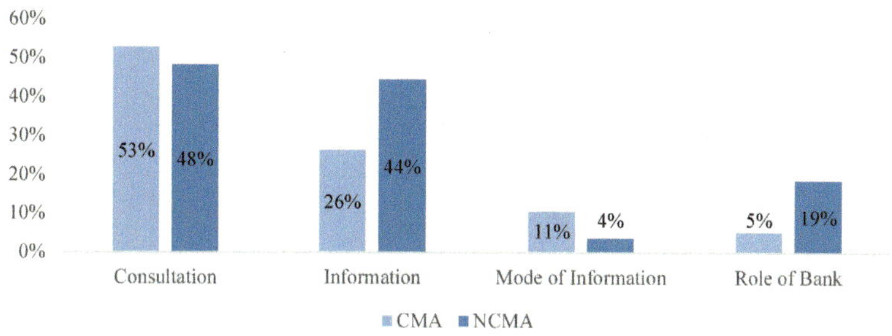

Source: This figure presents the main thematic categories of companies' reported bank expectations by capital market activity, coded and assigned using thematic content analysis. The full overview of coded reported expectations can be seen in Appendix A, Table 16. Note: "NCMA" denotes not capital market active and "CMA" denotes capital market active.

Taking a closer look at the subcategories reported in Figure 12, one can see that capital market active companies primarily would like to receive general consultation. In contrast, companies not active in capital markets are more specific in regard to the type of consultation. They would like to receive consultation on KPI choice, followed by promotional loans, reporting and rating optimization. Moreover, as mentioned above, the demand for information is significantly higher for companies not active in capital markets. They would like to receive information primarily on SFI use, encompassing experiences and use cases with other customers to learn from, as well as general information. However, if capital market active companies would like to receive information on SF use, they would like it to be best practice examples, as seen in Appendix A, Table 16.

Figure 12. Bank Expectation Subcategories by Capital Market Activity

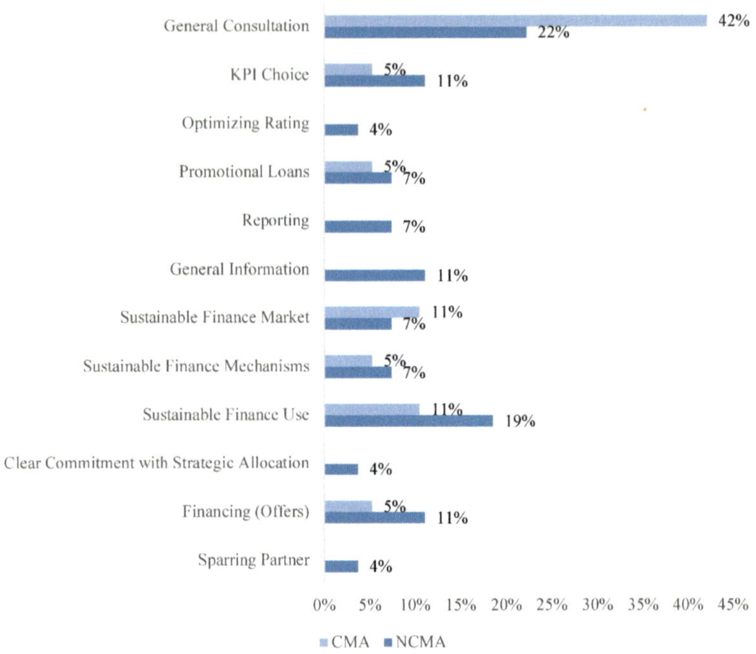

Source: This figure presents the subcategories of companies' reported bank expectations by capital market activity, coded and assigned using thematic content analysis. The full overview of coded reported expectations can be seen in Appendix A, Table 16. Note: "NCMA" denotes not capital market active and "CMA" denotes capital market active.

Furthermore, companies active and not active in capital markets would like to receive information on the sustainable finance market, including a market overview and their financing partners' expectations. In regard to the sustainable finance mechanism, companies active in capital markets would like to receive information on framework conditions, as seen Appendix A, Table 16. In contrast, companies not active in capital markets would like to receive information on the differences between green and conventional instruments, as well as the impact of a sustainability rating on financing conditions.

As seen in Figure 12, almost one-fifth of companies not active in capital markets that believe in their banks' support also stated very precise expectations for their banks. Primarily, they would like to receive concrete financing offers. Moreover, they would like their bank to have a clear commitment and to function as their sparring partner for a successful sustainability transition. Finally, a few companies also reported their preferred mode of information. These include a wide range of suggestions from personal talks, questionnaires, workshops and presentations to events (see Appendix A, Table 16).

Overall, the qualitative analysis allowed for a deeper understanding of companies' expectations regarding the form of their banks' support and complements the quantitative results. Companies not active in capital markets would like to receive both, consultation and information. In regard to consultation, they would like to receive guidance on KPI choice and reporting, which is in line with their reported barriers in Section 5.2.2. Moreover, they would like to receive information on SFI use and receive concrete financing offers, which supports the findings from section 5.2.2 and 5.3.1 that companies not active in capital markets perceive the lack of experience and knowledge as a barrier and have been recommended SFI use less than companies active in capital markets. Furthermore, their demand for a clear commitment from their bank and for them to be their sparring partner mirrors their currently high uncertainty regarding their banks' ability to support them in their sustainability transition, as seen in section 5.3.1, Figure 9. Finally, their interest in promotional loan consultation is discussed further in section 5.4 on promotional loan use.

3.5.3.3 Enabling Factors of SMEs Not Active in Capital Markets

Regarding the SME share of companies not active in capital markets, it is striking that none of the companies have been recommended to use SFIs by their bank, in contrast to 28 % of all companies not active in capital markets (see Appendix A, Table 13). This suggests that from their banks' perspective it is either not feasible to offer SFIs or that they do not think that it would be an attractive or viable option for their clients. Furthermore, SMEs have a lower share (33 %) that believe their bank can support them in their sustainability transition, compared to the full sample of companies not active in capital markets (47 %). This contradicts the assumption that SMEs not active in capital markets might benefit from their close house bank relations in terms of a strong trust and thus easier implementation of SFIs. The observed behavior could be due to a lack of knowledge and uncertainty regarding how their house banks can support them in their sustainability transition. This is discussed in further detail in section 6. Finally, SME's bank rating is on average similar to all of the companies not active in capital markets, with 33 % rating their banks' support as very good and 67 % as average.

3.5.4 Promotional Loans

Promotional loans are a financing instrument that is usually linked to a certain topic and offers companies more favorable loan conditions compared to a conventional loan. They are often provided through public financial institutions, such as the European Investment Bank ((EIB), 2023) and KFW (2024a). For instance, KFW (2024a) offers promotional loans for investments in companies' sustainability transition in line with the EU taxonomy, in energy and resource efficiency, as well as renewable energies and the reduction of greenhouse gas emissions. Promotional loans have favorable financing conditions in the form of attractive interest rates, easier access to credit when KFW assumes part of the credit risk, or even an investment grant.

The aim is to foster sustainability investments by lowering companies' financial barriers to implement their transition strategy. Promotional loans could be particularly attractive for companies not active in capital markets, as they have lower sustainability data requirements than a sustainability-linked or green loan.[31] Furthermore, the loan application is processed through a company's bank, which means that they can benefit from their long-term trust relation. However, companies consequently also depend on their banks to support them in the application process. In the following section, the difference in promotional loan interest, knowledge and use between companies active and not active in capital markets, as well SMEs not active in capital markets, are analyzed.

3.5.4.1 Promotional Loan Interest, Knowledge and Use

The survey asked respondents whether they are familiar with or have already used a promotional loan in connection with sustainable finance. As seen in Figure 13, promotional loan knowledge is very similar for companies active (53 %) and not active (57 %) in capital markets. However, for both groups only slightly more than half of the companies are familiar with promotional loans connected with SFIs. Furthermore, it is striking that only companies not active in capital markets have used promotional loans so far. This suggests that promotional loans indeed offer an attractive financing opportunity for companies not active in capital markets. Capital market active companies might prefer to use capital market SFIs, such as a green or sustainability-linked bond, as they offer a potential reputational benefit, as explained in section 2.2.3.

31 For instance, the climate action promotional loan for medium-sized businesses by KFW (2024b) finances investments into the reduction, prevention and elimination of greenhouse gas emissions. Regarding the promotional loan's sustainability criteria requirements, companies have to adhere to a list of eligible investment categories and have to prove the appropriate use of the funds. However, they do not have to provide any company-level or project-level sustainability data, as would be the case for a green or sustainability-linked loan.

Figure 13. Promotional Loan Knowledge and Use by Capital Market Activity

a. Promotional Loan Knowledge

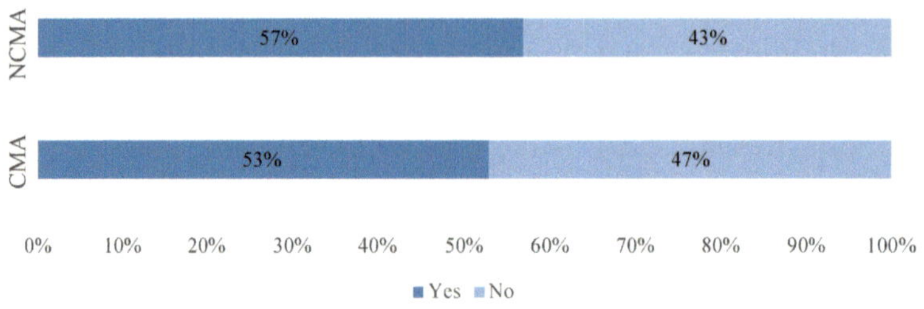

b. Promotional Loan Use

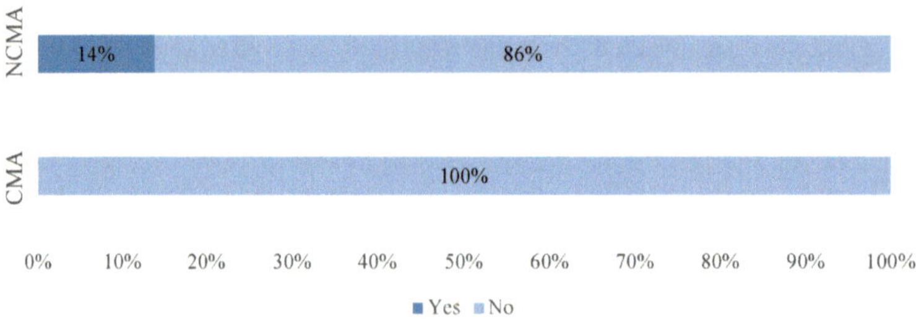

Source: This figure presents the share of companies that know and / or use promotional loans by capital market activity, based on the survey results reported in Appendix A, Table 17. Note: "NCMA" denotes not capital market active and "CMA" denotes capital market active.

In regard to promotional loan interest, one can see in Figure 14 that promotional loan interest is higher for companies not active in capital markets (83 %) compared to companies active in capital markets (62 %). This relation is supported by the logistic regression results which indicate a statistically significant negative association between being interested in promotional loans and being active in capital markets (see Appendix A, Table 18). This result further supports the finding that promotional loans are a particularly attractive financing instrument to foster sustainability transition investments for companies not active in capital markets. Finally, it is striking that almost one-fifth of companies active in capital markets (24 %) are unsure whether they are interested in promotional loans, as seen in Figure 14. This suggests that companies are uncertain whether they can use and how they can benefit from promotional loans connected to sustainable finance.

Figure 14. Promotional Loan Interest

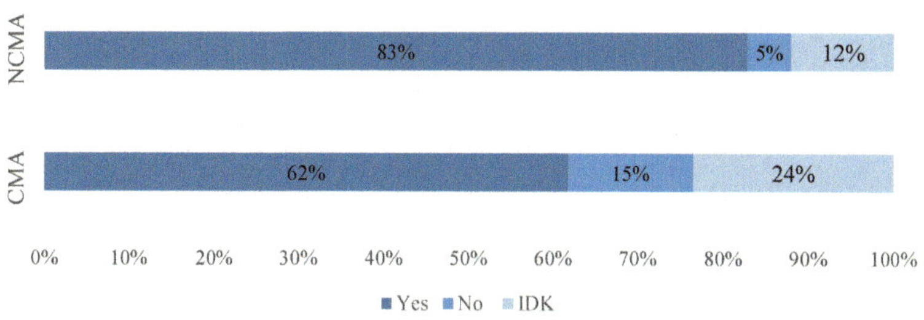

Source: This figure presents the share of companies that are interested in promotional loans by capital market activity, based on the survey results reported in Appendix A, Table 17. Note: "NCMA" denotes not capital market active and "CMA" denotes capital market active.

3.5.4.2 Promotional Loans and SMEs Not Active in Capital Markets

Regarding the SME share that is not active in capital markets, one can see that promotional loan knowledge is significantly lower (33 %) compared to all of the companies not active in capital markets (53 %) (see Appendix A, Table 17). Moreover, none of SMEs not active in capital markets have used a promotional loan connected to sustainability transition investments so far. This is an important observation, as promotional loans could be particularly helpful for SMEs, providing a more cost-sensitive option to foster sustainability transition investments compared to a sustainable finance loan. Compared to a sustainability-linked or green loan, the data requirements in terms of sustainability data collection and monitoring are lower and the process already more standardized. The promotional loan interest among SMEs not active in capital markets is comparatively a bit lower (67 %) than for all companies not active in capital markets (83 %), as seen in Appendix A, Table 17. Nevertheless, more than half are interested in promotional loans in contrast to only one-third knowing about promotional loans connected to sustainable finance in advance of the survey. This observation suggests that SMEs do not have sufficient knowledge regarding promotional loan use and is further discussed in the following section.

3.6 Discussion

The survey results show that companies not active in capital markets experience lower regulatory pressure and transition risk. Moreover, they experience uncertainty in regard to further sustainability regulations, but expect a linkage between credit conditions and sustainability criteria to be likely, whilst the loss of financing access is seen as more unlikely. An important difference to companies active in capital markets is that they cannot benefit from reputational advantages of SFIs in the same manner, as explained in section 5.1. Consequently, companies not active in capital markets could be best incentivized to use SFIs by a pricing advantage.

SFIs such as green or sustainability-linked loans have the potential to offer such a pricing advantage, but also have precise and binding sustainability data and reporting requirements that are challenging for companies not active in capital markets to comply with. Regarding the implementation of SFIs, companies not active in capital markets demonstrate to have insufficient data availability and monitoring, as well as a lack of sustainable finance knowledge and experience. This is particularly the case for SMEs not active in capital markets. A potential explanation based on the preceding analysis is that they perceive lower regulatory pressure and transition risk, whilst the costs to obtain sustainability data and implement a SFIs are relatively higher. This is reflected in the low share of companies that have an ESG rating and the low share of SFI users. Consequently, SFIs for companies not active in capital markets, and especially for SMEs, should be adapted in terms of their data requirements accordingly. Companies not active in capital markets in particular asked for more flexibility of SFIs to be able to adapt them to their financing needs and investment projects, as explained in section 5.2.

A form of SFI that could be particularly attractive for companies not active in capital markets, and who are currently unable to meet sustainability data requirements of green or sustainability-linked loans, are promotional loans. The data requirements for promotional loans are lower, in terms of sustainability data collection and monitoring, compared to a green or sustainability-linked loan. Moreover, they offer a clear pricing or risk advantage compared to a conventional loan, whilst fostering investments into companies' sustainability transition. A study by Brüggemann et al. (2023) shows that especially SMEs often use promotional loans to finance their transition projects, compared to large companies. The survey results reflect this, with the majority of companies not active in capital markets being interested in promotional loans connected to sustainability. However, more than half of the companies not active in capital markets are currently not familiar with said promotional loans, as seen in Section 6.1 and 6.2. As promotional loans are usually processed through a company's bank, they play an important role in supporting companies to use promotional loans to foster sustainability investments.

The diversity and different financing conditions of promotional loans connected to sustainability investments can be overwhelming for companies. For instance, KFW (2024a) currently has ten different promotional loans and grants connected to sustainable finance, with varying conditions, including promotional loans tailored to SMEs, as well as to sustainability technologies. Therefore, banks play a crucial role in aiding companies to find the best option for their sustainability investment plans and in supporting them in the subsequent application process. Nevertheless, this approach relies on banks' willingness to support companies in their promotional loan use, even though interest margins earned with promotional loans are considered as low by banks (Handke, 2011). However, the promotional loan process can also offer banks the opportunity to develop a closer relationship with their corporate clients and to reduce information asymmetry by developing a credit history (Handke, 2011). Furthermore, supporting companies to finance their sustainability transition with the help of a promotional loan falls into the mandate of the majority of particularly regional banks. Apart from profit-making, cooperative and savings banks have the mandate to support the business of their members (Schmidt & Tyrell, 2004) and to serve the common good in line with their public mandate (DSGV, 2017) respectively, as explained in Section 3.1.

In general, the survey results demonstrate the importance of banks' support to use SFIs and promotional loans. In contrast to the assumption that companies not active in capital markets might benefit from their close relation with their house banks (see section 3.3), the opposite appears to be true. Companies not active in capital markets have a lower SFI recommendation and higher uncertainty regarding their banks' support for their sustainability transition. This observation is even stronger for SMEs not active in capital markets, of which none have been recommended SFI use and only 33 % believe that their bank can support them in their sustainability transition (see section 5.2.3).

This reflects how particularly regional banks appear to be lagging behind in the integration of sustainability in their lending processes and the support of SFIs. This is supported by the fact that only 19 % of regional banks currently require sustainability data from their borrowers (Strube et al., 2023a) and 82 % do not offer any sustainability-linked loan (Strube et al., 2023b). Consequently, regional banks need to improve their sustainable finance support. However, the problem is not limited to regional banks, as even among all bank groups, only 13 % of SMEs state that their sustainability performance was a topic in their credit negotiations (Gerstenberger, 2024). This emphasizes that, in general, SMEs require a more tailored sustainable finance support than larger companies (Hinsche, 2024), taking their current level of sustainability data collection and relatively higher financial costs into consideration.

Based on the survey results, banks and in particular regional banks should advance and improve their sustainable finance support for companies not active in capital markets. The survey results show that companies are asking for a clear commitment, concrete financing offers and for their banks to be a sparring partner in acquiring the funds to finance their sustainability transition. It is striking that companies not active in capital markets and their banks are currently not making sufficient use of their, often long-term, (house) bank relationship. The advantage of an in-depth knowledge of the company's business, which is otherwise very costly to obtain given the prevalent information asymmetry, as well as trust built on years of experience together, should be used to foster sustainability investments. Banks should encourage their clients to make use of SFIs to invest in their sustainability transition, provide necessary information and consultation, and support them in the implementation.

In regard to the type of SFIs, the study demonstrates that sustainability-linked or green loans' data and reporting requirements might be difficult to align with the current level of data availability and relatively high costs of implementation for companies not active in financial markets, and particularly SMEs. This is supported by the fact that regional banks think that sustainability-linked loans are only conditionally suitable (Strube et al., 2023b) and that only 31 % of SMEs think that SFIs offer an understandable, transparent and accessible financing option (Scharf, 2022).

In the long run, companies not active in capital markets, including SMEs, will have to report on their sustainability performance due to the CSRD, SFDR and the accompanying trickle-down effect, as explained in section 2.2. Even if SMEs should be exempted from certain sustainability disclosure regulations, the trickle-down effect will eventually lead to all companies having to report certain sustainability data points and thus create the desired transparency. Currently, however, the availability of sustainability data is still insufficient and hinders sustainability investments, as this study showed. Yet, the overarching goal of sustainable finance is to foster investments into sustainability to advance the economy's sustainability transition and to meet our climate targets. In order to successfully achieve the European Green Deal and global climate targets, sustainability investments need to be realized now and should not wait until sufficient data collection and monitoring are provided. Therefore, sustainable finance instruments need to be adapted to the current data availability and monitoring capabilities of companies not active in capital markets, particularly SMEs.

An alternative option for companies not active in capital markets is to use, at least temporarily, promotional loans, which have lower data requirements than green or sustainability-linked loans, as explained above. A potential adaptation could be to require companies to collect certain sustainability performance indicators in a defined time frame, in order to receive a promotional loan, as proposed and explained by Hinsche (2024). This could incentivize and progress data collection and monitoring, as long as the financial advantage of the promotional loan is higher than the costs of acquiring sustainability data. But ultimately, promotional loans should continue to support investments into companies' sustainability transition and not investments into sustainability data collection, to advance the real economy's progress to achieve the European Union's Green Deal climate target until 2030. Furthermore, in the course of promotional loan applications, particularly SMEs could receive information from their house banks regarding sustainability data requirements that they can expect in the upcoming years, how this can affect their financing and how to prepare accordingly, to decrease insufficient sustainability awareness and sustainable finance knowledge.

Apart from sustainability data requirements, the findings show that companies not active in capital markets can be primarily incentivized to use SFIs by a pricing advantage. Promotional loans can offer a clear pricing or risk advantage, however, the funds for the required promotional loans are provided by the state. In contrast, green and sustainability-linked loans mobilize private sector investments into sustainability, independently from public funds. This is crucial, as one of the main aims of sustainable finance is to mobilize the required private sector sustainability investments in addition to public sector sustainability investments. However, a fundamental prerequisite, in order for green and sustainability-linked loans to be able to systemically offer a pricing advantage compared to a conventional instrument, is a clear established link between a company's or asset's sustainability and financial risk.

As the current market mechanism and structures do not price environmental pollution yet, they fail to direct investments into environmentally sustainable activities and companies' sustainability transition. Furthermore, research so far fails to establish a clear link between sustainability and financial risk (NGFS, 2020; NGFS, 2022). Consequently, the state must intervene to ensure that the necessary sustainability investments are realized in a timely manner, in order to avoid higher damages and costs caused by the climate crisis in the future. Promotional loans can constitute a temporary option for the state to intervene, in the form of directly providing the necessary funds. However, from a social market economy perspective, the preferred solution would be for the state to only intervene in the form of regulations and to return to market-based structures. This would be possible, for instance, by determining a price for environmental pollution or in regard to sustainable finance by introducing risk-weighted adjustment factors, based on a company's sustainability, to capital requirements as part of pillar I of the Basel framework (Deutsche Bundesbank, 2023).

Otherwise, sustainable finance is currently relying on public pressure to transition and the voluntary nature of companies. The results emphasize that companies not active in capital markets cannot benefit from reputational effects in capital markets and can therefore be primarily incentivized to use SFIs by a clear pricing advantage. Consequently, in order to foster sustainability investments by companies relying on bank-based financing and to avoid a dependency on promotional loans, two important adjustments are necessary: Firstly, SFIs need to be improved in terms of their accessibility and feasibility for companies relying on bank-based financing. Secondly, a clear link between a company's sustainability performance and financial risk needs to be established, in order to ensure a pricing incentive for companies to invest into their sustainability transition.

3.7 Conclusion

This study analyzed how companies active and not active in capital markets differ in their SFI use and motivation, and whether the sustainable finance incentivization scheme might need to be adapted accordingly. Furthermore, the study evaluates how the characteristics of a house bank relation could be utilized for an efficient SFI use, with a special consideration of SMEs not active in capital markets. The research data was collected through a survey conducted in June 2023 with 700 invited corporate customers from DZ BANK AG. Subsequently, the analysis was performed using a mixed method approach, with correlation and logistic regression analysis for the quantitative analysis and a thematic content analysis for the qualitative research parts.

The survey results show that companies active and not active in capital markets differ in their motivation to use SFIs. Companies not active in capital markets perceive on average a lower regulatory pressure and transition risk. Moreover, they believe that a link between credit conditions and sustainability criteria is likely, but perceive the risk to lose financing access due to failure to achieve certain sustainability targets mostly as average. Also, in contrast to capital market active companies, companies not active in capital markets do not benefit from reputational advantages that arise due to the transparency of the capital market. Therefore, companies not active in capital markets can primarily be incentivized by a potential pricing advantage of SFIs compared to a conventional financing instrument.

Companies active and not active in capital markets also differ in regard to the implementation of SFIs. Companies not active in capital markets have a significantly lower SFI knowledge and a lower share that has an ESG rating. This is supported by companies' perceived barriers to SFI use, which demonstrate that companies not active in capital markets perceive particularly company requirements and implementation as barriers. The respective barriers include data collection, comparability, KPI choice and reporting, as well as knowledge barriers such as insufficient experience and consulting. Generally, the implementation results suggest that particularly data availability and SFI knowledge pose a challenge for companies not active in capital markets to use SFIs.

Finally, companies not active in capital markets also differ in terms of their bank support and SFI enabling factors. They experience high uncertainty regarding their banks' ability to support them in their sustainability transition and rate their banks' current support predominantly as average. Furthermore, only a small share of companies not active in capital markets have been recommended SFI use by their bank, compared to capital market active companies. However, their desired bank support in the form of more information on sustainable finance use, mechanism and market, as well as consultation regarding KPI choice, promotional loans and reporting, shows that companies not active in capital markets are interested in their banks taking a more proactive role. This is supported by their demand for concrete SFI financing offers and for their banks to demonstrate a clear commitment to sustainability and to support them as a sparring partner in their sustainability transition.

Additionally, this study analyzed differences in motivation, implementation and enabling factors inherent to SMEs not active in capital markets. The survey results show that SMEs not active in capital markets perceive lower regulatory pressure, transition risk and risk to lose financing access in case of failure to achieve sustainability targets. The latter could be attributed to SMEs' trust in their established banking relations with their house banks. Furthermore, data availability is an even more pressing issue for SMEs not active in capital markets, as none reported to have an ESG rating and only 50 % have a carbon footprint. In regard to bank support, SMEs not active in capital markets demonstrate high uncertainty about how their bank could support them in their sustainability transition and none have been recommended SFI use by their bank. This emphasizes the important role of (regional) banks to improve their sustainable finance support particularly for SMEs not active in capital markets.

To conclude, this paper contributes to the existing literature by demonstrating how companies active and not active in capital markets differ in their motivational, implementation and enabling factors to use SFIs based on a mixed methods research approach. Furthermore, this study suggests how the currently implemented sustainable finance incentive structure could be adapted to the characteristics of companies not active in capital markets and particularly SMEs. In regard to limitations, it should be noted that the share of SMEs in the sample is comparably small, as the survey was distributed to corporate customers of DZ BANK AG and not through regional cooperative bank branches. Thus, further research focusing on regional bank clients, including cooperative and savings bank clients, could provide even more insights into house bank relation characteristics in relation to sustainable finance instrument use.

In terms of policy recommendations, the research results suggest that the currently implemented sustainable finance incentive structure indeed needs to be adapted to the differing characteristics of companies not active in capital markets, and even more in the case of SMEs not active in capital markets. Furthermore, the paper discusses potential pathways to increase sustainability investments for companies not active in capital markets. The results indicate that companies, which rely on bank-based financing, can be primarily incentivized by a pricing advantage. In order to ensure a systemic pricing advantage, a clear link between companies' sustainability and financial risk has to be established. However, as research has failed to identify a clear link between sustainability and financial risk so far, the state might have to intervene in order to ensure the necessary sustainability investments in a timely manner.

From a social market economy perspective, the preferred option would be to introduce a price for environmental pollution or, for instance, risk-weighted adjustment factors, based on a company's sustainability, with respect to capital requirements (e.g. Basel framework). Thereby, the state would only intervene in the form of a regulatory adjustment and could subsequently return to market-based structures. In contrast, promotional loans rely on the state intervening by providing liquidity in the form of public funds and should therefore only be used temporarily, until a link between sustainability and financial risk is established, or the state introduces regulatory adjustments accordingly. Finally, the paper results emphasize the need for banks to step up their sustainable finance support and become a sparring partner to their corporate customers, providing information and consultation regarding the financing of their sustainability transition.

References

Allen, F., & Gale, D. (2000). *Comparing financial systems.* MIT press.

Bachelet, M. J., Becchetti, L., & Manfredonia, S. (2019). The green bonds premium puzzle: The role of issuer characteristics and third-party verification. *Sustainability, 11(4).* https://doi.org/10.3390/su11041098

Behr, P., & Schmidt, R. H. (2016). The German banking system: Characteristics and challenges. In T. Beck and B. Casu (Eds.), *The Palgrave handbook of European banking (pp. 541–566).* Palgrave Macmillan London. https://doi.org/10.1057/978-1-137-52144-6

Berrada, T., Engelhardt, L., Gibson, R., & Krueger, P. (2022). The economics of sustainability linked bonds. *Swiss Finance Institute Research Paper No. 22–26.* https://dx.doi.org/10.2139/ssrn.4059299

Brüggemann, A., Grewenig, E., Römer, D., & Schwartz, M. (2023). *KfW-Klimabarometer 2023.* KfW Research. https://www.kfw.de/PDF/Download-Center/Konzernthemen/Research/PDF-Dokumente-KfW-Klimabarometer/KfW-Klimabarometer-2023.pdf

Bundesverband mittelständische Wirtschaft. (2023). *Der Mittelstand ist Garant für Stabilität und Fortschritt.* Retrieved November 21, 2023, from https://www.bvmw.de/de/der-verband/über-uns/zahlen-fakten

Capasso, G., Gianfrate, G., & Spinelli, M. (2020). Climate change and credit risk. *Journal of Cleaner Production, 266.* https://doi.org/10.1016/j.jclepro.2020.121634

Carbone, S., Giuzio, M., Kapadia, S., Krämer, J. S., Nyholm, K., & Vozian, K. (2021). The low-carbon transition, climate commitments and firm credit risk. *European Central Bank Working Paper Series No. 2631.* https://www.ecb.europa.eu/pub/pdf/scpwps/ecb.wp2631~00a6e0368c.en.pdf

Creswell, J. D., & Creswell, J. W. (2018). *Research design. qualitative, quantitative, and mixed methods approaches* (fifth edition). SAGE.

Deutsche Bank. (2022). *Green Asset Ratio: die Nachhaltigkeits-Kennziffer für Banken.* Retrieved November 21, 2023, from https://www.deutsche-bank.de/ms/results-finanzwissen-fuer-unternehmen/zahlungsverkehr/09-2022-green-asset-ratio-die-nachhaltigkeits-kennziffer-fuer-banken.html

Deutsche Bundesbank. (2023). *Nachhaltigkeitsrisiken in der Bankenaufsicht.* https://www.bundesbank.de/resource/blob/908142/135778eb15c61c27b515e2ba955aa176/mL/2023-04-nachhaltigkeit-bankenaufsicht-data.pdf

Deutsche Bundesbank. (2024). *Banks (MFIs) in Germany.* https://www.bundesbank.de/resource/blob/816066/77911f8f365aae5c7fa3382ae47c5d0a/mL/i-3-aktiva-und-passiva-nach-bankengruppen-data.pdf

Deutscher Sparkassen- und Giroverband. (2017). *Legal structure of savings and retail banks in Europe.* https://www.dsgv.de/content/dam/dsgv-de/sparkassen-finanzgruppe/downloads/190410ESBG-perspectives.pdf

DZ BANK. (2023). *Balance sheet as at 31 December 2023.* Retrieved June 20, 2024, from https://www.annualreport.dzbank.com/en/financial-report/consolidated-financial-statements

Elsas, R. (2005). Empirical determinants of relationship lending. *Journal of Financial Intermediation, 14(1), 32–57.*

Elsas, R., & Krahnen, J.P., (2004). Universal banks and relationships with firms. In J. P. Krahnen and R. H. Schmidt (Eds.), *The German financial system* (pp. 197–232). Oxford University Press.

European Banking Authority (2022). *Environmental, social and governance pillar 3 disclosures.* Retrieved June 19, 2024, from https://www.eba.europa.eu/publications-and-media/press-releases/eba-publishes-binding-standards-pillar-3-disclosures-esg

European Banking Authority. (2023). *On the role of environmental and social risks in the prudential framework.* https://www.eba.europa.eu/sites/default/files/document_library/Publications/Reports/2023/1062711/Report%20on%20the%20role%20of%20environmental%20and%20social%20risks%20in%20the%20prudential%20framework.pdf

European Central Bank. (2020). *Guide on climate related and environmental risk.* https://www.bankingsupervision.europa.eu/ecb/pub/pdf/ssm.202011finalguideonclimate-relatedandenvironmentalrisks~58213f6564.en.pdf

European Central Bank. (2022a). *2022 climate risk stress test.* https://www.bankingsupervision.europa.eu/ecb/pub/pdf/ssm.climate_stress_test_report.20220708~2e3cc0999f.en.pdf

European Central Bank. (2022b). *Walking the talk – banks gearing up to manage risks from climate change and environmental degradation.* https://www.bankingsupervision.europa.eu/ecb/pub/pdf/ssm.thematicreviewcerreport112022~2eb322a79c.en.pdf

European Commission. (2020). *Renewed sustainable finance strategy and implementation of the action plan on financing sustainable growth.* https://finance.ec.europa.eu/publications/renewed-sustainable-finance-strategy-and-implementation-action-plan-financing-sustainable-growth_en

European Commission. (2024a). *The European Green Deal.* Retrieved June 19, 2024, from https://commission.europa.eu/strategy-and-policy/priorities-2019-2024/european-green-deal_en

European Commission. (2024b). *2030 Climate Target Plan.* Retrieved June 19, 2024 from https://ec.europa.eu/info/law/better-regulation/have-your-say/initiatives/12265-2030-Climate-Target-Plan_en

European Commission. (2024c). *European Climate Law.* Retrieved June 19, 2024, from https://climate.ec.europa.eu/eu-action/european-climate-law_en#:~:text=The%20European%20Climate%20Law%20writes,2030%2C%20compared%20to%201990%20levels

European Commission. (2024d). *EU taxonomy for sustainable activities.* Retrieved June 19, 2024, from https://finance.ec.europa.eu/sustainable-finance/tools-and-standards/eu-taxonomy-sustainable-activities_en

European Commission. (2024e). *Corporate sustainability reporting.* Retrieved June 19, 2024, from https://finance.ec.europa.eu/capital-markets-union-and-financial-markets/company-reporting-and-auditing/company-reporting/corporate-sustainability-reporting_en

European Commission. (2024f). *Sustainability-related disclosure in the financial services sector.* Retrieved June 19, 2024, from https://finance.ec.europa.eu/sustainable-finance/disclosures/sustainability-related-disclosure-financial-services-sector_en

European Financial Reporting Advisory Group. (2024). *Voluntary ESRS for non-listed small- and medium-sized enterprises (VSME ESRS).* Retrieved June 24, 2024 from https://www.efrag.org/Assets/Download?assetUrl=%2Fsites%2Fwebpublishing%2FSiteAssets%2FVSME%2520ED%2520January%25202024.pdf

European Investment Bank. (2024). *Loans.* Retrieved June 20, 2024, from https://www.eib.org/en/products/loans/index.htm

European Parliament. (2022). *Sustainable economy: Parliament adopts new reporting rules for multinationals.* https://www.europarl.europa.eu/news/en/press-room/20221107IPR49611/sustainable-economy-parliament-adopts-new-reporting-rules-for-multinationals

Fakis, A., Hilliam, R., Stoneley, H., & Townend, M. (2014). Quantitative analysis of qualitative information from interviews: A systematic literature review. *Journal of Mixed Methods Research, 8(2),* 139–161. https://doi.org/10.1177/1558689813495111

Federal Financial Supervisory Authority. (2020). *BaFin guidance notice on dealing with sustainability risks.* Retrieved June 19, 2024, from https://www.bafin.de/SharedDocs/Downloads/EN/Merkblatt/dl_mb_Nachhaltigkeitsrisiken_en.html

Federal Financial Supervisory Authority. (2023). *Minimum requirements for risk management.* Retrieved June 19, 2024, from https://www.bafin.de/SharedDocs/Downloads/EN/Rundschreiben/dl_rs_0523_marisk_ba_en.html

Fischer, K. H., & Pfeil, C. (2004). Regulation and competition in German banking: An assessment. In J. P. Krahnen and R. H. Schmidt (Eds.), *The German financial system (pp. 291–349).* Oxford University Press.

Flögel, F., Schepelmann, P., Zademach, H. & Zörner, M. (2023). Injecting climate finance into SME lending in Germany: Opportunities for and limitations of regional savings and cooperative Banks. *ZFW – Advances in Economic Geography.* https://doi.org/10.1515/zfw-2022-0011

Franke, G., & Krahnen, J. P. (2017). SME funding without banks? On the interplay of banks and markets. *SAFE White Paper No. 44.*

Friede, G., Busch, T., & Bassen, A. (2015). ESG and financial performance: aggregated evidence from more than 2000 empirical studies. *Journal of sustainable finance & investment, 5(4),* 210–233. https://doi.org/10.1080/20430795.2015.1118917

Fuest, C., Hainz, C., Wackerbauer, J., Stitteneder, T., (2020). *Sustainable Finance – eine kritische Würdigung der deutschen und europäischen Vorhaben.* Ifo-Institut. https://www.ifo.de/publikationen/2020/monographie-autorenschaft/sustainable-finance

Gerstenberger, J., Grewenig, E., & Lo, V. (2023). *Vielfältige Hemmnisse bremsen Klimaschutzinvestitionen im Mittelstand.* KfW Research. https://www.kfw.de/PDF/Download-Center/Konzernthemen/Research/PDF-Dokumente-Fokus-Volkswirtschaft/Fokus-2023/Fokus-Nr.-440-September-2023-Klimaschutzhemmnisse.pdf

Gerstenberger, J. (2024). *Bisher nur wenige KMU von Banken aus Nachhaltigkeitsinformationen angesprochen – Bedarf dürfte aber zunehmen.* KfW Research. https://www.kfw.de/PDF/Download-Center/Konzernthemen/Research/PDF-Dokumente-Fokus-Volkswirtschaft/Fokus-2024/Fokus-Nr.-453-Februar-2024-Nachhaltigkeit-Kredit.pdf

Gianfrate, G., & Peri, M. (2019). The green advantage: exploring the convenience of issuing green bonds. *Journal of cleaner production, (219),* 127–135. https://doi.org/10.1016/j.jclepro.2019.02.022

Greitens, J., (2023). Sustainable Finance and small and medium enterprises: Germany's bank-based financial system and EU disclosure requirements. *Intereconomics, 58(4),* 222–226.

Greene, J. C., Caracelli, V. J., & Graham, W. F. (1989). Toward a conceptual framework for mixed-method evaluation designs. *Educational evaluation and policy analysis, 11(3*), 255–274. https://doi.org/10.3102/01623737011003255

Hackethal, A. (2004). German banks and banking structure. In J. P. Krahnen and R. H. Schmidt (Eds.), *The German financial system* (pp. 71–105). Oxford University Press.

Hackethal, A., & Schmidt, R.H., (2000). Finanzsystem und Komplementarität. *Working Paper Series: Finance & Accounting No. 50.*

Hainz, C., & Wiegand, M. (2013). Financing of the german economy during the financial crisis. *CESifo DICE Report, 11(1),* 48–54.

Handke, M. (2011). *Die Hausbankbeziehung: institutionalisierte Finanzierungslösungen für kleine und mittlere Unternehmen in räumlicher Perspektive.* LIT Verlag Münster.

Hardie, I. & Howarth, D. (Eds.) (2013). *Market-based banking and the international financial crisis.* Oxford. https://doi.org/10.1093/acprof:oso/9780199662289.001.0001

Hinsche, I. C. (2021). A greenium for the Next Generation EU Green Bonds analysis of a potential green bond premium and its drivers. *Center for Financial Studies Working Paper,* (663). https://dx.doi.org/10.2139/ssrn.3965664

Hinsche, I.C. (2024). Sustainable finance instruments and support – one size does not fit all. Understanding companies' individual sustainable finance needs and providing tailored sustainable finance support. (*Publication in process*).

Kabir, M. N., Rahman, S., Rahman, M. A., & Anwar, M. (2021). Carbon emissions and default risk: International evidence from firm-level data. *Economic Modelling, 103.* https://doi.org/10.1016/j.econmod.2021.105617

Kapraun, J., Latino, C., Scheins, C., & Schlag, C. (2021). (In)-credibly green: which bonds trade at a green bond premium?. In *Proceedings of Paris December 2019 Finance Meeting EUROFIDAI-ESSEC.* https://dx.doi.org/10.2139/ssrn.3347337

Kreditanstalt für Wiederaufbau. (2023). *KfW Mittelstandspanel 2023.* Retrieved June 20, 2024, from https://www.kfw.de/Über-die-KfW/KfW-Research/KfW-Mittelstandspanel.html

Kreditanstalt für Wiederaufbau. (2024a). *Energy efficiency, corporate environmental protection and renewable energies.* Retrieved June 20, 2024, from https://www.kfw.de/inlandsfoerderung/Companies/Energy-and-the-environment/

Kreditanstalt für Wiederaufbau. (2024b). *Klimaschutzoffensive für Unternehmen.* Retrieved June 24, 2024, from https://www.kfw.de/inlandsfoerderung/Unternehmen/Energie-Umwelt/Förderprodukte/Klimaschutzoffensive-für-den-Mittelstand-(293)/

Kuckartz, U. (2014). Mixed Methods: Methodologie, Forschungsdesigns und Analyseverfahren. Springer-Verlag. https://doi.org/10.1007/978-3-531-93267-5

Löher, J., Rieger-Fels, M., Nielen, S., Schröder, C., (2022). *Die Förderung nachhaltiger Finanzierung durch die EU – Auswirkungen auf den Mittelstand.* IfM-Materialien Nr. 294. https://www.ifm-bonn.org/fileadmin/data/redaktion/publikationen/ifm_materialien/dokumente/IfM-Materialien-294_2022.pdf

Morgan, D. L. (2014). *Integrating qualitative and quantitative methods: A pragmatic approach.* SAGE. https://doi.org/10.4135/9781544304533

Neagu, F., Tatarici, L., Dragu, F., & Stamate, A. (2024). Are green loans less risky? Micro-evidence from a European emerging economy. *Journal of Financial Stability, 70.* https://doi.org/10.1016/j.jfs.2023.101208

Network for Greening the Financial System. (2020). *A status report on financial institutions' experiences from working with green, non-green and brown financial assets and a potential risk differential.* https://www.ngfs.net/sites/default/files/medias/documents/ngfs_status_report.pdf

Network for Greening the Financial System. (2022). *Capturing risk differentials from climate-related risks.* https://www.ngfs.net/sites/default/files/medias/documents/capturing_risk_differentials_from_climate-related_risks.pdf

Rismanchi, S., McDaniels, J., Ochiai, I., Palmer, M., Idler, M., Portilla, A. (Ed.), Gibbs, S. (Ed.), & Monroe, M. F. (Ed.). (2022). *Climate and capital: views from the institute of international finance.* Institute of International Finance. https://www.iif.com/portals/0/Files/content/32370132_climate_and_capital_-_perspectives_from_the_iif_final.pdf

Safiullah, M., Kabir, M. N., & Miah, M. D. (2021). Carbon emissions and credit ratings. *Energy Economics, 100.* https://doi.org/10.1016/j.eneco.2021.105330

Scharf, E. (2022). *Sustainable Finance in der mittelständischen Unternehmensfinanzierung Deutschland – ein zusätzlicher Bestandteil in der Finanzierungsstrategie.* (Unpublished doctoral dissertation). University Cottbus-Senftenberg. https://doi.org/10.26127/BTUOpen-6018

Schmidt, R.H. (2019). On the change of the German financial system. *SAFE White Paper No. 61.*

Schmidt, R.H., Tyrell, M. (2004). What constitutes a financial system in general and the german financial system in particular?. In J. P. Krahnen and R. H. Schmidt (Eds.), *The German financial system* (pp. 19–67). Oxford University Press.

Schwartz, M., Gerstenberger, J., (2019). *Mittelstand mit großer Treue zur Hausbank.* KfW Research. https://www.kfw.de/PDF/Download-Center/Konzernthemen/Research/PDF-Dokumente-Fokus-Volkswirtschaft/Fokus-2019/Fokus-Nr.-243-Februar-2019-Mittelstand-und-Hausbanken.pdf

Sharpe, S. A. (1990). Asymmetric Information, Bank Lending and Implicit Contracts: A Stylized Model of Customer Relationships. *The Journal of Finance, 45(4),* 1069–1087. https://doi.org/10.2307/2328715

Strube, D., Mayer-Friedrich, & M. D., Streuer, O. (2023a). Quo Vadis, Nachhaltigkeit? Eine empirische Untersuchung der Nachhaltigkeitsintegration im Kreditmanagement von Volksbanken und Sparkassen. *Corporate Finance, (09–10),* 221–226.

Strube, D., Mayer-Friedrich, & M. D., Streuer, O. (2023b). Bewertung, Umsetzung und Perspektiven der Integration von Nachhaltigkeitsaspekten in der Managementpraxis von Regionalbanken. *Corporate Finance, (11–12),* 270–277.

Walther, U. (2023). *Climate stress tests: are banks fit for the green transition?.* Deutsche Bank Research. https://www.dbresearch.com/PROD/RPS_EN-PROD/PROD0000000000526206/Climate_stress_tests%3A_Are_banks_fit_for_the_green_.PDF?undefined&realload=OpesygUtqtzxvMXKvNDVo9yjgsFjYIVfbufAWIgtjioHB6L3/fB2UlmmG9haiplm

Tang, D. Y., & Zhang, Y. (2020). Do shareholders benefit from green bonds?. *Journal of Corporate Finance, 61,* 101427. https://dx.doi.org/10.2139/ssrn.3259555

Appendix A: Tables

Table 2. Summary Statistics – Companies' Sustainability Characteristics

	Observations	Percent of Data
Number of Companies	93	100 %
Carbon Footprint		
Yes	52	55.9 %
No	33	35.5 %
I don't know	8	8.6 %
ESG Rating		
Yes	21	22.6 %
No	53	57.0 %
I don't know	10	10.8 %
I don't know, unfamiliar with the term ESG	9	9.7 %
Company-Level Sustainability Targets		
Yes	65	69.9 %
No	25	26.9 %
I don't know	3	3.2 %
Sustainability Target Commitment Scheme		
Yes	12	12.9 %
No	65	69.9 %
I don't know	16	17.2 %

Source: This table presents the company sustainability characteristics of the 93 survey respondents.

Table 3. Summary Statistics – Respondents' Additional Information

	Observations	Percent of Data
Numer of Companies	93	100 %
Company Department		
Finance	86	94,5 %
Other Deparment	5	5,5 %
Gender		
Male	80	87,9 %
Female	9	9,9 %
Diverse	1	1,1 %
No Answer	1	1,1 %
Age Group		
20 to 29 years	2	2,2 %
30 to 39 years	21	23,1 %
40 to 49 years	28	30,8 %
50 to 59 years	28	30,8 %
60 years or older	12	13,2 %
Study / Work Experience in Sustainability		
Yes, study and work experience in sustainability	8	8,8 %
Yes, work experience in sustainability	27	29,7 %
No, neiter study nor work experience in sustainability	48	52,7 %
No Answer	8	8,8 %

Source: This table presents additional information regarding the 93 survey respondents, based on survey questions 26, 27, 28 and 29. Differences in the number of observations are due to the fact that the response was voluntary and not all survey participants answered these questions.

Table 4. Correlation Analysis Results

	CMA	
	Fisher's Exact	Cramér's V
Regulatory Pressure	0.555	0.1662
Transformation Risk	0.710	0.1234
Financing Access	0.832	0.1199
Financing Link	0.941	0.0907
Carbon Footprint	0.237	0.1710
ESG Rating	0.079*	0.2685
Company-Level Sustainability Targets	0.511	0.1237
Sustainability Target Commitment Scheme	0.275	0.1716
Unfamiliar with ESG	0.721	-0.0511
Unfamiliar with SFI	0.049**	0.2127
Barriers	0.273	0.1352
Bank SF Support Rating	0.278	0.2273
Bank SFI Recommendation	0.044**	0.2564
Banks Potential Role	0.624	0.1042
Promotional Loan Knowledge	0.829	0.0384
Promotional Loan Use	0.024**	0.2363
Promotional Loan Interest	0.087*	0.2384

Source: Fisher's exact test and Cramér's V calculation run in Stata using the data from Table 7, Table 9, Table 13 and Table 17. The number of observations is 92, as one recorded "no answer" option for capital market activity is excluded. Significance levels are denoted as follows: *** $p<.01$, ** $p<.05$, * $p<.1$.

Table 5. SFI Use and Company Size by Capital Market Activity

	Sample	
	CMA	Not CMA
Count	34	58
Company Size		
Up to €9 million	0	1
€10 to €49 million	4	5
€50 to €499 million	14	32
€500 million to €5 billion	6	17
Bigger than €5 billion	8	2
No Answer	2	1
Sustainable Finance Use		
Yes	9	4
No	22	38
Yes in Progress	1	5
IDK SFI	1	10
IDK	1	1

Source: This table presents the recorded data based on survey questions 1, 19 and 20 by capital market activity. Note. "CMA" means capital market active, "Not CMA" means not capital market active and "IDK" means I don't know.

Table 6. Logistic Regression Results – SFI Use and Company Size

<u>Logistic Regression: CMA – SFIUse</u>

CMA	Odds Ratio	Robust Std. Err.	z	P >|z|	95 % Confidence Interval		Significance / Comment
Yes	1	.	.	.	.	.	Baseline
No	.257	.17	-2.05	.04	.07	.941	**
Yes in Progress	.089	.112	-1.93	.054	.008	1.043	*
IDK SFI	.044	.054	-2.56	.01	.004	.481	**
IDK	.444	.687	-0.52	.6	.022	9.182	
Constant	2.25	1.359	1.34	.18	.688	7.353	
Number of obs	=	*92*			*Log pseudol.*	=	*-54.894267*
Wald chi2(4)	=	*8.77*			*Pseudo R2*	=	*.0942*
Prob > chi2	=	*.0670*					

<u>Logistic Regression: CMA – Company</u>

CMA	Odds Ratio	Robust Std. Err.	z	P >|z|	95 % Confidence Interval		Significance / Comment
< 49 M	1	.	.	.	.	.	Baseline
50 – 499 M	.656	.476	-0.58	.561	.159	2.716	
500 – 5 B	.529	.427	-0.79	.43	.109	2.568	
>5 B	6	6.157	1.75	.081	.803	44.84	*
NA	3	4.176	0.79	.43	.196	45.921	
Constant	.667	.433	-0.62	.532	.187	2.379	
Number of obs	=	*92*			*Log pseudol.*	=	*-55.112019*
Wald chi2(4)	=	*8.78*			*Pseudo R2*	=	*.0906*
Prob > chi2	=	*.0668*					

Source: Logistic regression analysis with robust standard errors run in Stata using data from Table 5. The dependent variable is a binary variable for which 1 denotes capital market activity and 0 no capital market activity. The independent variables are in this case SFI Use and Company Size respectively. Significance levels are denoted as follows: *** p<.01, ** p<.05, * p<.1.

Table 7. Motivational Factors by Capital Market Activity and SME Share

	Sample		Percentage		SME Share	
	CMA	Not CMA	CMA	Not CMA	Not CMA	Not CMA
Count	34	58	100 %	100 %	6	100 %
Transition Risk						
Little	3	7	9 %	12 %	2	33 %
Average	10	14	29 %	24 %	2	33 %
Strong	14	29	41 %	50 %	1	17 %
Very Strong	7	8	21 %	14 %	1	17 %
Regulatory Pressure						
Little	0	4	0 %	7 %	1	17 %
Average	13	19	38 %	33 %	3	50 %
Strong	14	23	41 %	40 %	1	17 %
Very Strong	7	12	21 %	21 %	1	17 %
Credit Link						
Very Unlikely	1	2	3 %	3 %	0	0 %
Unlikely	4	4	12 %	7 %	2	33 %
Average	7	14	21 %	24 %	1	17 %
Likely	15	25	44 %	43 %	2	33 %
Very Likely	7	13	21 %	22 %	1	17 %
Financing Access						
Very Low	3	3	9 %	5 %	0	0 %
Low	10	13	29 %	22 %	2	33 %
Average	11	24	32 %	41 %	3	50 %
High	8	15	24 %	26 %	0	0 %
Very High	2	2	6 %	3 %	1	17 %

Source: This table presents the recorded data based on survey questions 14, 15, 16, 17 and 20 by capital market activity in the first column. "CMA" means capital market active and "Not CMA" means not capital market active. The second column shows the respective percentage with the two groups CMA and Not CMA as the respective baseline. The third column presents only the SME share of companies Not CMA.

Table 8. Logistic Regression Results – Motivational Factors

Logistic Regression: CMA – Regulatory Pressure

CMA	Odds Ratio	Robust Std. Err.	z	P >|z|	95 % Confidence Interval		Signifi-cance / Comment
Low	1	.	.	.	.	.	PFP
Average	1	.	.	.	.	.	Baseline
Strong	.89	.442	-0.24	.814	.336	2.358	
Very Strong	.853	.511	-0.27	.79	.263	2.763	
Constant	.684	.248	-1.05	.294	.337	1.391	
Number of obs	=	*88*			*Log pseudol.*	=	*-58.65975*
Wald chi2(2)	=	*.09*			*Pseudo R2*	=	*.0008*
Prob > chi2	=	*.9569*					

Logistic Regression: CMA – Transformation Risk

CMA	Odds Ratio	Robust Std. Err.	z	P >|z|	95 % Confidence Interval		Signifi-cance / Comment
Low	1	.	.	.	.	.	Baseline
Average	1.667	1.349	0.63	.528	.341	8.14	
Strong	1.126	.864	0.16	.877	.25	5.066	
Very Strong	2.042	1.771	0.82	.411	.373	11.175	
Constant	.429	.297	-1.22	.222	.11	1.67	
Number of obs	=	*92*			*Log pseudol.*	=	*-59.906354*
Wald chi2(3)	=	*1.37*			*Pseudo R2*	=	*.0115*
Prob > chi2	=	*.7120*					

Logistic Regression: CMA – Financing Access

CMA	Odds Ratio	Robust Std. Err.	z	P >|z|	95 % Confidence Interval		Signifi-cance / Comment
Very Low	1	.	.	.	.	.	Baseline
Low	1.026	.899	0.03	.977	.184	5.718	
Average	.611	.52	-0.58	.563	.115	3.238	
High	.711	.629	-0.39	.7	.125	4.031	
Very High	1.333	1.687	0.23	.82	.112	15.918	
Constant	.75	.576	-0.37	.708	.166	3.379	
Number of obs	=	*92*			*Log pseudol.*	=	*-59.946244*
Wald chi2(4)	=	*1.29*			*Pseudo R2*	=	*.0108*
Prob > chi2	=	*.8623*					

Logistic Regression: CMA – Financing Link

CMA	Odds Ratio	Robust Std. Err.	z	P >|z|	95 % Confidence Interval		Signifi-cance / Comment
Very Unlikely	1	.	.	.	.	.	Baseline
Unlikely	2	2.844	0.49	.626	.123	32.464	
Average	1	1.316	0.00	1	.076	13.201	
Likely	1.2	1.529	0.14	.886	.099	14.589	
Very Likely	1.077	1.42	0.06	.955	.081	14.275	
Constant	.5	.616	-0.56	.574	.045	5.587	
Number of obs	=	*92*			*Log pseudol.*	=	*-60.23298*
Wald chi2(4)	=	*.74*			*Pseudo R2*	=	*.0061*
Prob > chi2	=	*.9469*					

Source: Logistic regression analysis with robust standard errors run using data from Table 7. Further details see Table 6. Significance levels: *** p<.01, ** p<.05, * p<.1."PFP" = predicts failure perfectly.

Table 9. Implementation Factors by Capital Market Activity and SME Share

	Sample		Percentage		SME Share	
	CM A	Not CMA	CMA	Not CMA	Not CMA	Not CMA
Count	34	58	100 %	100 %	6	100 %
Carbon Footprint						
Yes	19	33	56 %	57 %	3	50 %
No	10	22	29 %	38 %	3	50 %
IDK	5	3	15 %	5 %	0	0 %
ESG Rating						
Yes	12	9	35 %	16 %	0	0 %
No	14	39	41 %	67 %	2	33 %
IDK	4	5	12 %	9 %	1	17 %
IDK ESG Term	4	5	12 %	9 %	3	50 %
Sustainability Targets						
Yes	24	40	71 %	69 %	3	50 %
No	8	17	24 %	29 %	2	33 %
IDK	2	1	6 %	2 %	1	17 %
Incentive Scheme						
Yes	7	5	21 %	9 %	1	17 %
Management compensation	3	2	-	-	-	-
Management reporting	0	1	-	-	-	-
No	22	43	65 %	74 %	4	67 %
IDK	5	10	15 %	17 %	1	17 %
Unfamiliar with SFI						
Yes	1	10	3 %	17 %	1	17 %
No	33	48	97 %	83 %	5	83 %
Barriers						
Yes	17	21	50 %	36 %	2	33 %
No	17	37	50 %	64 %	4	67 %

Source: This table presents the recorded data based on survey questions 1, 2, 20, 21, 22, 23 and 24 by capital market activity in the first column. "CMA" means capital market active and "Not CMA" means not capital market active. The second column shows the respective percentage with the two groups CMA and Not CMA as the respective baseline. The third column presents only the SME share of companies Not CMA. Note. "IDK" = I don't know.

Table 10. Logistic Regression Results – Implementation Factors I

Logistic Regression: CMA – Carbon Footprint

CMA	Odds Ratio	Robust Std. Err.	z	P >|z|	95 % Confidence Interval		Significance / Comment
Yes	1.267	.609	0.49	.623	.494	3.248	
No	1	.	.	.	.	.	Baseline
I don't know	3.667	3.037	1.57	.117	.723	18.595	
Constant	.455	.174	-2.06	.04	.214	.964	**
Number of obs	=	*92*			*Log pseudol.*	=	*-59.302853*
Wald chi2(2)	=	*2.47*			*Pseudo R2*	=	*.0214*
Prob > chi2	=	*.2910*					

Logistic Regression: CMA – ESG Rating

CMA	Odds Ratio	Robust Std. Err.	z	P >|z|	95 % Confidence Interval		Significance / Comment
Yes	3.714	2.016	2.42	.016	1.282	10.764	**
No	1	.	.	.	.	.	Baseline
I don't know	2.229	1.657	1.08	.281	.519	9.573	
I don't know, unfamiliar	2.229	1.657	1.08	.281	.519	9.573	
Constant	.359	.112	-3.27	.001	.194	.663	***
Number of obs	=	*92*			*Log pseudol.*	=	*-57.306143*
Wald chi2(3)	=	*6.30*			*Pseudo R2*	=	*.0544*
Prob > chi2	=	*.0981*					

Logistic Regression: CMA – CLST

CMA	Odds Ratio	Robust Std. Err.	z	P >|z|	95 % Confidence Interval		Significance / Comment
Yes	1.275	.642	0.48	.629	.476	3.419	
No	1	.	.	.	.	.	Baseline
I don't know	4.25	5.545	1.11	.267	.329	54.825	
Constant	.471	.203	-1.75	.08	.202	1.095	*

Number of obs	=	*92*	*Log pseudol.*	=	*-59.921326*
Wald chi2(2)	=	*1.26*	*Pseudo R2*	=	*.0112*
Prob > chi2	=	*.5324*			

Logistic Regression: CMA – STCS

CMA	Odds Ratio	Robust Std. Err.	z	P >|z|	95 % Confidence Interval		Significance / Comment
Yes	2.736	1.765	1.56	.119	.773	9.688	
No	1	.	.	.	.	.	Baseline
I don't know	.977	.597	-0.04	.97	.295	3.234	
Constant	.512	.135	-2.54	.011	.305	.858	**

Number of obs	=	*92*	*Log pseudol.*	=	*-59.298665*
Wald chi2(2)	=	*2.54*	*Pseudo R2*	=	*.0215*
Prob > chi2	=	*.2813*			

Source: Logistic regression analysis with robust standard errors run in Stata using data from Table 9. Further details see Table 6. Significance levels: *** p<.01, ** p<.05, * p<.1. "CLST" means company-level sustainability targets and "STCS" means sustainability target commitment scheme.

Table 11. Logistic Regression Results – Implementation Factors II

Logistic Regression: CMA – Unfamiliar with ESG

CMA	Odds Ratio	Robust Std. Err.	z	P >|z|	95 % Confidence Interval		Significance / Comment
No	1	.	.	.	.	.	Baseline
Yes	1.413	1.007	0.49	.627	.35	5.712	
Constant	.566	.13	-2.48	.013	.361	.888	**
Number of obs	=	*92*			*Log pseudol.*	=	*-60.485032*
Wald chi2(1)	=	*.24*			*Pseudo R2*	=	*.0019*
Prob > chi2	=	*.6273*					

Logistic Regression: CMA – Unfamiliar with SFI

CMA	Odds Ratio	Robust Std. Err.	z	P >|z|	95 % Confidence Interval		Significance / Comment
No	1	.	.	.	.	.	Baseline
Yes	.145	.157	-1.79	.074	.018	1.205	*
Constant	.688	.156	-1.65	.099	.44	1.074	*
Number of obs	=	*92*			*Log pseudol.*	=	*-58.098981*
Wald chi2(1)	=	*3.19*			*Pseudo R2*	=	*.0413*
Prob > chi2	=	*.0739*					

Logistic Regression: CMA – Barriers

CMA	Odds Ratio	Robust Std. Err.	z	P >|z|	95 % Confidence Interval		Significance / Comment
Yes	1.762	.777	1.28	.199	.742	4.181	
No	1	.	.	.	.	.	Baseline
Constant	.459	.135	-2.64	.008	.258	.818	***
Number of obs	=	*92*			*Log pseudol.*	=	*-59.765225*
Wald chi2(1)	=	*1.65*			*Pseudo R2*	=	*.0138*
Prob > chi2	=	*.1989*					

Source: Logistic regression analysis with robust standard errors run in Stata using data from Table 9. Further details see Table 6. Significance levels: *** p<.01, ** p<.05, * p<.1.

Table 12. Perceived Barriers by Capital Market Activity

Main Categories	Subcategories Level 1	Subcategories Level 2	Number of Observations	
			CMA	NCMA
Applicability	Company Characteristics	*Company purpose*	1	0
		Financing structure	1	1
		Industry	0	1
	Financing Need	*Insufficient flexibility*	0	1
		Use Case	0	1
Company Requirements	Administrative Work	*Add. work capacities needed*	1	0
		General add. effort	4	3
		Reporting	1	3
	Knowledge	*Insufficient consulting*	1	0
		No experience	0	1
		Regulatory uncertainty	0	2
Economic Efficiency	Cost	*Costs higher than benefits*	1	2
		Higher costs	3	0
		Insufficient promotional loans	1	1
	Risk	*Greenwashing risk*	1	0
		Regulatory risk	0	1
		Risk of failure to achieve targets	3	1
Implementation	Instrument	*Data collection*	0	2
		KPI choice & tracking	1	3
		Size	0	1
	Standards & Regulations	*Data availability*	0	3
		Data comparability	0	1
		Investor requirements	1	0

Source: This table presents the recorded perceived barriers based on survey questions 2 and 20 by capital market activity. "CMA" means capital market active and "Not CMA" means not capital market active. 17 companies CMA and 21 companies NCMA reported barriers. The number of perceived barriers exceeds the number of companies, as some companies reported more than one barrier. The qualitative answers were categorized using thematic content analysis based on Kuckartz (2014).

Table 13. Enabling Factors by Capital Market Activity and SME Share

	Sample		Percentage		SME Share	
	CMA	Not CMA	CMA	Not CMA	Not CMA	Not CMA
Count	34	58	100 %	100 %	6	100 %
Bank Recommendation						
Yes	18	16	53 %	28 %	0	0 %
No	15	38	44 %	66 %	4	67 %
IDK	1	4	3 %	7 %	2	33 %
Bank Believe						
Yes	19	27	56 %	47 %	2	33 %
No	6	10	18 %	17 %	2	33 %
IDK	9	21	26 %	36 %	2	33 %
Bank Support						
Very Bad	3	2	9 %	3 %	0	0 %
Bad	5	6	15 %	10 %	0	0 %
Average	9	28	26 %	48 %	4	67 %
Good	14	18	41 %	31 %	0	0 %
Very Good	3	4	9 %	7 %	1	33 %

Source: This table presents the recorded data based on survey questions 11, 12, 13 and 20 by capital market activity in the first column. "CMA" means capital market active and "Not CMA" means not capital market active. The second column shows the respective percentage with the two groups CMA and Not CMA as the respective baseline. The third column presents only the SME share of companies Not CMA.

Table 14. Enabling Factors by Capital Market Activity excl. SFIDK

	Sample		Percentage	
	CMA	Not CMA	CMA	Not CMA
Count	33	48	100 %	100 %
Bank Recommendation				
Yes	18	16	55 %	33 %
No	14	28	42 %	58 %
IDK	1	4	3 %	8 %
Bank Believe				
Yes	18	23	55 %	48 %
No	6	10	18 %	21 %
IDK	9	15	27 %	31 %
Bank Support				
Very Bad	3	0	9 %	0 %
Bad	5	3	15 %	6 %
Average	9	24	27 %	50 %
Good	13	17	39 %	35 %
Very Good	3	4	9 %	8 %

Source: This table presents the recorded data from Table 13, excluding companies that were unfamiliar with SFI before the survey (SFIDK).

Table 15. Logistic Regression Results – Enabling Factors

Logistic Regression: CMA – Bank Support

CMA	Odds Ratio	Robust Std. Err.	z	P >|z|	95 % Confidence Interval		Significance / Comment
Very Bad	1	.	.	.	.	.	Baseline
Bad	.556	.612	-0.53	.594	.064	4.812	
Average	.214	.213	-1.55	.122	.03	1.508	
Good	.519	.511	-0.67	.505	.075	3.577	
Very Good	.5	.598	-0.58	.562	.048	5.22	
Constant	1.5	1.377	0.44	.659	.248	9.065	
Number of obs	=	*92*			*Log pseudol.*	=	*-58.181787*
Wald chi2(4)	=	*4.52*			*Pseudo R2*	=	*.0399*
Prob > chi2	=	*.3402*					

Logistic Regression: CMA – Bank Recommendation

CMA	Odds Ratio	Robust Std. Err.	z	P >|z|	95 % Confidence Interval		Significance / Comment
Yes	2.85	1.316	2.27	.023	1.153	7.047	**
No	1	.	.	.	.	.	Baseline
I don't know	.633	.738	-0.39	.695	.065	6.215	
Constant	.395	.121	-3.03	.002	.216	.72	***
Number of obs	=	*92*			*Log pseudol.*	=	*-57.586603*
Wald chi2(2)	=	*5.78*			*Pseudo R2*	=	*.0498*
Prob > chi2	=	*.0555*					

Logistic Regression: CMA – Bank Role

CMA	Odds Ratio	Robust Std. Err.	z	P >|z|	95 % Confidence Interval		Significance / Comment
Yes	1.173	.704	0.27	.791	.362	3.803	
No	1	.	.	.	.	.	Baseline
I don't know	.714	.468	-0.51	.608	.198	2.583	
Constant	.6	.312	-0.98	.325	.217	1.66	
Number of obs	=	*92*			*Log pseudol.*	=	*-60.096509*
Wald chi2(2)	=	*.98*			*Pseudo R2*	=	*.0084*
Prob > chi2	=	*.6125*					

Source: Logistic regression analysis with robust standard errors run in Stata using data from Table 13. Further details see Table 6. Significance levels: *** p<.01, ** p<.05, * p<.1.

Table 16. Companies' Bank Expectations by Capital Market Activity

Main Categories	Subcategories Level 1	Subcategories Level 2	Number of Observations CMA	Number of Observations NCMA
Consultation	General Consultation		8	6
	KPI Choice		1	3
	Optimizing Rating		0	1
	Promotional Loans		1	2
	Reporting		0	2
Information	General Information		0	3
	Sustainable Finance Market	*Expectation of bank / capital market participants*	1	1
		Market Overview	1	1
	Sustainable Finance Mechanisms	*Comparison to conv. financing*	0	1
		Impact of sustainability on rating / financing	0	1
		Information on conditions	1	0
	Sustainable Finance Use	*Best Practice*	2	0
		Experience with other customers	0	4
		Use Cases	0	1
Mode of Information	Event		1	0
	Personal Talks		1	0
	Presentation		1	0
	Questionnaire		0	1
	Workshop		1	0
Role of Bank	Clear Commitment with Strategic Allocation		0	1
	Financing (Offers)		1	3
	Sparring Partner		0	1

Source: This table presents the recorded expectations based on survey questions 12 and 20 by capital market activity. "CMA" means capital market active and "Not CMA" means not capital market active. 19 companies CMA and 27 companies NCMA reported expectations. The number of expectations exceeds the number of companies, as some companies reported more than one expectation. The qualitative answers were categorized using thematic content analysis based on Kuckartz (2014).

Table 17. Promotional Loan Factors by Capital Market Activity and SME Share

	Sample		Percentage		SME Share	
	CMA	Not CMA	CMA	Not CMA	Not CMA	Not CMA
Count	34	58	100 %	100 %	6	100 %
PL Knowledge						
Yes	18	33	53 %	57 %	2	33 %
No	16	25	47 %	43 %	4	67 %
PL Use						
Yes	0	8	0 %	14 %	0	0 %
No	34	50	100 %	86 %	6	100 %
PL Interest						
Yes	21	48	62 %	83 %	4	67 %
No	5	3	15 %	5 %	1	17 %
I don't know	8	7	24 %	12 %	1	17 %

Source: This table presents the recorded data based on survey questions 9, 10 and 20 by capital market activity in the first column. "CMA" means capital market active and "Not CMA" means not capital market active. The second column shows the respective percentage with the two groups CMA and Not CMA as the respective baseline. The third column presents only the SME share of companies Not CMA.

Table 18. Logistic Regression Results – Promotional Loan Factors

Logistic Regression: CMA – Promotional Loan Interest

CMA	Odds Ratio	Robust Std. Err.	z	P >|z|	95 % Confidence Interval		Significance / Comment
Yes	.263	.205	-1.71	.086	.057	1.211	*
No	1	.	.	.	.	.	Baseline
I don't know	.686	.617	-0.42	.675	.118	4.001	
Constant	1.667	1.224	0.70	.487	.395	7.029	
Number of obs	=	*92*			*Log pseudol.*	=	*-58.057085*
Wald chi2(2)	=	*4.91*			*Pseudo R2*	=	*.0420*
Prob > chi2	=	*.0860*					

Logistic Regression: CMA – Promotional Loan Knowledge

CMA	Odds Ratio	Robust Std. Err.	z	P >|z|	95 % Confidence Interval		Significance / Comment
No	1	.	.	.	.	.	Baseline
Yes	.852	.372	-0.37	.714	.362	2.005	
Constant	.64	.206	-1.39	.166	.341	1.203	
Number of obs	=	*92*			*Log pseudol.*	=	*-60.534806*
Wald chi2(1)	=	*.13*			*Pseudo R2*	=	*.0011*
Prob > chi2	=	*.7141*					

Logistic Regression: CMA – Promotional Loan Use

CMA	Odds Ratio	Robust Std. Err.	z	P >|z|	95 % Confidence Interval		Significance / Comment
No	1	.	.	.	.	.	Baseline
Yes	1	.	.	.	.	.	PFP
Constant	.68	.152	-1.72	.085	.439	1.054	*
Number of obs	=	*84*			*Log pseudol.*	=	*-56.691203*
Wald chi2(0)	=	.			*Pseudo R2*	=	*.0000*
Prob > chi2	=	.					

Source: Logistic regression analysis with robust standard errors run in Stata using data from Table 17. Further details see Table 6. Significance levels: *** p<.01, ** p<.05, * p<.1. "PFP" = predict failure perfectly.